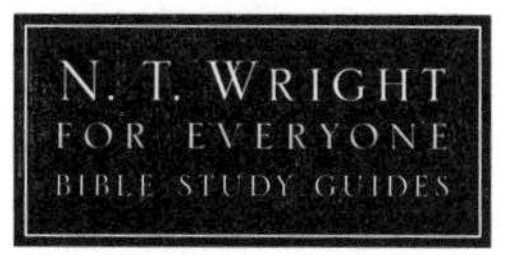

HEBREWS

13 STUDIES FOR INDIVIDUALS AND GROUPS

N. T. WRIGHT

WITH PATTY PELL

An imprint of InterVarsity Press
Downers Grove, Illinois

InterVarsity Press
P.O. Box 1400, Downers Grove, IL 60515-1426
World Wide Web: www.ivpress.com
E-mail: email@ivpress.com

InterVarsity Press® is the book-publishing division of InterVarsity Christian Fellowship/USA®, a movement of students and faculty active on campus at hundreds of universities, colleges and schools of nursing in the United States of America, and a member movement of the International Fellowship of Evangelical Students. For information about local and regional activities, write Public Relations Dept., InterVarsity Christian Fellowship/USA, 6400 Schroeder Rd., P.O. Box 7895, Madison, WI 53707-7895, or visit the IVCF website at <www.intervarsity.org>.

Design: Cindy Kiple
Cover image: Paul Knight/Trevillion Images

ISBN 978-0-8308-2195-2

Printed in the United States of America ∞

InterVarsity Press is committed to protecting the environment and to the responsible use of natural resources. As a member of Green Press Initiative we use recycled paper whenever possible. To learn more about the Green Press Initiative, visit <www.greenpressinitiative.org>.

P 18 17 16 15 14 13 12 11 10 9 8

Y 25 24 23 22 21 20 19 18

Contents

Getting the Most Out of Hebrews

Half the fun of Christmas morning, especially for young children, is the exciting packages in glittering wrapping, with ribbons and bows, all telling you something about how wonderful the present itself will be. Many small children are so excited by the wrapping and the beautiful boxes that they almost ignore the present itself.

The writer of the letter of Hebrews is anxious that the people it is written to should not make that same mistake. The wrapping of the old covenant and its sacrificial system had come off the present; and the present was Jesus himself, God's own, unique son, sent to fulfill everything the law and the prophets had spoken of. They could move on from the earlier stages of God's purpose and gladly live out the new one which had dawned. Hebrews is written to urge its readers to not go back to their old ways.

We don't know who wrote the letter of Hebrews, but we do know it was written to Jewish Christians (who of course formed the nucleus of the earliest church). In the very last chapter, Hebrews 13, we have small indications of the situation of the writer and the readers. Verse 19, which sounds similar to what Paul says in Philemon 22, may indicate that the writer is in prison, though nothing elsewhere in the letter leads us to suspect that. Maybe he is simply engaged in difficult work which prevents him from coming to them at the moment.

The sudden mention of Timothy in 13:23, and of his being released, links this letter to Paul's world, but frustratingly doesn't help us get much further with identifying its writer or place of origin. The mention of those from Italy in 13:24 doesn't necessarily mean that the writer was in Italy at the time; it might easily indicate that there was a small community, wherever he was, who had come from Italy—consisting perhaps of those, like the people mentioned in Acts 18:2, who had been expelled from Rome by Claudius. Saying "Italy" instead of "Rome" may well be a note of caution, so as not to put Christians there in jeopardy should the letter fall into the wrong hands. (For more on this letter, also see my *Hebrews for Everyone,* published by SPCK and Westminster John Knox. This guide is based on that book and was prepared with the help of Patty Pell, for which I am grateful.)

This letter seems to be written not in the very earliest period of the church, but perhaps some time between A.D. 50 and A.D. 70, possibly even after that. For many Jewish Christians things were not easy. Lots of their family members and friends and neighbors had not accepted Jesus as the long-awaited Messiah, and they regarded them as dangerous, misguided and disloyal to all that God had said earlier on. All sorts of pressure would have been put on them to try and make them go back to where they had been before, to abandon this new-found movement with its strange claims and to take up again a position of living under God's law, the law given through Moses.

We know from chapter 10 (verses 32-34) that persecution was a problem for the recipients of this letter. And the writer seeks to further encourage his readers in chapter 11 with examples of those who held to their faith, often in the midst of very difficult circumstances.

Thus, Hebrews was written to show that you can't go back to an earlier stage of God's purposes, but must instead go forward, must press on eagerly from within the new stage to the one that is yet to come. The letter is a call to not play with the wrapping instead of with the brilliant present itself.

SUGGESTIONS FOR INDIVIDUAL STUDY

1. As you begin each study, pray that God will speak to you through his Word.

2. Read the introduction to the study and respond to the "Open" question that follows it. This is designed to help you get into the theme of the study.

3. Read and reread the Bible passage to be studied. Each study is designed to help you consider the meaning of the passage in its context. The commentary and questions in this guide are based on my own translation of each passage found in the companion volume to this guide in the For Everyone series on the New Testament (published by SPCK and Westminster John Knox).

4. Write your answers to the questions in the spaces provided or in a personal journal. Each study includes three types of questions: observation questions, which ask about the basic facts in the passage; interpretation questions, which delve into the meaning of the passage; and application questions, which help you discover the implications of the text for growing in Christ. Writing out your responses can bring clarity and deeper understanding of yourself and of God's Word.

5. Each session features selected comments from the For Everyone series. These notes provide further biblical and cultural background and contextual information. They are designed not to answer the questions for you but to help you along as you study the Bible for yourself. For even more reflections on each passage, you may wish to have on hand a copy of the companion volume from the For Everyone series as you work through this study guide.

6. Use the guidelines in the "Pray" section to focus on God, thanking him for what you have learned and praying about the applications that have come to mind.

SUGGESTIONS FOR GROUP MEMBERS

1. Come to the study prepared. Follow the suggestions for individual study mentioned above. You will find that careful preparation will greatly enrich your time spent in group discussion.

2. Be willing to participate in the discussion. The leader of your group will not be lecturing. Instead, she or he will be asking the questions found in this guide and encouraging the members of the group to discuss what they have learned.

3. Stick to the topic being discussed. These studies focus on a particular passage of Scripture. Only rarely should you refer to other portions of the Bible or outside sources. This allows for everyone to participate on equal ground and for in-depth study.

4. Be sensitive to the other members of the group. Listen attentively when they describe what they have learned. You may be surprised by their insights! Each question assumes a variety of answers. Many questions do not have "right" answers, particularly questions that aim at meaning or application. Instead the questions push us to explore the passage more thoroughly.

   When possible, link what you say to the comments of others. Also, be affirming whenever you can. This will encourage some of the more hesitant members of the group to participate.

5. Be careful not to dominate the discussion. We are sometimes so eager to express our thoughts that we leave too little opportunity for others to respond. By all means participate! But allow others to also.

6. Expect God to teach you through the passage being discussed and through the other members of the group. Pray that you will have an enjoyable and profitable time together, but also that as a result of the study you will find ways that you can take action individually and/or as a group.

7. It will be helpful for groups to follow a few basic guidelines. These guidelines, which you may wish to adapt to your situation, should be read at the beginning of the first session.

   - Anything said in the group is considered confidential and will not be discussed outside the group unless specific permission is given to do so.

- We will provide time for each person present to talk if he or she feels comfortable doing so.
- We will talk about ourselves and our own situations, avoiding conversation about other people.
- We will listen attentively to each other.
- We will be very cautious about giving advice.

Additional suggestions for the group leader can be found at the back of the guide.

God's One and Only Son

Hebrews 1

The ancient world did not have printing presses such as we do in the modern world, but it had equivalents, particularly for making coins. The emperor would employ an engraver who carved the royal portrait, and suitable words or abbreviations, on a stamp, or die, made of hard metal. The engraver used the stamp to make a coin, so that the coin gave the exact impression, indeed expression, of what was on the stamp.

The writer of Hebrews begins the letter with this idea. It is as though the exact imprint of the Father's very nature and glory has been precisely reproduced in the soft metal of the Son's human nature.

OPEN

How do you see people in the surrounding culture trying to experience and expand their spirituality?

STUDY

1. *Read Hebrews 1.* This chapter is a grand and formal opening to this letter to the Hebrews.

What do we learn in particular about Jesus in verses 1-4?

2. How does the writer invite us in verses 1-4 to look at the whole sweep of biblical history and see it coming to a climax in Jesus?

3. In verse 5, two Old Testament passages are quoted: Psalm 2:7 and 2 Samuel 7:14. These two passages were frequently used by the early Christians when they were struggling to say what had to be said about Jesus. How do these quotes further explain who Jesus is?

4. The writer quotes from two psalms (97:7 and 104:4) in verses 6-7. How do these verses contrast Jesus and angels?

5. In verses 8-9, Psalm 45:6-7 is being quoted. The psalm addresses the king as if he can be called God, but the writer of Hebrews applies this psalm to Jesus, the Messiah. What will the reign of the Messiah be like according to this psalm?

6. When you think of the condition of the world today, where do you long to see the reign of Jesus?

7. Why might the writer of Hebrews have chosen to include the quotes from Psalm 102:25-27 in verses 10-12?

8. A third psalm is quoted in verse 13: Psalm 110. Once again, in verses 13-14 the writer contrasts Jesus with the angels, though in a different way. What is the role of the angels compared to that of the Messiah?

9. As mentioned in the introduction, many of the Jewish believers in the early church had family members who had not accepted that Jesus was the Messiah, and they regarded the Jewish believers as dangerously misguided and disloyal. Great pressure was exerted on the Jewish believers to turn back to the law, which according to Jewish tradition had been given to Moses by angels on Mount Sinai.

   In what ways do verses 5-14 help establish Jesus' superiority over the law?

10. Not many readers today, perhaps, will be tempted to abandon Christianity in favor of some form of Judaism—though it is important for us to understand why that was such an obvious pressure in the early days. But many today, including many in the churches, seem dissatisfied with what they have, and are eager to expand their spiritual horizons (as they might see it) to include angels, saints and other interesting distractions.

    What specific ways are you and your church or faith community tempted to expand your spiritual horizons?

11. The angels, the law and the prophets were all part of God's preparation, part of the brilliant and beautiful wrapping in which the ultimate present, God's gift of his own self in the person of the Son, would be contained. How can you pay closer attention to who Jesus is and to the role of worship and service to which he has called you, instead of playing with the "wrapping"?

PRAY

Spend time in worship giving praise to the Messiah. Focus on Jesus as the ultimate climax to all of history, and give specific prayers of thanks for the aspects of his reign.

2

Jesus as the Truly Human Being

Hebrews 2

Imagine being in a little motorboat, some way out from shore, needing to find your way along the coast to the right harbor. You need to keep the engine running and a firm hand on the tiller. If you don't, there is no guarantee that you will drift in the right direction, and every probability that you will drift in the wrong one—perhaps onto a rocky shore or out to the wild ocean.

Hebrews 2 is a warning many believers need. It is all too easy to suppose that we can take the pressure off and allow other people to do the praying, the thinking, the serious business; we'll go along for the ride, we'll stop putting so much effort into it, we'll go with the flow. The problem is that if we haven't got our own motor running and our own hand on the tiller, we may drift further and further away without realizing it.

OPEN

Describe a time when someone gave you a warning that you didn't pay much attention to. What happened?

STUDY

1. *Read Hebrews* 2. As mentioned before, according to Jewish tradition the law came to Moses through angels—and look what happens if people ignore *that*. Now: what will happen if they refuse to listen to something even more important and powerful? God may have to conclude that they really aren't interested in being rescued, in being saved from the sin and injustice which rages around them like an angry sea. That's why, in this passage and frequently later on, Hebrews insists not just that Christians must stick with what they've got, rather than abandoning it, but also that they must pay *closer* attention, must go deeper into the truth and life which is theirs because they belong to the Messiah.

   In what different ways, according to 2:1-4, was the message of salvation in Christ emphasized?

2. How does this compare and contrast with the message that came through angels?

3. What evidence is there in your life or in your Christian community that the message of Jesus is true and powerful?

4. In what ways does the writer speak about both the *future* role of Jesus in God's new creation and his *present* position in verses 5-9?

5. In a parliamentary democracy, voters in each area elect someone to *represent* them in the central councils of state. They can't all be there themselves so they find an appropriate way of appointing someone who is there *on their behalf*, carrying their hopes, fears, needs and aspirations, in his or her own person. Thus, because the representative is there and they are not, he or she also acts as their *substitute*, doing for them what, for various reasons, they can't do for themselves.

   How is Jesus being portrayed as the representative in verses 5-9?

6. What does it mean to you on a daily basis that Jesus Christ has already dealt with death on our behalf and is already ruling the world as its rightful Lord?

7. What different family images do you find in Hebrews 2:10-18?

8. This passage of Hebrews depicts Jesus as the kind of older brother who, without a trace of patronizing or looking down his nose at us, comes to find us where we are, out of sheer love and goodness of heart, and to help us out of the mess.

   How does the writer of Hebrews say in verses 10-18 that Jesus rescues humanity?

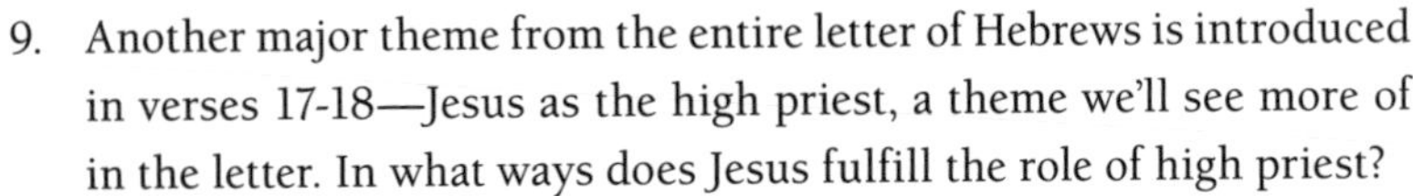

9. Another major theme from the entire letter of Hebrews is introduced in verses 17-18—Jesus as the high priest, a theme we'll see more of in the letter. In what ways does Jesus fulfill the role of high priest?

10. Looking at 2:10-18, in what ways is Jesus like a pioneer?

11. Which image from chapter 2 (such as representative, older brother, high priest, pioneer) connects with you the most and why?

12. How does this image help you to "keep your hand on the tiller" of your boat and continue to live in faith?

PRAY

Take some time to sit in silence and meditate on the image of Jesus in this passage that resonates with you. What does Jesus seem to be saying to you through this image?

NOTE ON HEBREWS 2:5-9

The phrase "son of man," which to a Jewish reader could simply mean "a typical human being," could also, to someone familiar with the book of

Daniel (7:13; 8:17) or the teaching of Jesus, mean "the Messiah"—highlighting the fact that the Messiah is now to be seen as the true, typical, authentic and representative human being. This is what Hebrews has in mind, as we can see from the last line of the quotation about God placing everything under his feet.

This passage also highlights how Jesus has already attained the status which God marked out for humans in general. Here we meet a point which we shall discover to be typical of the way Hebrews understands the Old Testament. Psalm 8, quoted in Hebrews 2:6-8, speaks of humankind in general as set in authority over the world, with "everything subject to him." But, says Hebrews, this clearly hasn't happened yet. Humans are not ruling the world in a way that brings God's order and justice to bear on the whole of creation. Everything is still in a state of semi-chaos. How then can this psalm be taken seriously?

The answer is that it *has* happened—in the case of Jesus. He is the representative of the human race. He has gone ahead of the rest of us into God's future, the future in which order and justice—saving order, healing justice—will come into the world.

Hold On Tight!

Hebrews 3

Enthusiastic beginnings, grumbling when things got tough, and then provision of enough to go on with describes more or less the wanderings of the children of Israel in the wilderness after they had come out of Egypt.

At this point in Hebrews there is something of the same narrative sequence. There has been discussion of Moses and the giving of the law, and now the writer talks about the wilderness wanderings, the forty years they all spent in the desert before, finally, they were allowed to enter the land they had been promised. During that time they went through what the writer of Psalm 95 calls "the great bitterness," the time when the people faced the test of whether or not they were going to trust God to provide for them, and they in turn put God to the test by demanding signs of his presence and care. Some even wanted to go back to Egypt and slavery thinking they'd at least be fed there.

The author of Hebrews wants to challenge readers to remember that previous generation who walked through the wilderness so they don't make the same mistakes.

OPEN

Give an example of when you were really passionate about something but over time that passion faded away. Why did the passion fade?

STUDY

1. *Read Hebrews 3.* What does the writer mean when he says in verse 1 that his readers share the call from heaven?

2. How does the writer compare and contrast Moses and Jesus in the first six verses of chapter 3?

3. Most first-century Jews, when presented with the idea of "God's house," would think at once of the temple. But Hebrews and Paul, and also some other radical Jewish groups of the period, thought of the true "house" not as a building of bricks and mortar but as a community of people. The people who make up this house are described in verse 6 as a bold, confident family. They are people who, as verse 1 says, are willing to confess their belief in Jesus.

   Why are we sometimes unwilling to state this belief to others?

4. The writer of Hebrews uses Psalm 95, which chronicles the desert wanderings, to make his point in verses 7-11. How is the experience of the Israelites wandering in the desert similar to and different from the position the early Christians were in?

5. What is the main challenge the writer of Hebrews is making to the early believers in verses 12-13?

6. Many of the people in the wilderness stopped believing that God was really with them, really leading them. They simply stopped believing in God's promises and instead believed a lie. Hebrews is concerned with something similar—whether or not Jewish Christians continue to follow and trust Jesus, or waiver and drift back to the law.

   What old ways are you tempted to return to instead of continuing to trust God in Christ?

7. In what ways can we guard against drifting away and hardening our hearts?

8. What does it mean to share the life of Christ, the Messiah (v. 14), in the context of this chapter?

9. The writer returns to the desert wanderings with three probing questions in verses 16, 17 and 18. What point is the writer trying to make with these questions?

10. Psalm 95:7-8 (quoted in Hebrews 3:7-8 and repeated in 3:15) emphasizes that people face a choice. The challenge becomes more urgent with the word *today*. Along with the other early Christians, the writer believed passionately that God had acted once for all in Jesus the Messiah, and that as a result the new day had dawned for which Israel had been waiting. They had been living in "tomorrow mode" for long enough. Now it was "today mode," the moment when suddenly it was all happening. If they would remember that, they would stay on track.

    How can a focus on the fact that Jesus is at work right now in our world, bringing God's kingdom reign to earth, help us live more faithfully as followers of Jesus?

11. The writer of the Hebrews thinks it could be all too easy to be spiritually complacent. "We're not like Gentiles." "We've got the law from Moses." "We are from the lineage of Abraham." But the author of Hebrews wants us to note that it was in fact the people of Israel

who complained, who rebelled and who were punished by God as a result. So we ought not to think we are above these sorts of problems or attitudes. We too could fall. This warning, the writer is insisting, isn't for the person standing next to you. It's for you. Yes, you.

Why might we be tempted to think we couldn't fall or drift away from Christ?

12. How can we fight spiritual complacency?

PRAY

Pray about how you are tempted to drift back to old ways of relying on other things or people besides Jesus. Ask God to keep you from complacency and to help you keep a firm, tight grip on him.

Getting Through to the Sabbath Rest

Hebrews 4:1-13

In biblical theology there is a principle of "one day in seven," or possibly "one year in seven," or some variation on these, which is built into creation from the beginning. By the time of Jesus, the parts of the Mosaic law which dealt with sabbath observance had become such a tightly drawn legal system that people were forgetting their purpose, which was to help people by giving them rest, not to add burdens to them by forbidding things like healing. Jesus had to break through all that, as we see in the Gospels, but nowhere does the New Testament deny that the principle set out in Genesis 1 remains important: a day of rest once a week, corresponding to God's day of rest at the end of creation. In Hebrews chapter 4 the idea of God's rest on the seventh day of creation comes into its own in a different way.

OPEN

Describe what a perfectly restful day would be like for you.

STUDY

1. *Read Hebrews 4:1-13.* The writer has already used Psalm 95 to talk about the "rest" which the Israelites had been promised once they reached their destination (see Hebrews 3:15). In Hebrews 4:3, the author quotes Psalm 95 again, alongside examples of other kinds of rest.

   What two other examples or types of rest are described in 4:1-10?

2. How are the three "rests" different from one another?

3. The writer of Hebrews speaks about "entering the rest" five times in verses 1-13. What prevents someone from entering the "rest"?

4. What different things can cause us to trip and fall into unbelief?

5. Verse 10 says that anyone who enters the future rest will take a rest from all their works. What kind of works does the writer have in mind?

6. All of us face the challenge to trust God rather than to trust the way we feel or the things we see in front of us. How can we keep before our eyes the promise of God's eventual, and eternal, "rest"?

7. At the time Hebrews was written, the author may not have known about other books and letters that are in our New Testament—indeed some may not even have been written at this point. Was the author then referring just to the Old Testament when he mentions "God's word" in 4:12, or something more? Explain.

8. What does God's word do as seen in verses 11-13?

9. How does this help stem the steady erosion of belief that results in unbelief?

10. What obstacles keep you from spending time prayerfully and thoughtfully with Scripture and with Jesus, the written and living Word of God, who can touch you gently and powerfully?

If we open ourselves, day by day and week by week, to the message of Scripture, its grand sweep and its small details, and allow the faithful preaching of Jesus and his achievement to enter our consciousness and soak down into our imagination and heart, then the admittedly uncomfortable work of God's word will be happening on a regular basis, showing us (as we say) where we really are, what's going on deep inside.

11. While God's word is essential to our spiritual growth and for us to know what's going on deep inside, what else is needed and helpful in our lives for this?

12. What can you do specifically this week to allow the word of God to cleanse and heal you as it is described in verses 11-13?

PRAY

Take a few minutes to read through Psalm 95. Use the words of the psalm to direct you to Jesus and guide your prayer time.

NOTE ON HEBREWS 4:12

The way the New Testament writers use the phrase "God's word" suggests that they meant more (not less) than the Old Testament. They also meant the message which Jesus announced—that God's kingdom was coming to birth in and through his work—and then the message *about* Jesus and what he'd done, essentially the same message but from a new perspective. However, since the point of what Jesus had done was precisely that it fulfilled the prophecies of the Old Testament, which is after all what this letter is mostly about, we can put the two together quite easily. "God's word" seems to mean "the ancient scriptures, and the message about how they all came true in Jesus."

The Son Becomes the Priest

Hebrews 4:14–5:14

There was a son who inherited a business from his father. It sounds like a rather grand thing—the son comes in to sit in a splendid office and enjoy the lifestyle of business lunches, golf outings, foreign trips and all the rest—but it wasn't a bit like that. The father made sure that the son learned the business from the ground up. He had to work in the workshops along with the hardened mechanics. He had to visit the suppliers to see where the raw materials came from, and find out for himself how hard it was to get them at the right price. He had to go out as a salesman into the suspicious world that wasn't convinced it wanted the product. And he had to share the work of the financial department as they spent day after day crunching the complicated numbers. Only when he had thoroughly understood every aspect of how the business worked was he even given an office of his own.

Now he would have to learn both how to lead and how to manage a workforce as well as how to represent the business in the wider world. He had to learn what it meant to be the son of his father. This story goes some way toward explaining some of the oddest phrases in the whole letter of Hebrews, which are found in chapter 5.

OPEN

Talk about a difficult lesson you've learned and how you learned it. How did this experience give you compassion for others who are in similar situations?

STUDY

1. *Read Hebrews 4:14–5:14.* How does Jesus fulfill the role of a high priest as explained in verses 4:14–5:10?

   Don't make the mistake that some Christians have made of imagining that Jesus, having become human in the incarnation, stopped being human after his death. One of the central beliefs of the early Christians, not least in this letter and those of Paul, is that Jesus remains fully and gloriously human, and that it is as a human being that he rules the world. When he represents us before the Father, he isn't looking down on us from a great height and being patronizing about those poor creatures down there who can't really do much for themselves. He can truly sympathize. He has been here. He knows exactly what it's like.

2. How do these same verses say that Jesus surpassed the function of the high priest of Israel?

3. Once Jesus was resurrected he did not simply go to a convenient resting place in some spiritual sphere where he could remain, satisfied with having accomplished his earthly work. According to verses 4:14, where is Jesus now and what is he presently doing?

4. How does it affect you knowing that Jesus can sympathize with your weaknesses (4:15)?

5. In light of this, what does it look like for believers to approach the throne of grace with confidence (4:16)?

6. There is evidence that Jews may have criticized the early Christian movement, and Jesus himself, for apparently snatching at a position which belonged, uniquely and forever, to the temple in Jerusalem. How does Hebrews 5:4-6 address this concern?

We will hear more about Melchizedek in Hebrews 6–7. For the moment we can say that he meets Abraham briefly in Genesis 14:18-20. He was a priest of the Most High God, but obviously not of Aaron's priesthood, since Aaron (along with Moses) lived hundreds of years later.

7. What scenes from Jesus' life are called to mind by 5:7-8?

8. How does this help explain what it meant for Jesus to learn to be a son?

9. Verses 11-14 of chapter 5 are a remarkable rebuke that bursts upon us, and must have burst upon its first hearers, like a sudden cold shower. The writer clearly wants to wake the readers up with a double challenge. Of what is the writer accusing the believers?

10. What is the nature of "maturity" that the writer has in mind?

11. When is it hard for you to distinguish between behavior that is right and behavior that isn't?

12. How can we grow in our ability to distinguish the two?

The word for *justice* is a tricky one wherever we meet it in the New Testament; it's often translated "righteousness," but that gives people the impression that it's all about behaving yourself in a rather self-consciously religious fashion, which certainly isn't what Hebrews (or the other early Christians) had in mind. *Justice* doesn't quite catch the full flavor, either, but at least it makes the point that the purposes of God in the gospel are focused on God's longing to put the world right, and to put people right as part of that work. The writer here longs for people to understand the entire message of God's healing, restoring, saving justice. He wants them to be able to handle this message in relation to their own lives, their communities and the wider world.

PRAY

Practice praying with confidence as you approach the throne of grace. Spend a few minutes praying and meditating on the truth that Jesus sympathizes with you.

NOTE ON HEBREWS 5:8-9

Although Jesus was God's Son, he learned the nature of obedience through what he suffered. One might have thought (the writer seems to be saying) that being God's Son would simply be a matter of sharing God's rule of the world, living in glory and bliss. Not so. The God who is the Father of Jesus is the God who made the world in the first place, and he remains deeply committed to his creation, even though it has become wayward and corrupt. Jesus must learn what it means to be his Father's obedient Son; and that will mean suffering, not because God is a sadist who simply wants to see his dear Son having a rough time of it, but because the world which God made and loves is a dark and wicked place and the Son must suffer its sorrow and pain in order to rescue it.

When it says that Jesus was made complete and perfect, it doesn't mean that he was imperfect before in the sense of being sinful. Rather he needed to attain the full stature of sonship through experiencing the pain and grief of the Father himself over his world gone wrong. He became truly and fully what in his nature he already was.

Keep Up the Good Work

Hebrews 6

Most of us have started projects and have gotten bogged down. Often we discover that there are several distinct phases to the process: the initial burst of enthusiasm and the excitement of something quite new, the gradual seeping away of energy as we reach the hard grind of carrying on, and then the days, and perhaps the weeks and even years, when we get out of bed without enthusiasm, without desire to work on the project, wishing we could have some other novelty to excite us but realizing that there is a goal ahead which will make it all worthwhile if only we can put one foot in front of another until we get there.

Living as a Christian is often like that, and the writer of Hebrews knows that his readers may be in just that situation.

OPEN

What projects have you gotten bogged down with and why?

STUDY

1. *Read Hebrews 6.* What is meant by each of the basic teachings of the Christian faith found in verses 1-2?

2. Why are these things we shouldn't have to go back over again once we've begun our Christian life?

3. Sometimes, of course, Christians never learned these things properly in the first place. What steps could you or your fellowship take to make sure people have a good grasp of why people are baptized, what precisely the resurrection is and why we should believe it, what "dead works" are and why we should repent of them?

4. Verses 4-5 offer a lavish description of what happens when you become a Christian. Expand on what is meant by each phrase.

5. The writer is saying that he is *not* going to go back over all the same ground again. Rather, he wants to go deeper, to teach them more developed and wide-ranging truths. How does the metaphor about the land in verses 7-8 illustrate his reasons for this?

6. Verse 6 raises an interesting question, which the writer doesn't pursue here: is it possible first to become a genuine Christian and then to lose everything after all? To this question Paul, in Romans 5–8, gives the emphatic answer "No!" In Hebrews the writer quickly goes on to say that he doesn't think his readers come into the category he's describing (6:9), but he chooses not to unpack this wider theological question.

   The normal way of holding what he says together with what Paul says is that the people described in verses 4 and 5 are those who have become church members, and have felt the power of the gospel and the life that results from it through sharing the common life of Christian fellowship but who have never really made it their own, deep down inside.

   The question the writer poses for all of us is: What might entice us or some within our Christian fellowship to turn our backs on the faith and join in the general tendency to sneer at the gospel and the church?

7. In 6:10-12 the writer encourages his readers to continue strong in their active love for others. How would you compare your level of energy and enthusiasm for acts of love and service now, compared to when you first became a Christian? Explain.

8. What specific act of love or service could you engage in this week?

9. In Hebrews 6:1 the author talks about the foundation in the Christian life of repentance from dead works and of faith toward God. Now in 6:9-12 he encourages energetic participation in that life and warns against laziness. How can we balance the truths of God's faithfulness and our own human effort in daily life as believers?

10. The "two unchangeable things" mentioned in 6:18 are God's promise to Abraham and the oath he swore by himself that he would keep the promise (6:13-14, 17). God can't lie in either of them. This is why the promise can and must be regarded as firm and secure; and this, in turn, explains what lies underneath the exhortations in the previous passage to hold on to hope and to persevere in faith.

    The rest of the chapter explores the life of Abraham, the classic biblical example of faithful patience. How does the life of Abraham in verses 13-20 encourage the believers?

11. "Behind the curtain" (6:19) refers to the great moment, once a year, when the high priest goes into the temple, behind the last curtain, into the innermost sanctuary of the temple, into the holy of holies. There, on what Jews believed was the holiest spot on earth, the high priest would make atonement for the people. Jesus, through his death, resurrection and ascension, went into the very presence of the loving Father, and we are attached to him as though by a great cable. He is there, in the very presence of God, like an anchor. As long as we don't let go of the cable, we are anchored to the presence of God.

    How is Jesus in this way our anchor in the storms of life?

12. Christian faith isn't optimism, a vague sense that things will probably turn out right. Christian faith is trusting—and going on trusting through thick and thin—in the God who made unbreakable promises and will certainly keep them.

    Where in your life do you need to keep on trusting God's promises?

PRAY

Pray in silence for a few moments and meditate on God's promises. Ask God to speak his promises to you and then listen for his voice.

NOTE ON HEBREWS 6:9-12

Ever since the Reformation in the sixteenth century, many Christians have been taught, quite rightly, that nothing we can do can earn God's favor. Grace remains grace; God loves us because he loves us, not because we manage to do a few things to impress him, or to notch up a few points on some heavenly scorecard. But at the same time the whole New Testament insists that what Christians *do* matters a great deal.

Yes, there are undoubtedly times when, like the children of Israel beside the Red Sea, we need the message that says, "The Lord will fight for you; all you need to do is to be still" (Exodus 14:14). But these are the exceptional moments, the particular situations, often in times of emergency, when there is nothing we can or should do, and we must trust that God will do it all. But the normal Christian life is one of energy, enthusiasm, faithful effort and patient hard work.

When Paul tells the Philippians to "work out their own salvation with fear and trembling," he at once adds, "because God is at work in you" (Philippians 2:12-13). The energy to do all that we are called to do comes itself from God working within us in the power of the Holy Spirit.

7

The Permanent Priesthood of Jesus

Hebrews 7

Sometimes when you are working on a particular subject or studying a topic, you will come across something that you do not understand or know. Maybe it is a name or a place. So, you might go to the relevant dictionary or reference materials and look it up. Suddenly, from a small question about a single person or topic, a whole new area of thought, history or culture opens up in front of you. You can get a view of the wide sweep of the ancient world, and when you come back to the original task, you carry with you all the information about that one person or topic. What started off as a small puzzle in the middle of your work has turned into a lighthouse sending rays of light flashing over the rest of the subject.

That is the effect that Hebrews wants to create with the discussion of Melchizedek in chapter 7. This passage takes us into what seems at first sight a technical, almost bizarre discussion of a short reference in Genesis, but leads us to a place where the rays of light are flashing over the entire topic.

OPEN

Talk about a time when you discovered a "better" way to do something. Perhaps it was a new way to build something, a better way to organize or a more compassionate approach to a problem. How did you feel about this discovery?

STUDY

1. *Read Hebrews 7.* The writer of Hebrews has quoted Psalm 110:4, tantalizingly, three times already (5:6, 10 and 6:20). He, like many early Christians, has realized that Jesus has been appointed by God to a position at his right hand, waiting for his kingdom to be complete (Psalm 110:1). According to the psalm, the Messiah, the one to whom all things are put into subjection, is appointed by God as a priest forever, according to the order of Melchizedek. To find out what the psalmist meant, the writer of Hebrews, in 7:1-10, reviews some key points from Genesis 14, the only other passage in the whole Bible where Melchizedek is mentioned.

   What do we learn about Melchizedek from Hebrews 7:1-10?

2. Levi, one of the twelve sons of Jacob and a great-grandson of Abraham, founded the priestly tribe of Israel. How does 7:4-10 make the case that Melchizedek's priesthood is superior to Levi's?

Some people have thought that the writer of Hebrews, finding in the text no mention of Melchizedek's parents or ancestors (or his birth or death), has concluded that Melchizedek didn't have any. This is unnecessary and unlikely. The point is that no mention is made of where he got his priesthood—in particular, there is no mention that he inherited it through his family as priests of Levi did. It is as though, the writer says, Melchizedek is just there—a permanent fixture.

3. How are Melchizedek and Jesus similar as seen in these verses?

4. A first-century Jew would have found it striking that one person could be both king and priest since there was a clear division between those two roles in the history of Israel. Discovering more about Melchizedek, and so discovering what Psalm 110 meant when talking of the Messiah as a priest as well as a king, is a way to increase and deepen our sense of trust and assurance as we lean the full weight of our future hope on Jesus and on him alone.

   In what different ways or areas of your life do you gain assurance knowing that Jesus is king but is also our high priest?

5. What further contrasts are outlined in verses 11-19 between Jesus' priesthood and the priesthood of Levi and his descendant Aaron?

6. The word often translated as "perfection" in 7:11 and 19 can also be translated as "completeness." It is when everything has been put into place for the final great purpose to be achieved. What is this great purpose (verses 11-19)?

7. The word *better* (or at least the Greek word which it here translates) occurs more times in Hebrews than in the whole of the rest of the New Testament put together. The writer is constantly contrasting—not something bad with something good, but something good with something better. He is not saying that the ancient Israelite system was a bad thing, with its temple, its law and its priesthood of Levi. What he is saying is that something new has arrived in and through Jesus which is *even better* than what went before.

   What was the purpose of the old religious system?

8. What examples have you seen of God, through the new system in Jesus, bringing this world to completion?

9. In chapters 4 and 5, we noted one half of the meaning of Jesus' high priesthood. He is a truly human being, tempted in every respect just as we are. Now, in verses 20-28, we discover the other half of the picture.

What does Jesus' superiority to other priests mean for our salvation?

10. Some Christians face the danger of forgetting just how central and vital Jesus himself was and is to every aspect of Christian faith. How do we tend to forget the centrality of Jesus?

11. This chapter of Hebrews should bring us to a place of gratitude and hope after we truly grasp the work of Jesus in his death and resurrection. In what ways can you express your gratitude to Jesus this week?

PRAY

Use short expressions of praise and gratitude for all that Jesus is and for all that he has accomplished for the world and for you individually.

The Promise of a New Covenant

Hebrews 8

Years ago there was a toy which simulated the game of football. It was a table-top version that was played with plastic figures an inch or two high. It was played by flicking the figures with a finger, so that they would hit the ball and try to get it into the opponent's goal in the usual way. You could become quite good at the game, particularly if you were small and have active little fingers. But if you ever saw an actual football match you would never mistake the table-top variety for the real thing.

Supposing, however, that the game was given to a family who had not only never seen a real football match but who didn't know that such a thing existed. They might imagine that table-top football was the reality; this was all there was. They wouldn't know that it was a copy of the real thing, and gained most of its meaning, and its appeal for most people, because it was reminding them of the true, grown-up version.

Something like this, only more so, lies at the heart of the contrast Hebrews now draws in chapter 8 and will go on drawing.

OPEN

Why are people sometimes satisfied with a copy or a lower-quality product rather than the real thing?

STUDY

1. *Read Hebrews 8.* How does the writer describe the present and continuing role of Jesus in verses 1-6?

2. What do you think and feel in response to this?

3. In the Bible heaven is not simply a "spiritual," in the sense of nonphysical, dimension. It is God's space, God's realm, which interlocks with our realm in all sorts of ways. The Israelites believed that the temple in Jerusalem was the place above all where heaven and earth met, quite literally. When you went into the temple, especially when you went into the holy of holies in the middle of it, you were actually going into heaven itself.

   What evidence does the writer of Hebrews provide that the tabernacle was a copy of the real thing (Hebrews 8:5 and Exodus 25:40)?

4. This passage draws together for the last time the contrast between Jesus and the priesthood before him. How do verses 1-6 outline this final contrast?

5. The readers of Hebrews are encouraged not to cling to the copy. This must have presented a particular challenge to those Jewish Christians who all their lives had looked to the Jerusalem temple as the focus of devotion, the place of pilgrimage, the very house of God, and to the priests who served there.

   How do you see people today choosing to focus on a "copy" instead of on the reality of Jesus?

6. In verses 7-13, we are faced with the longest single biblical quotation so far in a letter which has more than its fair share. In what particular ways does the writer use this text from Jeremiah 31:31-34 to continue the theme of something "better"?

7. What reasons do these verses give for the necessity of a new covenant?

8. The promises God made to Abraham and his family, and the require-

ments that were laid on them as a result, came to be seen in terms either of the agreement that a king would make with a subject people, or sometimes of the marriage bond between husband and wife. One regular way of describing this relationship was "covenant," which can thus include both promises and law. The original covenant with Abraham was renewed with Moses at Mount Sinai with the giving of the Law. Jeremiah 31 promised that after the punishment of exile God would make a new covenant with his people, forgiving them and binding them to him more intimately.

Do you find that external constraints (like the law) or internal changes (like of mind and heart) better help you do what's right? Why?

9. What does verse 12 highlight about the new covenant?

10. What does it mean to you that God forgets your sins?

11. How would using the text from Jeremiah have strengthened the writer's argument for the importance of holding on to Jesus instead of going back to the apparent safety of Judaism?

12. How does it help you want to hold on to Jesus?

PRAY

Read several times the passage from Jeremiah 31 used in this chapter of Hebrews. Use the text as a guide for your prayers.

The Sacrifice of the Messiah

Hebrews 9

When a large city is in the midst of a complicated construction project, alternative arrangements have to be made in order to allow the daily traffic to get through while the project is in process. Ordinary life has to go on and people still have to get to work. So, in addition to the eventual plan—the great design in the mind of the planners and somewhere no doubt in a model under a glass case in City Hall—there have to exist all sorts of preparatory and intermediate plans. While the work is going on, the city needs to build extra temporary roads going this way and that, which they will then demolish when the final stage is complete. No doubt this work, too, subdivides into several stages.

The main point to which Hebrews now comes, in one sense, is that God has all along had a master plan for how the world would be put right. Yet, for reasons that people may only be dimly aware of, this cannot be done all at once. Temporary arrangements have to be made to keep things flowing, to regulate ongoing human life, until the appointed time.

OPEN

Why do we sometimes favor the old over the new?

STUDY

1. *Read Hebrews 9:1-14.* Describe the structures and functions of the tabernacle that the writer recounts in verses 1-10.

2. Having brought up the new covenant of Jeremiah 31 in the last chapter, the writer of Hebrews is now reminding his readers of some key aspects of the old covenant. How does the double structure of the tabernacle, which was reflected in the temple in Jerusalem, serve as a picture or parable of the two "ages," the two periods of time, within the long purposes of God?

3. What do we learn about the sacrificial system from verses 11-14?

4. In what ways is the new covenant "better" or more superior to the former things in verses 11-14?

5. The God whom Israel has always worshiped but whose saving plan was still in the preliminary stage had revealed once and for all through Jesus' death and resurrection the way into his presence, the way by which his people could serve him gladly and joyfully without the slightest shadow or stain on their consciences (9:14). Many Christian people, still today, forget that they are called to that kind of joyful service, free from any motivation caused by guilt or fear.

   Why do you suppose that such a liberating and healing message would be so hard to believe and remember?

6. *Read Hebrews 9:15-28.* In what ways, according to the writer of Hebrews, does the way a will works help us understand how a covenant works?

7. The idea of no pardon without bloodshed can seem primitive or barbaric. Yet our modern society tolerates, even fosters, so many things that previous generations, and other civilizations today, would consider barbaric.

   The point of sacrifice within the Old Testament system was a combination of at least three things: (1) humans offering to God something which represented their own true selves, (2) the outpouring of life to signify dealing with sin, and (3) the effects of both of these in the cleansing or purifying of the worshiper. Now we go a stage further, even more mysteriously, into the heart of the second of these. Somehow, it seems, the blood of the sacrificial animals was pointing forward to a deeper truth still: that at the heart of the sacrificial system there lies the self-giving love of God himself.

How does Jesus' sacrifice reveal God's love to us?

8. Continuing his theme of what is now "better," what more does the writer of Hebrews have to say in verses 23-28 about why Jesus' sacrifice is superior to those of the old covenant?

The writer of Hebrews explains that the heavenly sanctuary, like the earthly one, needed purifying, albeit in a superior fashion. This is bound to seem puzzling at first glance. Why should the heavenly sanctuary need to be purified? What could have been wrong with it? The answer, it seems, is that there wasn't anything wrong with the heavenly sanctuary itself, but that it needed to be made ready for the arrival of people with whom there had been a very great deal wrong—namely, sinful human beings. We can't come into the presence of a holy God that way, but we were nonetheless promised that somehow we would. Jesus, then, purifies the heavenly sanctuary itself so that when other human beings are welcomed into it they will find, as the Israelites found in the earthly sanctuary, that everything there too bears the mark of God's self-giving love.

9. The word in 9:26 that is translated as the "end" or "close" of the ages literally refers to something which joins on to something else, and so makes one or both of them complete. How do verses 26-28 tell us Christ's work is ultimately fulfilled?

10. If you thought you needed to marry your spouse every year, every month or every week in order to be married, it would mean you

hadn't really understood what the wedding ceremony was about in the first place. What does it tell us about Christ's sacrifice that it was something that only happened once for all?

11. What difference does this hope we have in Christ make to you now?

12. How does the complete sacrifice of Jesus strengthen your faith?

PRAY

Look back over this chapter and ponder what Christ has done for us. Let this guide your praise, worship and thanksgiving.

NOTE ON HEBREWS 9:24

Verse 24 speaks, literally, of Jesus appearing "before God's face." This was a powerful idea in Jewish tradition: seeing God's face was such a devastatingly awesome experience that even the angels which flanked God's presence had to veil their faces (Isaiah 6:2). Now Jesus has gone in to see the Father's face, and has done so on our behalf, against the day when we will share that glorious vision and do so unafraid, because of the blood which has purified us through and through.

Come to Worship

Hebrews 10

The shopping was all done, and all the food and drink had been brought back into the house. All the telephone calls had been made. The house was cleaned, straightened and decorated. The food was prepared. Then, at last, the people began to arrive. Friends, neighbors and family all turned up. It was a party!

Hebrews has now, if it can be put this way, done the shopping, made the telephone calls and cleaned the house. At last the invitation goes out: come to the party! Chapter 10 is the invitation to a party that the writer of Hebrews has been preparing. The writer has been collecting key passages from Scripture, calling up ideas and images both familiar and unfamiliar, shaping and polishing the exposition. It leads to chapter 10: come to worship!

OPEN

Are you ever reluctant to join others in worship? Why or why not?

STUDY

1. *Read Hebrews 10:1-18.* The problem with the sacrifices and offerings of the old covenant, says Hebrews, wasn't that they were physical, "earthly" in that sense. After all, Jesus' own sacrifice was just as earthly and physical as the animal sacrifices in the temple. What was the problem instead (vv. 1-4)?

2. How does the use of Psalm 40 in verses 5-10 point to something new and better?

3. For much of the world, and for much of history, the act of sitting down (v. 12) meant that you had finished your work. Most people stood to work and sat down to rest. That is the contrast being made between the work of the priests in the old covenant who stood to make sacrifices in the temple and the work of Jesus in the new covenant who sat down at the right hand of God (vv. 11-18).

   How is the truth that Jesus has fully completed the purposes of God a comfort to the believers Hebrews is addressing?

   We have a sense, here in chapter 10, of several strands of thought in the letter as a whole being drawn together and fitting into the eventual big picture the writer has all along been holding in his mind. The picture of Jesus as the Messiah, the truly human being, the great high priest after the order of Melchizedek, the one who has offered the perfect sacrifice through which the sin-forgiving new covenant has been established at last—all these belong together. The argument of the letter is about Jesus at every point. The result of discovering, with the help of the Old Testament, what Jesus has achieved is to realize that he has fulfilled God's purposes as set out in scripture, so that the only wise place to be is with him, rather than with those who cling to the signposts instead of the reality.

4. *Read Hebrews 10:19-39.* What, as seen in 10:22-23, should characterize us as we draw near to God in worship?

5. How are we dependent on God and his work for each of these?

6. What can we gain from joining others in worship (vv. 24-25)?

The danger of people thinking they could be Christians all by themselves was, it seems, present in the early church just as today. This may not have been due to people failing to realize what a corporate thing Christianity was and is, nor because they were lazy or didn't like the other Christians in their locality. Rather it could very well be that when there is a threat of persecution (see 10:32-34), it's much easier to escape notice if you avoid meeting together with other worshipers. Much safer just not to turn up. There's no place for that, declares Hebrews.

7. Which part of Hebrews 10:19-25 is most difficult for you to embrace in your own life and why?

8. We find some rather severe warnings in 10:26-31. Put into your own words the kind of person the author is referring to when he talks about those who "sin deliberately and knowingly" (v. 26) and "trample the son of God underfoot" (v. 29)?

9. Many of us are so unused to thinking of God's judgment at all that we bend over backwards to downplay warnings like this one. What difference would it make in our thinking about God and how he relates to humans if God didn't judge people who have systematically ordered their lives so as to become an embodiment of injustice and malice?

10. In 10:26-39 we get the clearest indication of the situation of the believers to whom this letter is addressed and the persecution they faced. Hebrews 10:26-31 is a warning about those who have come close to Christian faith, perhaps sharing in the life of Christian worship, and then turn around and publicly deny it all.

    Persecution or other troubles have tempted some, and can tempt us, to declare that Christ and the whole Christian life are worthless. What can help us resist such temptation?

11. What kinds of difficulties were the original readers of Hebrews facing (vv. 32-39)?

12. How is Habakkuk 2:3-4 (quoted in Hebrews 10:37-38) used to help the believers face their circumstances?

13. How do these words help you?

PRAY

The writer of Hebrews calls the believers to come and worship in complete assurance of faith. Spend several minutes worshiping God. Use Psalm 40 or some worship music to help you focus on praise and thanksgiving.

NOTE ON HEBREWS 10:1

Many readers have wondered if perhaps the writer is using ideas that had been made famous by the philosopher Plato. In particular, the idea of something being a "shadow" rather than a "real form" sounds like his well-known picture of the Cave, in which people who haven't yet been enlightened think they're looking at reality but are in fact only looking at shadows cast by objects that remain out of sight.

This appearance, though, is superficial. The contrast the writer is making is not, like Plato, the contrast between physical objects and nonphysical ideas, or "forms." As verse 1 insists, it is the contrast between the *present* and the *future* realities. Jesus, who has gone ahead of us into God's future reality, will reappear when that future reality bursts into the present for the whole world.

NOTE ON HEBREWS 10:26-31

The question of who precisely such warnings are aimed at is one which bothered the early church from the second and third century onward, and ought still to concern us today. Some saw it as referring to anyone who, at any point after baptism, committed any serious sin. That's why, in the third and fourth centuries in particular, many prominent church attenders put off baptism until the last possible moment—either before death, or, if they were called to ministry, before ordination! They were frightened lest, by subsequent sinning of whatever kind, they might forfeit their entire salvation. Others read it more in light of what happened when persecution arouse. Such passages as this, it was thought, applied principally to people who, under threat of physical violence or death, were prepared to blaspheme against Jesus and revile him.

Many in our day tend to react in the opposite way. We don't want to imagine God being angry with anyone. We are probably as greatly deceived as were those in earlier centuries who treated these passages as a warning not so much against sinning as against baptism.

It is absolutely basic to both Judaism and Christianity that there will come a time when the living God will bring his just and wise rule to bear fully and finally on the world. On that day those who willfully stand out against his rule, live a life which scorns the standards which emerge in creation itself and in God's good intention for it, and spurn all attempts at reformation or renewal, will face a punishment of destruction. We who have got as far at least as reading Hebrews, and trying to see what it might mean for us, should be all the more eager that there will never come a time when we might turn our backs wholesale on God in this way.

11

What Faith Really Means

Hebrews 11

Our little group of climbers walked through the mist not realizing that anyone else was there. We kept moving, knowing that we would face some difficult climbing, including a rocky crag, later on. When we reached a small plateau, the sky cleared and we noticed that there was another large group of climbers ahead of us. They must have started several hours earlier and appeared to have negotiated the crag successfully. I took out a set of binoculars to see the group ahead of us a little more clearly. There was a sparkle of light from where the climbers were. Sure enough: ice axes. Now we knew just what we would be facing and just what was needed to cope with it—and that it was possible to make it.

Hebrews has now reached a plateau from which there is an excellent view of those who have gone on before. Looking at them, the readers can discover for themselves what is up ahead, what they will need to cope with it, and the fact that when they get there themselves there will be a great welcome.

OPEN

Who are your spiritual heroes, strong believers who have faced difficult things faithfully? What about them is so encouraging to you?

STUDY

1. *Read Hebrews 11:1-22.* Explain how faith and hope are linked, as described in Hebrews 11:1?

2. What do we learn about faith through Abel and Enoch in 11:4-6?

3. Hebrews wants its readers to learn that faith is not a general religious attitude to life. It is not simply believing difficult or impossible things for the sake of it, as though simple credulity was itself a virtue. So what do we learn about what faith really is from Noah, Abraham and Sarah in 11:7-12?

4. Hebrews mentions a city for the first time in verse 10. This emerges as a main theme in the last chapters of Hebrews. In light of God's promises to Abraham and the kind of life he led, what is meant by the city mentioned here?

5. How does this city relate to the topic of faith that has been under discussion?

Faith, it now emerges, is not only the assurance of unseen realities, and the backbone of hope, as in verse 1; it is not only the belief that God exists and rewards those who seek him, as in verse 6; it is also the badge that marks people out as members already of God's true people. Precisely because this faith is also hope, their membership, and their inheriting of God's promises, does not yet appear in public. Faith enables this standing, this "righteousness," to be affirmed in the present time. Hebrews thus agrees more or less exactly with what Paul means by "justification by faith," one of the New Testament's most powerful, encouraging and comforting doctrines.

6. In 11:13-16 the writer says God wasn't ashamed to be called the God of the people mentioned so far in chapter 11. Why might some think God would be ashamed to be called "their God"?

7. Hebrews 11:17-19 recalls the story of Abraham and Isaac (from Genesis 22) and 11:20-22 mentions Isaac and Joseph (from Genesis 27 and 48–50). What further themes about faith, obedience and hope are developed in these stories?

8. *Read Hebrews 11:23-40.* What encouragement do you draw from the example of Moses in verses 23-31?

9. In verses 32-40, there is a long catalog of people who faced terrifying situations, and in many cases were persecuted to within an inch

of their lives if not beyond. Why, if God was at work in the lives of Gideon, Barak, Samson, and those who were stoned and so on—why, if God was calling them and was with them, did they have to go through all that?

10. What does the writer mean by saying in 11:38 that the world didn't deserve them?

11. The writer of Hebrews wanted his readers to think through the sort of faith their forebears had had, and see how the long purposes of God, cherished and believed in the face of impossibilities, dangers and even death itself, are finally fulfilled in the events concerning Jesus, and the new life they have as a result.

    Considering the heroes of faith in this chapter, what might it mean, specifically, to live by faith in God's future world while the society all around is living as though the present world is all there is or all there will be?

12. Describe one way that you can live by faith in this coming week and trust that God will give you strength to live this way.

PRAY

Pray for strength and courage to live by faith as defined and illustrated in Hebrews 11. Pray about the specific ways you could live by faith in the situation you mentioned in the last question. Pray for boldness, strength and trust in that circumstance.

NOTE ON HEBREWS 11:10 AND 16

As mentioned, the writer introduces the image of the city in Hebrews 11:10 and 16, which he develops further in later chapters. The focal point of the promise in chapter 11 is about the land. In Hebrews 12:12 it is the heavenly Jerusalem. In 13:14 it is the future city, contrasted with any city to which one might give allegiance here on earth, and perhaps particularly the earthly Jerusalem itself. What does the writer have in mind?

Jerusalem was of course the holy city, David's ancient capital. But in Jewish writings roughly contemporary with the New Testament, there were pointers to a deeper reality, to the belief that God had established a "true" or heavenly Jerusalem, waiting for the day when heaven and earth would be remade. This is picked up in the great description of the new Jerusalem in Revelation 21–22.

Looking to Jesus

Hebrews 12

If you've ever run in a race, you may find the opening verses of chapter 12 bringing back memories. I remember one cross-country race in which, mile after mile, I was almost alone, with only the few other runners around me for company. But then, when we came round the last turn and into the final few hundred yards of the course, that all changed. Crowds of people were cheering, waving flags, holding signs, clapping and shouting words of encouragement. The noise reached a great roar as we crossed the finishing line itself.

Several aspects of this climactic chapter in Hebrews draw on the same image of the Christian pilgrimage as a long-distance race. Those who have gone before us, from Abel and Abraham right through to the unnamed heroes and heroines noted at the end of chapter 11, haven't simply disappeared. They are there at the finishing line, cheering us on, surrounding us with encouragement and enthusiasm, willing us to do what they did and finish the race in fine style.

OPEN

Think of a competition you were involved in, whether athletic or otherwise. What helped you finish or what caused you to drop out? Explain.

STUDY

1. *Read Hebrews 12.* In verses 1-2, the writer uses athletic imagery. Describe the things he mentions that would help someone run a foot-race with efficiency and success.

2. How do each of these parallel or relate to the Christian life?

3. How would verses 2-3 about Jesus' experience and work have served as an encouragement for the early believers in their context?

4. According to verses 4-11, how is discipline from God evidence that we are his beloved children?

The truth of verse 11 is offered so that we can cling to it when things are difficult. There is much sorrow in an ordinary human life; sorrow which was, of course, shared by the Man of Sorrows as he identified completely with us, a point Hebrews has already made forcefully (5:7-10). Again and again, when we find ourselves thwarted or disappointed, opposed or vilified, or even subject to physical abuse and violence, we may in faith be able to hear the gentle and wise voice of the Father, urging us to follow him more closely, to trust him more fully, to love him more deeply.

5. How have you seen this to be true in your own life or the lives of others?

6. Hebrews 12:12-17 recalls the story told in Genesis 25–27 about Isaac's twin sons, Jacob (the younger) and Esau (the older). Esau had been out hunting in the countryside and when he came back home Jacob was cooking a meal. Esau was famished with hunger; Jacob refused to give him food unless he gave him the rights of the firstborn son, in other words, the principal share of the inheritance from their father Isaac. Esau, it seems, happily swore away his birthright in exchange for the food—something he bitterly regretted later. Jacob doesn't exactly come out of the story with his hands clean, but the focus here is on the folly of Esau.

   In addition to warning against the immoral or worldly-minded decisions of Esau, verses 12-17 also strongly caution against coasting as a Christian, not seeking spiritual healing, continuing to live in conflict and allowing bitterness to take root in our relationships.

   Which of these do you see as most critical to avoid and why?

7. Hebrews 12:18-21 refers to Mount Sinai and Exodus 19 where the people were warned not to touch the mountain and where Moses received the Ten Commandments and the warnings the people were given during that episode. The contrast between Mount Sinai and Mount Zion (or Sion as it is sometimes spelled) in verses 18-24 is not suggesting that holiness doesn't matter any more. How instead are the two mountains contrasted?

8. In verses 18-24 the writer of Hebrews picks up the theme (begun in Hebrews 11:10) of the new Jerusalem, the new city we anticipate and hope for. While there is still much to look forward to, in what senses does the writer suggest here that we have already arrived at this heavenly city?

The Old Testament story which began with Abraham, Moses and Mount Sinai reached its glorious conclusion with the entry into the Promised Land, the establishment of the monarch and finally the building of the temple on Mount Zion. Now, Hebrews is saying, take that story as a whole, and see it as the equivalent of Mount Sinai; it is the complete story of the old covenant. You need to come into the Promised Land (Hebrews 3–4); you need to benefit from the ministry of the true high priest (Hebrews 5–7); you need to realize that you are within the new covenant, where the ultimate sacrifice has already been made, through which you can approach the very presence of God himself (Hebrews 8–10).

9. How does 12:25-29 bring us back full circle to what the writer began with in Hebrews 2:1-4?

10. The central theme that the writer wants to leave with the readers before the concluding instructions of chapter 13 is a true picture of God and of people in relation to God. What is that picture?

11. Verses 28 tells us our response should be one of gratitude and worship. Why are these proper responses to the kind of God pictured by the writer?

12. How can and should we express these this week?

PRAY

Sit in silence and meditate on the character of God and what he has done in your own life. Speak short sentences of praise as offerings and sacrifices.

NOTE ON HEBREWS 12:15-17

The warning here takes its place alongside those in 6:4-8 and 10:26-31: a warning that to turn back to the ways of the world after tasting at least the fringe benefits of the new life may result in a fixed and unalterable condition of the heart and mind. According to 6:4, it is impossible to restore such people to repentance; this seems to be what 12:17 is saying as well. We should be cautious about suggesting that someone who genuinely wants to repent of their sin and get right with God will ever be refused; but we should be equally cautious about imagining that someone who enjoys Christian fellowship but then plays fast and loose with the consequent moral responsibilities will be able to come back in whenever and however they feel like it. Decisions and actions have consequences.

NOTE ON HEBREWS 12:25-29

The really worrying thing in this passage is that the quaking earth at Sinai is not replaced with some calm, flat transition to God's new covenant and new world, but with something even more tumultuous—not only an earthquake but also, so to speak, a heavenquake. As Revelation 21 insists, for there to be new heavens and a new earth, the present heavens, as well as the present earth, must undergo their own radical change, almost like a death and new birth.

Hebrews uses a different image for this same transition, but the end result is the same. Heaven and earth alike must be "shaken" in such a way that everything transient, temporary, secondary and second-rate may fall away. Then that which is of the new creation, based on Jesus himself and his resurrection, will shine out the more brightly. The new creation will, of course, include all those who belong to the new covenant and, through them, the new world which God had always promised.

13

The God of Peace Be with You

Hebrews 13

There is a diary of a clergyman who had been a prisoner of war during 1940 to 1945 in a German prison. I found it a fascinating account of daily life, but frustrating to read, because the Germans would not let people write things in diaries which might be subversive. The result is that quite a few references to current events in the diary were written in a sort of code. The writer would refer obliquely to events or hint at things he knew about the progress of the war, which other prisoners would have picked up at once, but which other readers, without help, could not fathom.

Chapter 13 of Hebrews is not as oblique as all that, but to understand it we need to put ourselves in the situation it refers to. It is quite possible, then, that both writer and readers knew that there was an increasingly tense situation brewing up for followers of Jesus in and around Jerusalem itself. Whether or not this refers to the time when the Jews in Palestine were in revolt against Rome, it is impossible to tell. But certainly that great war (A.D. 66-70), which ended in the destruction of Jerusalem and the temple, would fit very well.

OPEN

As you think about your past, present and future, which of the three weighs on you more than the others or which gives you more cause for hope? Explain.

STUDY

1. *Read Hebrews 13.* At the end of the first section (vv. 1-8) the writer makes a grand statement about Jesus. In looking over the whole letter to the Hebrews, what has it revealed about Jesus in each of these ways—yesterday and today and forever?

2. How does getting our picture right about Jesus in these ways affect the way we engage the practical-life issues raised in 13:1-7?

3. How does 13:1 act as a unifying theme for all the practical matters found in 13:2-7?

4. Look at the topics mentioned in verses 1-7: hospitality, those in prison, marriage, money and Christian leaders. What's a practical way you could follow up in one of these areas this week?

5. What similarities between Jesus and the sacrificial animals of the sin offering does the author highlight in verses 10-14?

6. Once again in 10:14 the writer mentions the future city we have. How does this help us hold lightly to the material goods, position, prestige, accomplishments, family or the other sources of self-worth we get in this world?

7. The writer may have been speaking about the tabernacle in the wilderness during Moses' day rather than the Jerusalem temple to avoid mentioning too directly the central institution of Judaism which Jesus declared to be under God's judgment and whose sacrificial system he replaced. Or it may be that the temple had already been destroyed by the Romans. In either case, the point is that the followers of Jesus should be happy to leave the city and its temple even though their fellow Jews may regard them as traitors.

   With the old sacrificial system defunct, what does 13:15-16 say about the different ways we can bring a continual sacrifice of praise to God?

8. The present mood, particularly in Western society, in which all authority seems suspect, and all power is assumed to corrupt people, gives an extra excuse to people who want to do their own thing rather than submit in any way to someone else. And yet, verses 17-25 suggest there are appropriate structures of responsibility within God's church.

How is the relationship between leaders in the church and the rest of God's people described in these verses?

9. What truths are learned in verses 17-25 about the work of the kingdom?

10. The crowning glory of this final passage is the great blessing in verses 20-21, which is still used regularly in many churches, especially in the Easter season. How do these verses bring Hebrews to a culmination?

11. As you think back over the themes of Hebrews, what truths or challenges have been the most significant for you?

12. How has your life of faith been changed by your journey through this letter?

PRAY

Pray the words of 13:20-21 several times. Pray them as a blessing over family, friends and fellow Christians.

Guidelines for Leaders

My grace is sufficient for you.
(2 Corinthians 12:9)

If leading a small group is something new for you, don't worry. These sessions are designed to flow naturally and be led easily. You may even find that the studies seem to lead themselves!

This study guide is flexible. You can use it with a variety of groups—students, professionals, coworkers, friends, neighborhood or church groups. Each study takes forty-five to sixty minutes in a group setting.

You don't need to be an expert on the Bible or a trained teacher to lead a small group. These guides are designed to facilitate a group's discussion, not a leader's presentation. Guiding group members to discover together what the Bible has to say and to listen together for God's guidance will help them remember much more than a lecture would.

There are some important facts to know about group dynamics and encouraging discussion. The suggestions listed below should equip you to effectively and enjoyably fulfill your role as leader.

PREPARING FOR THE STUDY

1. Ask God to help you understand and apply the passage in your own life. Unless this happens, you will not be prepared to lead others. Pray too for the various members of the group. Ask God to open

your hearts to the message of his Word and motivate you to action.

2. Read the introduction to the entire guide to get an overview of the topics that will be explored.

3. As you begin each study, read and reread the assigned Bible passage to familiarize yourself with it. This study guide is based on the For Everyone series on the New Testament (published by SPCK and Westminster John Knox). It will help you and the group if you have on hand a copy of the companion volume from the For Everyone series both for the translation of the passage found there and for further insight into the passage.

4. Carefully work through each question in the study. Spend time in meditation and reflection as you consider how to respond.

5. Write your thoughts and responses in the space provided in the study guide. This will help you to express your understanding of the passage clearly.

6. It may help to have a Bible dictionary handy. Use it to look up any unfamiliar words, names or places. The glossary at the end of each New Testament for Everyone commentary may likewise be helpful for keeping discussion moving.

7. Reflect seriously on how you need to apply the Scripture to your life. Remember that the group members will follow your lead in responding to the studies. They will not go any deeper than you do.

LEADING THE STUDY

1. At the beginning of your first time together, explain that these studies are meant to be discussions, not lectures. Encourage the members of the group to participate. However, do not put pressure on those who may be hesitant to speak—especially during the first few sessions.

2. Be sure that everyone in your group has a study guide. Encourage the group to prepare beforehand for each discussion by reading the

introduction to the guide and by working through the questions in each study.

3. Begin each study on time. Open with prayer, asking God to help the group to understand and apply the passage.

4. Have a group member read aloud the introduction at the beginning of the discussion.

5. Discuss the "Open" question before the Bible passage is read. The "Open" question introduces the theme of the study and helps group members to begin to open up, and can reveal where our thoughts and feelings need to be transformed by Scripture. Reading the passage first will tend to color the honest reactions people would otherwise give—because they are, of course, supposed to think the way the Bible does. Encourage as many members as possible to respond to the "Open" question, and be ready to get the discussion going with your own response.

6. Have a group member read aloud the passage to be studied as indicated in the guide.

7. The study questions are designed to be read aloud just as they are written. You may, however, prefer to express them in your own words.

   There may be times when it is appropriate to deviate from the study guide. For example, a question may have already been answered. If so, move on to the next question. Or someone may raise an important question not covered in the guide. Take time to discuss it, but try to keep the group from going off on tangents.

8. Avoid answering your own questions. An eager group quickly becomes passive and silent if members think the leader will do most of the talking. If necessary repeat or rephrase the question until it is clearly understood, or refer to the commentary woven into the guide to clarify the context or meaning.

9. Don't be afraid of silence in response to the discussion questions. People may need time to think about the question before formulating their answers.

10. Don't be content with just one answer. Ask, "What do the rest of you think?" or "Anything else?" until several people have given answers to the question.

11. Try to be affirming whenever possible. Affirm participation. Never reject an answer; if it is clearly off-base, ask, "Which verse led you to that conclusion?" or again, "What do the rest of you think?"

12. Don't expect every answer to be addressed to you, even though this will probably happen at first. As group members become more at ease, they will begin to truly interact with each other. This is one sign of healthy discussion.

13. Don't be afraid of controversy. It can be very stimulating. If you don't resolve an issue completely, don't be frustrated. Explain that the group will move on and God may enlighten all of you in later sessions.

14. Periodically summarize what the group has said about the passage. This helps to draw together the various ideas mentioned and gives continuity to the study. But don't preach.

15. Conclude your time together with the prayer suggestion at the end of the study, adapting it to your group's particular needs as appropriate. Ask for God's help in following through on the applications you've identified.

16. End on time.

Many more suggestions and helps for studying a passage or guiding discussion can be found in *How to Lead a LifeGuide Bible Study* and *The Big Book on Small Groups* (both from InterVarsity Press/USA).

Other InterVarsity Press Resources from N. T. Wright

The Challenge of Jesus

N. T. Wright offers clarity and a full accounting of the facts of the life and teachings of Jesus, revealing how the Son of God was also solidly planted in first-century Palestine. *978-0-8308-2200-3, 202 pages, hardcover*

Resurrection

This 50-minute DVD confronts the most startling claim of Christianity—that Jesus rose from the dead. Shot on location in Israel, Greece and England, N. T. Wright presents the political, historical and theological issues of Jesus' day and today regarding this claim. Wright brings clarity and insight to one of the most profound mysteries in human history. Study guide included. *978-0-8308-3435-8, DVD*

Evil and the Justice of God

N. T. Wright explores all aspects of evil and how it presents itself in society today. Fully grounded in the story of the Old and New Testaments, this presentation is provocative and hopeful; a fascinating analysis of and response to the fundamental question of evil and justice that faces believers. *978-0-8308-3398-6, 176 pages, hardcover*

Evil

Filmed in Israel, South Africa and England, this 50-minute DVD confronts some of the major "evil" issues of our time—from tsunamis to AIDS—and puts them under the biblical spotlight. N. T. Wright says there is a solution to the problem of evil, if only we have the honesty and courage to name it and understand it for what it is. Study guide included. *978-0-8308-3434-1, DVD*

Small Faith—Great God

N. T. Wright reminds us that what matters is not how much faith we have as Who our faith is in. Wright looks at the character of the faith God calls us to. He unfolds how dependence, humility and mystery all have a role to play. But the author doesn't ignore the messiness and difficulties of life, when hard times come and the unexpected knocks us down. He opens to us what faith means in times of trial and even in the face of death. Through it all he reminds us, it's not great faith we need: it is faith in a great God. *978-0-8308-3833-2, 176 pages, hardcover*

Justification: God's Plan and Paul's Vision

In this comprehensive account and defense of the crucial doctrine of justification, Wright also responds to critics who have challenged what has come to be called the New Perspective. Ultimately, he provides a chance for those in the middle of and on both sides of the debate to interact directly with his views and form their own conclusions. *978-0-8308-3863-9, 279 pages, hardcover*

Colossians and Philemon

In Colossians, Paul presents Christ as "the firstborn over all creation," and appeals to his readers to seek a maturity found only Christ. In Philemon, Paul appeals to a fellow believer to receive a runaway slave in love and forgiveness. In this volume N. T. Wright offers comment on both of these important books. *978-0-8308-4242-1, 199 pages, paperback*

Table of Contents

Introduction

When it comes to college football, Notre Dame *is* history.

Among its many traditions is the pregame walk from the locker room down to the field, where every single player touches the overhanging sign at the bottom of the stairway, which reads: "Play like a champion today."

There's the leprechaun mascot, the "Touchdown Jesus" mural, and the Golden Dome.

The school boasts the most famous song in American sports, the "Victory March," perhaps the game's most iconic name, and enough national championships to require two hands to count.

It is the only collegiate program to have an exclusive national television contract and Hollywood makes movies about both its legends and mere overachievers.

It's where running back George Gipp was more than just the subject of the most famous pep talk in history; he was possibly the best player to ever suit up for the Fighting Irish.

Yes, that includes the seven Heisman Trophy winners: Angelo Bertelli (1943), John Lujack (1947), Leon Hart (1949), John Lattner (1953), Paul Hornung (1956), John Huarte (1964), and Tim Brown (1987).

All of them are already inducted into the College Football Hall of Fame, which was conveniently built in South Bend because, well, where else would you put it?

Only at Notre Dame can someone like Dan Devine compile a record of 53–16–1, win a national championship, and not place in the program's all-time top five winning percentage list. His .764 winning percentage may be considered great, but is still not as great as Knute Rockne's .881, Frank Leahy's .855, Ara Pareghian's .836, Elmer Layden's .770, or Lou Holtz's .765—numbers most people not familiar with the program first assume must be typos.

Only at Notre Dame can the game's most legendary sports writer come up with the immortal words Grantland Rice used for the *New York Herald-Tribune* on October 19, 1924: "Outlined against a blue-gray October sky the Four Horsemen rode again. In dramatic lore they are known as famine, pestilence, destruction, and death. These are only aliases. Their real names are Stuhldreher, Miller, Crowley, and Layden."

Only at Notre Dame is nothing about football ever considered ordinary. ■

"The Four Horsemen" on the practice field in South Bend, Indiana, in 1924. From left to right are: Don Miller, Elmer Layden, Jim Crowley, and Harry Stuhldreher.

SEASON PREVIEW

For Charlie Weis, Notre Dame's 2008 season could only be described as a pain, and not just because he sustained ligament damage in his right knee due to a sideline hit against Michigan.

In addition to the Fighting Irish not living up to expectations, a late-season swoon left the coach answering questions about job security through the team's trip to the Hawaii Bowl.

Yes Notre Dame, which had played in Bowl Championship Series games in both 2005 and 2006, improved from a three-win 2007, but at the end of the regular season the coach was 10–17 in his last 27 games, and the 15 losses over the past two seasons were the most in school history. Weiss' 28–21 record, for a .571 winning percentage, was slightly worse than his two predecessors, Tyrone Willingham and Bob Davie.

Additionally, Notre Dame had its first-ever defeat to a team with eight losses (Syracuse) and finished 7–6, despite a 4–1 start. After the 38–3 pounding to Southern California, new athletics director Jack Swarbrick said he needed time to evaluate the program.

Needless to say, the angst was felt by just about everyone involved.

Consequently, Weis met with Swarbrick for more than two hours over the direction of the program and what it would take to put Notre Dame back on top.

"The question you're ultimately asking yourself is: 'Is he in a position to help direct the changes in the program, to help steer it back to where he and I really want it to be?'" Swarbrick told The Associated Press. "That really focused on a discussion about a series of very specific things that constitute the plan going forward."

The first step just may have been the decisive 49–21 win against Hawaii, ending a nine-game losing streak in the postseason dating back to the 1994 Cotton Bowl game against Texas A&M.

"I think it's just going out on top," outgoing wide receiver David Grimes said about what kind of impact the seniors wanted to make in Hawaii. "Kind of take that bitter taste out of our mouth that we had this last month, and get the seniors something to be happy about."

Weis himself called it a "great step," but nothing short of another BCS appearance at the end of 2009 may guarantee that his reign in South Bend will continue, despite having yet another young team.

The season will begin at home against Nevada on September. 5 and includes seven games against bowl opponents from 2008, but only one BCS qualifier, Southern California. Of the four Pac-10 opponents, just one played in the postseason, although Notre Dame will face Washington State in a high profile neutral-site game at San Antonio.

No one knows how many wins Weis and his staff will need, but Swarbrick did state that he's not worried about the coach's ability to deal with the pressure.

"I think he's very good at sort of shutting out external distractions and focusing on what needs to be done," Swarbrick said. "I think one of his real strengths is that when things don't work, he's very willing to examine them and look for alternatives. He's very flexible." ■

Offense

IRISH
adidas
7

Offense

The Tuesday before Notre Dame played Navy during the 2008 season, Coach Charlie Weis was asked about fans being upset over the Fighting Irish losing three of the last four games.

If anything, he understood where they were coming from. When Weis was a student at South Bend roughly 30 years ago he once called the university president to complain about a loss.

"I think that I'd be perturbed, too, if I were them, to be honest with you," he said at the press conference, also announcing that he would be taking over the play-calling, supposedly because offensive coordinator Mike Haywood was attending a funeral for a family member in Houston that week. (At season's end Haywood accepted the head coaching job at Miami of Ohio.)

The change came after the 17–0 loss to Boston College, when quarterback Jimmy Clausen had four passes intercepted. It was the third time the offense had been shut out in two seasons, matching Notre Dame's total from the previous 19 years.

"I'm confident that the program is going to go where we all want it to go," Weis said. "That's as honest as I can be, because I think we have pretty good players. When you have pretty good players, you have a chance to be pretty good."

Despite some obvious struggles, there was cause for optimism especially given the level of young offensive talent and numerous returning starters, including

Clausen, who will be a junior in 2009.

Helping form the core of the offense will be junior wide receiver Golden Tate, sophomore wide receiver Michael Floyd, three returning running backs in Armando Allen, James Aldridge, and Robert Hughes, and sophomore tight end Kyle Rudolph.

Tate, a big-play threat, had a breakout season in 2008 with 58 receptions for 1,080 yards and 10 touchdowns, the fifth-best receiving season in program history.

Floyd finished with 48 catches for 719 yards and seven touchdowns to set school single-season freshman records in all three categories. With 29 catches, 340 yards, and two touchdowns, Rudolph also set Notre Dame records for freshmen tight ends.

With Weis calling the plays from the coaches' box because of knee problems, Notre Dame scored 41 points in the Hawaii Bowl—which fans hope is just a sign of what's to come. Among the school bowl records to fall that day were passing yards (Clausen 401), passing touchdowns (five), completion percentage (84.6), receiving yards (Tate 177), receiving touchdowns (three), longest pass (69 yards), and total offense (478 yards).

However, the offensive line will likely be the key, where the Fighting Irish will need to replace left tackle Mike Turkovich and find a place for 6-foot-8, 330-pound senior Sam Young, the prize of the 2006 recruiting class.

Although guard Trevor Robinson became just the fifth freshman ever to start on the Notre Dame offensive line in 2008, the unit cut the number of sacks allowed by more than half, from 58 in 2007 to 22.

Should that kind of improvement continue, expect the offense, especially with its deep-threat potential, to average better than its 24.7 points and 355.1 yards per game in 2008. ■

Defense

Defense

Although the numbers were influenced by the struggling offense, Notre Dame's defensive statistics in 2008 could only be described as average.

The 22.2 points allowed ranked 42nd out of the 119 teams that make up the Football Bowl Subdivision. The 134.2 rushing yards allowed (4.06 per carry) ranked 45th, and the 195.7 passing yards allowed were only slightly better at 43rd. Total defense was an unspectacular 39th.

Nine opponents scored 20 points or more and three exceeded 30 (although Pitt needed four overtimes to score 36).

It's a point of obvious concern especially considering the Fighting Irish lost a number of key starters, including free safety David Bruton, cornerback Terrail Lambert, linebacker Maurice Crum, and defensive linemen Pat Kuntz and Justin Brown.

If there was a strength to the 2008 unit it was the veteran secondary, which ranked No. 22 in pass-efficiency defense with a 109.73 rating. Leading the unit was Bruton, whom Coach Charlie Weis once described as a "skinny little track kid," but who was second in team tackles with 97 and also had four interceptions, two forced fumbles, and two fumble recoveries.

Linebacker Harrison Smith is expected to move back to safety to take Bruton's spot; cornerback depth is also a concern.

Another key player to replace is defensive lineman Pat Kuntz, who could line up both inside or outside in the 3-4 alignment. He finished with 42 tackles, including eight for a loss, and 3.5 sacks.

That's the negative. Here's the other side:

The Fighting Irish were 20th in the nation in third-down conversions allowed (57 of 174 opportunities, 32.8 percent).

Notre Dame established a more aggressive approach that should carry over to this year, one that proved to be successful against Hawaii in a 49–21 victory.

"I told the team that's the only thing I wanted [for Christmas]," Coach Charlie Weis said. "I just wanted to win a bowl game.

"I heard it a hundred times in the locker room after the game and they wanted to know what I was giving them for Christmas. I told them: 'A flight home.'"

Weis' staff will especially be looking for several sophomores to take more prominent roles in 2009, particularly up the middle with defensive tackle Ian Williams and middle linebacker Brian Smith. At 310 pounds, Williams is big enough to help clog up the lanes and keep blockers off inside linebackers like Maurice Crum.

The line as a whole should benefit from more depth, with Texas native Kapron Lewis-Moore expected to step up along with Ethan Johnson and Darius Fleming.

Last year Smith made 54 tackles—including four for a loss—two sacks, and two fumble recoveries. Kerry Neal will have a bigger opportunity at outside linebacker and two names to watch are athletic Steve Filer, who could take Harrison Smith's spot, and sophomore David Posluszny. ■

The Irish will miss the standouts of its secondary in 2009, including David Bruton (left), who had 97 tackles and four interceptions in 2008, and cornerback Terrail Lambert, both of whom have moved on to the NFL.

Player to Watch: Jimmy Clausen

When the carnage was complete, even Hawaii's Greg McMackin could only offer praise.

"That dang quarterback, he's going to be a Heisman Trophy guy," McMackin said following the 49–21 season-ending loss to Notre Dame. "He has his days, but today he was right on the money. Every throw was right on the money."

The coach was taking about Fighting Irish quarterback Jimmy Clausen who, in his final game as a sophomore, completed 22 of 26 passes for 401 yards with five touchdowns at the Hawaii Bowl.

The performance was so impressive that at halftime, when Clausen had 300 passing yards and three touchdowns, he had already eclipsed Brady Quinn's postseason school record of 286 yards set against Ohio State in the 2006 Fiesta Bowl.

"The guys came out here on a mission," Clausen said.

So did he.

Clausen was the most acclaimed California prep quarterback since John Elway and made the earliest start of any Notre Dame freshman quarterback in school history when he was in the lineup for Game 2 of the 2007 season. However, his freshman year saw a 3–9 season in which he passed for 1,254 yards and seven touchdowns with six interceptions.

Both he and the offense appeared to be turning a

The main focus in 2009 for Jimmy Clausen and the Notre Dame offense will be consistency. They have both shown flashes of brilliance in the past, including Clausen's record-breaking Hawaii Bowl performance, but now it is time to put it all together for an entire season.

corner with a 5–2 start in 2008, only to struggle down the stretch. While playing with the flu, he had four interceptions against Boston College, and despite a 291-yard performance with two touchdowns and no interceptions, Notre Dame lost to 3–8 Syracuse.

"We've been consistent here and there," Clausen told the *Los Angeles Times* prior to the 38–3 loss to Southern California. "But whether it's finishing the game or starting out fast in a game, it's just little things here and there that's making this team a 6–5 team [rather than] a 9–2 team."

"There came a turning point right about the two-thirds mark of the season where I think that Jimmy, along with several players on the offense, seemed to get out of synch so to speak," Coach Charlie Weis said. "I think that ever since the last part of the year right through December we have been working on getting back into synch."

It happened in the postseason when Notre Dame set nine school records and enjoyed its first postseason victory in 15 years. Clausen's 69-yard touchdown pass to Golden Tate was the longest offensive play of the season and the players shared MVP honors.

Should they pick up where they left off, the mere threat of the deep ball should pay dividends in 2009 when fans hope Clausen steps up like his predecessor and breaks a few more of Quinn's records.

"(He was) as accurate as I've ever seen," said McMackin, who used to coach in the NFL. "He was outstanding, his receivers were outstanding." ■

Notre Dame's win in the 2008 Hawaii Bowl erased a nine-game bowl losing streak, the longest in school history.

Jimmy Clausen lugs around the trophy after the Fighting Irish win in the Hawaii Bowl. The dominating win over the host team set the stage for a potential record-breaking 2009 for the young quarterback.

With his mom watching, linebacker Manti Te'o inks his name on the papers sending him to Notre Dame on National Signing Day. The Hawaiian linebacker chose Notre Dame over USC and UCLA and he joins a recruiting class that could have a major impact from day one.

2009 National Signing Day Class

E.J. Banks	ATH	5-11	181	McKees Rocks, Penn.
Alex Bullard	OL	6-3	275	Brentwood, Tenn.
Carlo Calabrese	LB	6-2	225	Verona, N.J.
Jordan Cowart	OL	6-2	225	Fort Lauderdale, Fla.
Tyler Eifert	TE	6-6	220	Fort Wayne, Ind.
Shaquelle Evans	WR	6-0	203	Inglewood, Calif.
Dan Fox	LB	6-4	219	Rocky River, Ohio
Jake Golic	TE	6-4	220	West Hartford, Conn.
Zach Martin	OL	6-5	270	Indianapolis, Ind.
Zeke Motta	LB	6-2	207	Vero Beach, Fla.
Theo Riddick	RB	5-10	185	Somerville, N.J.
Nick Tausch	K	6-1	180	Dallas, Texas
Manti Te'o	LB	6-2	225	Honolulu, Hawaii
Ben Turk	K	6-0	190	Fort Lauderdale, Fla.
Chris Watt	OL	6-3	280	Glen Ellyn, Ill.
Cierre Wood	RB	6-0	192	Oxnard, Calif.

The University of Notre Dame

Location: South Bend, Indiana

Founded: 1842

Enrollment: 11,603

Nickname: Fighting Irish

Colors: Gold and Blue

Mascot: Leprechaun

Stadium: Notre Dame Stadium (80,795 capacity)

Tickets: (574) 631-7356

Website: http://und.cstv.com/

Consensus National Championships (8): 1943, 1946, 1947, 1949, 1966, 1973, 1977, 1988

Other National Championships (3): 1924, 1929, 1930

Other Seasons Notre Dame Was Selected No. 1 by at Least One Service (10): 1919, 1920, 1927, 1938, 1953, 1964, 1967, 1970, 1989, 1993

Bowl Appearances: 29 (14–15)

First season: 1887

ND

2008 SEASON REVIEW

Robert Hughes and the Irish barely escaped an embarrassing opening-game loss at home to the San Diego Aztecs with a 21–13 win on September 6, 2008.

Game 1: Notre Dame 21, San Diego State 13

SOUTH BEND | Despite four turnovers and a lackluster running game against San Diego State's makeshift defensive line, Norte Dame scored two touchdowns in the fourth quarter to pull out the victory.

Safety David Bruton made the key play, forcing a fumble from Brandon Sullivan near the goal line and recovering it in the end zone to nullify a 4-yard touchdown run.

"They had a chance to put the game away," Notre Dame Coach Charlie Weis said.

Minutes after the fumble, Jimmy Clausen threw a 38-yard touchdown pass to Golden Tate. Clausen was 5 of 5 for 76 yards on the drive, as Notre Dame avoided losing back-to-back season openers at home for the first time since 1887–88.

	1st Qtr	2nd Qtr	3rd Qtr	4th Qtr	Final
SAN DIEGO ST	0	7	6	0	**13**
NOTRE DAME	0	7	0	14	**21**

SCORING PLAYS

SAN DIEGO ST–TD, R Lindley 1 YD RUN (L Yoshida KICK) 9:28 2nd Qtr

NOTRE DAME–TD, M Floyd 23 YD PASS FROM J Clausen (B Walker KICK) 13:46 2nd Qtr

SAN DIEGO ST–TD, D Mougey 15 YD PASS FROM R Lindley (PAT FAILED) 6:29 3rd Qtr

NOTRE DAME–TD, G Tate 38 YD PASS FROM J Clausen (B Walker KICK) 5:17 4th Qtr

NOTRE DAME–TD, D Grimes 6 YD PASS FROM J Clausen (B Walker KICK) 12:52 4th Qtr

GAME STATISTICS

	SAN DIEGO ST	NOTRE DAME
First Downs	19	20
Yards Rushing	15–71	34–105
Yards Passing	274	237
Sacks—Yards Lost	1–7	0–0
Passing Efficiency	29–59–1	21–34–2
Punts	9–30.2	5–39.8
Fumbles—Lost	1–1	2–2
Penalties—Yards	11–100	7–58
Time of Possession	29:08	30:52

INDIVIDUAL STATISTICS - RUSHING

SAN DIEGO ST–Brandon Sullivan 10–66, Atiyyah Henderson 2–12, Darren Mougey 1–MINUS 1, Ryan Lindley 2–MINUS 6. NOTRE DAME–Armando Allen 17–59, Robert Hughes 16–54, Eric Maust 1–MINUS 8.

INDIVIDUAL STATISTICS - PASSING

SAN DIEGO ST–Ryan Lindley 29–59–274– 1. NOTRE DAME–Jimmy Clausen 21–34–237– 2.

INDIVIDUAL STATISTICS - RECEIVING

SAN DIEGO ST–Darren Mougey 5–97, Matthew Kawulok 9–60, Roberto Wallace 4–40, Atiyyah Henderson 4–37, Vincent Brown 3–19, Justin Shaw 1–7, Alston Umuolo 1–7, Brandon Sullivan 2–7. NOTRE DAME–Golden Tate 6–93, David Grimes 5–35, Robert Hughes 3–32, Duval Kamara 1–28, Michael Floyd 1–22, Armando Allen 3–18, Kyle Rudolph 1–5, Will Yeatman 1–4.

ATTENDANCE: 80,795

Game 2: Notre Dame 35, Michigan 17

SOUTH BEND | Although Notre Dame coach Charlie Weis tore ligaments in his right knee after being hit along the sideline during the second quarter, the Fighting Irish took advantage of six turnovers, including four fumbles.

Jimmy Clausen, who was sacked eight times in the 2007 meeting, had two touchdown passes and two interceptions, but wasn't sacked. Michigan won the two previous meetings, 38–0 and 47–21.

"We definitely showed up against a good opponent and it's sweet," said Weis, on crutches most of the game after tearing the ACL and MCL in his left knee Saturday when he was hit in the second quarter along the sideline. "This was a big win for our program and our kids."

	1st Qtr	2nd Qtr	3rd Qtr	4th Qtr	Final
MICHIGAN	7	10	0	0	17
NOTRE DAME	21	7	0	7	35

SCORING PLAYS

NOTRE DAME–TD, R Hughes 2 YD RUN (B Walker KICK) 3:08 1st Qtr

NOTRE DAME–TD, D Kamara 10 YD PASS FROM J Clausen (B Walker KICK) 4:00 1st Qtr

NOTRE DAME–TD, G Tate 48 YD PASS FROM J Clausen (B Walker KICK) 10:09 1st Qtr

MICHIGAN–TD, S McGuffie 40 YD PASS FROM S Threet (K Lopata KICK) 13:04 1st Qtr

MICHIGAN–FG, K Lopata 23 YD 3:07 2nd Qtr

NOTRE DAME–TD, R Hughes 1 YD RUN (B Walker KICK) 6:13 2nd Qtr

MICHIGAN–TD, K Grady 7 YD RUN (K Lopata KICK) 9:19 2nd Qtr

NOTRE DAME–TD, B Smith 35 YD FUMBLE RETURN (B Walker KICK) 0:10 4th Qtr

GAME STATISTICS

	MICHIGAN	NOTRE DAME
First Downs	21	14
Yards Rushing	42–159	34–113
Yards Passing	229	147
Sacks—Yards Lost	0–0	0–0

Michael Floyd tries to break away from Michigan's Morgan Trent. Floyd finished with two catches for 10 yards in Notre Dame's commanding win over the Wolverines.

Passing Efficiency	19–28–2	10–21–2
Punts	4–52.8	6–43.8
Fumbles—Lost	7–4	3–0
Penalties—Yards	7–79	3–38
Time of Possession	32:12	27:48

INDIVIDUAL STATISTICS - RUSHING

MICHIGAN–Sam McGuffie 25–131, Zoltan Mesko 1–13, Steven Threet 5–8, Michael Shaw 2–5, Kevin Grady 4–4, Brandon Minor 3–1, Carlos Brown 1–0, Team 1–MINUS 3. NOTRE DAME–Robert Hughes 19–79, James Aldridge 9–28, Jimmy Clausen 2–5, Armando Allen 2–4, Team 2–MINUS 3.

INDIVIDUAL STATISTICS - PASSING

MICHIGAN–Steven Threet 16–23–175– 0, Nick Sheridan 3–5–54– 2. NOTRE DAME–Jimmy Clausen 10–21–147– 2.

INDIVIDUAL STATISTICS - RECEIVING

MICHIGAN–Martavious Odoms 6–56, Sam McGuffie 4–47, Greg Mathews 4–46, Zion Babb 2–45, Darryl Stonum 3–35. NOTRE DAME–Golden Tate 4–127, Duval Kamara 1–10, Michael Floyd 2–10, David Grimes 1–3, Robby Parris 1–0, Robert Hughes 1–MINUS 3.

ATTENDANCE: 80,795

Game 3: Michigan State 23, Notre Dame 7

EAST LANSING | Javon Ringer ran for 201 yards and two touchdowns to notch his second straight 200-yard performance.

Notre Dame had three turnovers, missed two field goals, and accumulated just 16 rushing yards.

Jimmy Clausen passed for 242 yards and a touchdown, but also had two interceptions and was sacked twice.

Michigan State won for the ninth time in 12 meetings, for 27 wins overall, second only to Southern California's 32.

	1st Qtr	2nd Qtr	3rd Qtr	4th Qtr	Final
NOTRE DAME	0	0	0	7	**7**
MICHIGAN ST	3	7	3	10	**23**

SCORING PLAYS

MICHIGAN ST–FG, B Swenson 45 YD 3:46 1st Qtr

MICHIGAN ST–TD, J Ringer 1 YD RUN (B Swenson KICK) 11:32 2nd Qtr

MICHIGAN ST–FG, B Swenson 26 YD 9:28 3rd Qtr

NOTRE DAME–TD, M Floyd 26 YD PASS FROM J Clausen (B Walker KICK) 0:09 4th Qtr

MICHIGAN ST–FG, B Swenson 23 YD 5:50 4th Qtr

MICHIGAN ST–TD, J Ringer 1 YD RUN (B Swenson KICK) 12:44 4th Qtr

GAME STATISTICS

	NOTRE DAME	MICHIGAN ST
First Downs	18	16
Yards Rushing	22–16	43–203
Yards Passing	242	143
Sacks—Yards Lost	3–34	0–0
Passing Efficiency	24–41–2	12–26–0
Punts	5–40.8	5–45.2
Fumbles—Lost	3–1	1–1
Penalties—Yards	5–24	6–65
Time of Possession	26:15	33:45

INDIVIDUAL STATISTICS - RUSHING
NOTRE DAME–Golden Tate 1–24, James Aldridge 4–13, Robert Hughes 5–9, Armando Allen 6–8, Team 1–MINUS 7, Jimmy Clausen 5–MINUS 31. MICHIGAN ST–Javon Ringer 39–201, Brian Hoyer 2–6, Team 2–MINUS 4.

INDIVIDUAL STATISTICS - PASSING
NOTRE DAME–Jimmy Clausen 24–41–242– 2. MICHIGAN ST–Brian Hoyer 12–26–143– 0.

INDIVIDUAL STATISTICS - RECEIVING
NOTRE DAME–Michael Floyd 7–86, Golden Tate 5–83, Kyle Rudolph 2–29, Robby Parris 4–22, Armando Allen 5–20, Will Yeatman 1–2. MICHIGAN ST–Mark Dell 4–80, B.J. Cunningham 1–22, Blair White 2–19, Garrett Celek 2–15, Deon Curry 1–4, Andrew Hawken 1–3, Javon Ringer 1–0.

ATTENDANCE: 76,366

Game 4: Notre Dame 38, Purdue 21

SOUTH BEND | The Notre Dame offense ran for 201 yards on 40 carries and Jimmy Clausen passed for a career-high 275 yards as the Fighting Irish matched their win total from 2007.

Notre Dame amassed 476 total yards of offense, its highest total since gaining 663 yards in a 38–31 win over Stanford on Nov. 26, 2005. Armando Allen Jr. ran for a career-high 134 yards on 17 carries and had a 21-yard run to set up his 16-yard touchdown. Desmond Tardy had 10 catches for 175 yards for Purdue.

"I said, 'Where you've been?'" Weis said about Allen.

Notre Dame came into the game averaging 78 rushing yards and had yet to score in the third quarter. Against the Boilermakers, the Irish had 90 rushing yards and three touchdowns in the third quarter alone.

Golden Tate reaches over Purdue's Torri Williams to make the play. Williams was able to hold Tate in check to the tune of only five catches, but Tate still had a touchdown. Michael Floyd caught six balls for 100 yards.

	1st Qtr	2nd Qtr	3rd Qtr	4th Qtr	Final
PURDUE	7	7	7	0	**21**
NOTRE DAME	0	14	21	3	**38**

SCORING PLAYS

PURDUE–TD, K Sheets 22 YD RUN (C Summers KICK) 5:56 1st Qtr

NOTRE DAME–TD, R Blanton 47 YD INTERCEPTION RETURN (B Walker KICK) 5:04 2nd Qtr

PURDUE–TD, A Valentin 4 YD PASS FROM C Painter (C Summers KICK) 10:14 2nd Qtr

NOTRE DAME–TD, G Tate 6 YD PASS FROM J Clausen (B Walker KICK) 12:25 2nd Qtr

NOTRE DAME–TD, A Allen 16 YD RUN (B Walker KICK) 2:04 3rd Qtr

NOTRE DAME–TD, K Rudolph 5 YD PASS FROM J Clausen (B Walker KICK) 8:23 3rd Qtr

PURDUE–TD, D Tardy 54 YD PASS FROM C Painter (C Summers KICK) 9:36 3rd Qtr

NOTRE DAME–TD, D Grimes 30 YD PASS FROM J Clausen (B Walker KICK) 13:36 3rd Qtr

NOTRE DAME–FG, B Walker 41 YD 4:34 4th Qtr

GAME STATISTICS

	PURDUE	NOTRE DAME
First Downs	23	23
Yards Rushing	17–103	40–201
Yards Passing	359	275
Sacks—Yards Lost	0–0	1–8
Passing Efficiency	29–55–1	20–35–0
Punts	4–39	2–46.5

Fumbles—Lost	0–0	0–0
Penalties—Yards	5–43	6–44
Time of Possession	24:34	35:26

INDIVIDUAL STATISTICS - RUSHING
PURDUE–Kory Sheets 13–87, Justin Siller 2–6, Curtis Painter 1–5, Frank Halliburton 1–5. NOTRE DAME–Armando Allen 17–134, James Aldridge 8–34, Robert Hughes 9–26, Jimmy Clausen 5–8, Team 1–MINUS 1.

INDIVIDUAL STATISTICS - PASSING
PURDUE–Curtis Painter 29–55–359– 1. NOTRE DAME–Jimmy Clausen 20–35–275– 0.

INDIVIDUAL STATISTICS - RECEIVING
PURDUE–Desmond Tardy 10–175, Greg Orton 9–90, Kory Sheets 5–56, Keith Smith 2–24, Brandon Whittington 1–8, Colton McKey 1–3, Aaron Valentin 1–3. NOTRE DAME–Michael Floyd 6–100, David Grimes 4–65, Golden Tate 5–64, Kyle Rudolph 3–32, Armando Allen 1–9, Duval Kamara 1–5.

ATTENDANCE: 80,795

Game 5: Notre Dame 28, Stanford 21

SOUTH BEND | Jimmy Clausen completed a career-best 29 passes for 347 yards, with three touchdowns, to lead Notre Dame. "I think it's a major step when the quarterback doesn't force balls down the field and is willing to throw to his flair control," Charlie Weis said. "I think that's a major step."

Defensive end Pat Kuntz had two sacks, an interception, and a fumble recovery, while Michael Floyd had five catches for 115 yards, including a 48-yard touchdown.

Notre Dame improved to 4–1, in contrast to the 0–5 start in 2007.

	1st Qtr	2nd Qtr	3rd Qtr	4th Qtr	Final
STANFORD	0	7	0	14	**21**
NOTRE DAME	7	14	7	0	**28**

SCORING PLAYS

NOTRE DAME–TD, A Allen 21 YD PASS FROM J Clausen (B Walker KICK) 7:04 1st Qtr

STANFORD–TD, T Gerhart 1 YD RUN (A Zagory KICK) 4:09 2nd Qtr

NOTRE DAME–TD, A Allen 3 YD RUN (B Walker KICK) 8:48 2nd Qtr

NOTRE DAME–TD, M Floyd 48 YD PASS FROM J Clausen (B Walker KICK) 11:20 2nd Qtr

NOTRE DAME–TD, K Rudolph 16 YD PASS FROM J Clausen (B Walker KICK) 10:30 3rd Qtr

STANFORD–TD, J Dray 1 YD PASS FROM T Pritchard (A Zagory KICK) 4:54 4th Qtr

STANFORD–TD, D Baldwin 10 YD PASS FROM T Pritchard (A Zagory KICK) 9:00 4th Qtr

GAME STATISTICS

	STANFORD	NOTRE DAME
First Downs	20	20
Yards Rushing	37–161	27–83
Yards Passing	182	347
Sacks—Yards Lost	5–48	1–12
Passing Efficiency	18–28–3	29–40–0
Punts	3–42	5–41.4
Fumbles—Lost	1–1	0–0
Penalties—Yards	9–56	8–75
Time of Possession	26:40	33:20

INDIVIDUAL STATISTICS – RUSHING

STANFORD–Toby Gerhart 13–104, Anthony Kimble 10–61, Delano Howell 3–15, Michael Thomas 2–9, Tavita Pritchard 9–MINUS 28. NOTRE DAME–Armando Allen 9–33, Harrison Smith 1–23, Robert Hughes 8–14, James Aldridge 5–9, Jimmy Clausen 4–4.

INDIVIDUAL STATISTICS – PASSING

STANFORD–Tavita Pritchard 18–28–182– 3. NOTRE DAME–Jimmy Clausen 29–40–347– 0.

INDIVIDUAL STATISTICS – RECEIVING

STANFORD–Ryan Whalen 8–91, Doug Baldwin 3–42, Austin Gunder 4–34, Coby Fleener 1–12, Anthony Kimble 1–2, Jim Dray 1–1. NOTRE DAME–Michael Floyd 5–115, Kyle Rudolph 5–70, Armando Allen 7–66, David Grimes 7–60, Golden Tate 3–30, Robert Hughes 1–4, Duval Kamara 1–2.

ATTENDANCE: 80,795

Game 6: No. 22 North Carolina 29, Notre Dame 24

CHAPEL HILL | Notre Dame quarterback Jimmy Clausen threw for 383 yards and two touchdowns as the Fighting Irish outgained North Carolina 472–322 and converted 10 of 16 third downs. However, the Tar Heels forced five turnovers and returned an interception for a touchdown.

Notre Dame led 17–9 at halftime, but four second-half turnovers contributed to the North Carolina comeback, topped by safety Trimane Goddard's fumble recovery in North Carolina territory with seconds remaining.

The Tar Heels, ranked for the first time in seven years and playing at home as a ranked team for the first time in a decade, hosted the Fighting Irish for the first time since 1975.

	1st Qtr	2nd Qtr	3rd Qtr	4th Qtr	Final
NOTRE DAME	7	10	7	0	24
NORTH CAROLINA (22)	3	6	13	7	29

SCORING PLAYS

NOTRE DAME–TD, G Tate 19 YD PASS FROM J Clausen (B Walker KICK) 4:33 1st Qtr

NORTH CAROLINA–FG, C Barth 41 YD 12:11 1st Qtr

NOTRE DAME–FG, B Walker 42 YD 2:07 2nd Qtr

NORTH CAROLINA–FG, C Barth 34 YD 9:38 2nd Qtr

NOTRE DAME–TD, M Floyd 7 YD PASS FROM J Clausen (B Walker KICK) 14:08 2nd Qtr

NORTH CAROLINA–FG, C Barth 42 YD 14:51 2nd Qtr

NORTH CAROLINA–TD, Q Sturdivant 32 YD INTERCEPTION RETURN (C Barth KICK) 0:12 3rd Qtr

NOTRE DAME–TD, J Aldridge 2 YD RUN (B Walker KICK) 4:17 3rd Qtr

NORTH CAROLINA–TD, R Houston 1 YD RUN 9:46 3rd Qtr

NORTH CAROLINA–TD, C Sexton 4 YD RUN (C Barth KICK) 0:05 4th Qtr

GAME STATISTICS

	NOTRE DAME	N. CAROLINA (22)
First Downs	27	21
Yards Rushing	30–89	32–121
Yards Passing	383	201
Sacks—Yards Lost	4–26	1–8
Passing Efficiency	31–48–2	18–32–0
Punts	1–35	4–38
Fumbles—Lost	4–3	1–0
Penalties—Yards	4–33	7–55
Time of Possession	33:05	26:55

INDIVIDUAL STATISTICS - RUSHING

NOTRE DAME–Armando Allen 11–60, James Aldridge 4–23, Robert Hughes 4–12, Jimmy Clausen 11–MINUS 6. NORTH CAROLINA–Shaun Draughn 17–91, Ryan Houston 8–28, Greg Little 2–7, Cam Sexton 3–MINUS 2, Team 2–MINUS 3.

Washington head coach Tyrone Willingham looks on as his Huskies get pummeled by Notre Dame. The former Irish coach had nothing to smile about after the 33–7 loss that dropped his team to 0–7. Willingham's termination, effective at the end of the season, was announced two days later.

INDIVIDUAL STATISTICS - PASSING

NOTRE DAME–Jimmy Clausen 31–48–383– 2. NORTH CAROLINA–Cam Sexton 18–32–201– 0.

INDIVIDUAL STATISTICS - RECEIVING

NOTRE DAME–Golden Tate 5–121, Michael Floyd 6–93, Duval Kamara 5–58, Armando Allen 7–47, Kyle Rudolph 3–30, David Grimes 4–19, Robert Hughes 1–15. NORTH CAROLINA–Hakeem Nicks 9–141, Brooks Foster 3–28, Richard Quinn 1–15, Kenton Thornton 1–5, Zach Pianalto 1–5, Anthony Elzy 1–4, Cooter Arnold 2–3.

ATTENDANCE: 60,500

Game 7: Notre Dame 33, Washington 7

SEATTLE | Washington did not cross midfield until six minutes remained, had just 51 total yards on 35 plays entering the fourth quarter, and only 5 passing yards at halftime.

Fans booed when Notre Dame ran a fake punt despite being up 24–0 in the third quarter as Harrison Smith took a direct snap and ran 35 yards to set up a field goal.

Winless Washington, led by former Notre Dame coach Tyrone Willingham, scored with 2:56 remaining to prevent its first shutout loss at home since 1976.

Willingham had been notified the previous week that he would be fired effective the end of the season. Two days after the Notre Dame loss the decision was made public.

	1st Qtr	2nd Qtr	3rd Qtr	4th Qtr	Final
NOTRE DAME	14	3	10	6	33
WASHINGTON	0	0	0	7	7

SCORING PLAYS

NOTRE DAME–TD, M Floyd 51 YD PASS FROM J Clausen (B Walker KICK) 2:25 1st Qtr

NOTRE DAME–TD, G Tate 21 YD RUN (B Walker KICK) 7:12 1st Qtr

NOTRE DAME–FG, B Walker 28 YD 3:50 2nd Qtr

NOTRE DAME–TD, J Aldridge 4 YD RUN (B Walker KICK) 2:05 3rd Qtr

NOTRE DAME–FG, B Walker 42 YD 10:29 3rd Qtr

NOTRE DAME–TD, J Aldridge 3 YD RUN (TWO-POINT CONVERSION FAILED) 2:27 4th Qtr

WASHINGTON–TD, D Goodwin 6 YD PASS FROM R Fouch (R Perkins KICK) 12:04 4th Qtr

GAME STATISTICS

	NOTRE DAME	WASHINGTON
First Downs	25	9
Yards Rushing	49–252	23–26
Yards Passing	207	98
Sacks—Yards Lost	2–22	4–41
Passing Efficiency	15–28–1	11–25–0
Punts	0–0	9–33
Fumbles—Lost	1–0	0–0
Penalties—Yards	7–55	5–50
Time of Possession	37:28	22:32

INDIVIDUAL STATISTICS - RUSHING

NOTRE DAME–James Aldridge 13–84, Armando Allen 15–62, Gary Gray 9–61, Harrison Smith 1–35, Robert Hughes 4–19, Golden Tate 2–11, Evan Sharpley 1–1, Jimmy Clausen 4–MINUS 21. WASHINGTON–Terrance Dailey 8–24, David Freeman 5–16, D, Andre Goodwin 2–14, Paul Homer 1–2, Ronnie Fouch 7–MINUS 30.

INDIVIDUAL STATISTICS - PASSING

NOTRE DAME–Jimmy Clausen 14–26–201– 1, Evan Sharpley 1–2–6– 0. WASHINGTON–Ronnie Fouch 11–25–98– 0.

INDIVIDUAL STATISTICS - RECEIVING

NOTRE DAME–Michael Floyd 4–107, Golden Tate 3–47, Duval Kamara 2–22, Robby Parris 3–19, George West 1–6, Robert Hughes 1–5, James Aldridge 1–1. WASHINGTON–D, Andre Goodwin 7–47, Cody Bruns 1–21,

Charles Hawkins 1–12, Paul Homer 1–9, Terrance Dailey 1–9.

ATTENDANCE: 70,437

Game 8: Pittsburgh 36, Notre Dame 33 (4 OT)

SOUTH BEND | In the longest game ever for either school, Conor Lee kicked a career-high five field goals, including all four Pittsburgh scores in overtime and the 22-yard game winner.

Pitt beat Notre Dame for just the third time in the last 11 meetings.

"To sum it up, we get in overtime, you don't score touchdowns, you know sooner or later something bad can happen," Notre Dame Coach Charlie Weis said.

The Fighting Irish scored a pair of touchdowns 83 seconds apart to open a 14-point halftime lead, but Pitt scored on its opening drive after the break and the Panthers defense limited Notre Dame to 7 yards on 10 plays in the third quarter.

Irish receivers Golden Tate and Michael Floyd combined for 211 yards and three touchdowns.

	1st Qtr	2nd Qtr	3rd Qtr	4th Qtr	OT	Final
PITTSBURGH	3	0	7	14	12	**36**
NOTRE DAME	3	14	0	7	9	**33**

SCORING PLAYS

NOTRE DAME–FG, B Walker 39 YD 5:22 1st Qtr

PITTSBURGH–FG, C Lee 35 YD 9:02 1st Qtr

NOTRE DAME–TD, M Floyd 18 YD PASS FROM J Clausen (B Walker KICK) 13:33 2nd Qtr

NOTRE DAME–TD, M Floyd 4 YD PASS FROM J Clausen (B Walker KICK) 14:56 2nd Qtr

PITTSBURGH–TD, L Stephens-Howling 4 YD RUN (C Lee KICK) 4:05 3rd Qtr

PITTSBURGH–TD, L McCoy 1 YD RUN (C Lee KICK) 3:57 4th Qtr

NOTRE DAME–TD, G Tate 6 YD PASS FROM J Clausen (B Walker KICK) 9:22 4th Qtr

PITTSBURGH–TD, J Baldwin 10 YD PASS FROM P Bostick (C Lee KICK) 12:38 4th Qtr

PITTSBURGH–FG, C Lee 22 YD OT

NOTRE DAME–FG, B Walker 22 YD OT

NOTRE DAME–FG, B Walker 26 YD OT

PITTSBURGH–FG, C Lee 32 YD OT

PITTSBURGH–FG, C Lee 26 YD OT

NOTRE DAME–FG, B Walker 48 YD OT

PITTSBURGH–FG, C Lee 22 YD OT

GAME STATISTICS

	PITTSBURGH	NOTRE DAME
First Downs	17	20
Yards Rushing	47–178	39–115
Yards Passing	168	271
Sacks—Yards Lost	2–11	1–6
Passing Efficiency	15–30–3	23–44–0
Punts	4–36.8	5–30.4
Fumbles—Lost	0–0	1–0
Penalties—Yards	8–53	6–60
Time of Possession	31:16	28:44

INDIVIDUAL STATISTICS - RUSHING

PITTSBURGH–LeSean McCoy 32–169, LaRod Stephens-Howling 8–23, Conredge Collins 1–4, Derek Kinder 1–1, Kevan Smith 1–MINUS 3, Aundre Wright 1–MINUS 4, Pat Bostick 3–MINUS 12. NOTRE DAME–Armando Allen

19–73, James Aldridge 8–25, Robert Hughes 8–25, Team 1–MINUS 2, Jimmy Clausen 3–MINUS 6.

INDIVIDUAL STATISTICS - PASSING

PITTSBURGH–Pat Bostick 14–27–164– 3, Kevan Smith 1–3–4– 0. NOTRE DAME–Jimmy Clausen 23–44–271–0.

INDIVIDUAL STATISTICS - RECEIVING

PITTSBURGH–Oderick Turner 2–42, T.J. Porter 1–37, Jonathan Baldwin 2–31, LeSean McCoy 2–23, LaRod Stephens-Howling 1–14, Derek Kinder 2–10, John Pelusi 2–7, Cedric McGee 1–4, Dorin Dickerson 1–2, Nate Byham 1–MINUS 2. NOTRE DAME–Golden Tate 6–111, Michael Floyd 10–100, Kyle Rudolph 2–26, Duval Kamara 2–21, Armando Allen 3–13.

ATTENDANCE: 80,795

Game 9: Boston College 17, Notre Dame 0

BOSTON | Paul Anderson intercepted Jimmy Clausen twice, running one back 76 yards for a touchdown, as Boston College won its sixth straight against its Catholic rival.

It was the first shutout in series history and the third for Notre Dame over the last two seasons, matching its total from the previous 19 years.

The victory tied the series between the schools at 9–9. Notre Dame dropped Boston College from its schedule after 2010.

	1st Qtr	2nd Qtr	3rd Qtr	4th Qtr	Final
NOTRE DAME	0	0	0	0	**0**
BOSTON COLLEGE	3	7	7	0	**17**

SCORING PLAYS

BOSTON COLLEGE–FG, S Aponavicius 27 YD 13:14 1st Qtr

BOSTON COLLEGE–TD, P Anderson 76 YD INTERCEPTION RETURN (S Aponavicius KICK) 8:41 2nd Qtr

BOSTON COLLEGE–TD, B Robinson 9 YD PASS FROM C Crane (S Aponavicius KICK) 4:33 3rd Qtr

GAME STATISTICS

	NOTRE DAME	BOSTON COLLEGE
First Downs	16	13
Yards Rushing	21–66	41–167
Yards Passing	226	79
Sacks—Yards Lost	1–12	1–3
Passing Efficiency	26–46–4	9–22–0
Punts	7–31.3	8–40.6
Fumbles—Lost	2–1	0–0
Penalties—Yards	6–58	9–90
Time of Possession	27:53	32:07

INDIVIDUAL STATISTICS - RUSHING

NOTRE DAME–Armando Allen 6–24, Jimmy Clausen 6–19, Robert Hughes 3–18, James Aldridge 5–3, Asaph Schwapp 1–2. BOSTON COLLEGE–Montel Harris 23–120, Chris Crane 9–40, Josh Haden 6–12, Team 3–MINUS 5.

INDIVIDUAL STATISTICS - PASSING

NOTRE DAME–Jimmy Clausen 26–46–226– 4. BOSTON COLLEGE–Chris Crane 9–22–79– 0.

INDIVIDUAL STATISTICS - RECEIVING

NOTRE DAME–Michael Floyd 5–69, Golden Tate 6–66, Armando Allen 9–47, Kyle Rudolph 4–29, Asaph Schwapp 1–10, Duval Kamara 1–5. BOSTON COLLEGE–Rich Gunnell 4–34, Brandon Robinson 2–26, Ryan Purvis 2–13, Justin Jarvis 1–6.

ATTENDANCE: 44,500

Game 10: Notre Dame 27, Navy 21

BALTIMORE | A year after Notre Dame had its record 43-game winning streak against Navy snapped, the Fighting Irish had to withstand a wild last-minute rally.

With the victory, Notre Dame became bowl eligible. It held the Midshipmen to 178 rushing yards, Navy's lowest total since October 14, 2006 (113 vs. Rutgers).

Notre Dame led 27–7 with 1:39 remaining when Navy scored twice and recovered two onside kicks.

"Before we get going, anyone want to be on my hands team next week?" Charlie Weis asked reporters after the game. "Any volunteers?"

The previous week, Weiss, who called offensive plays for the first time that season, fielded questions about his job security.

	1st Qtr	2nd Qtr	3rd Qtr	4th Qtr	Final
NOTRE DAME	7	3	14	3	**27**
NAVY	0	7	0	14	**21**

SCORING PLAYS

NOTRE DAME–TD, T Smith 14 YD BLOCKED PUNT RETURN (B Walker KICK) 8:57 1st Qtr

NAVY–TD, C Finnerty 22 YD RUN (M Harmon KICK) 12:21 2nd Qtr

NOTRE DAME–FG, B Walker 28 YD 15:00 2nd Qtr

NOTRE DAME–TD, A Allen 11 YD RUN (B Walker KICK) 5:29 3rd Qtr

NOTRE DAME–TD, R Hughes 7 YD RUN (B Walker KICK) 11:31 3rd Qtr

NOTRE DAME–FG, B Walker 36 YD 3:43 4th Qtr

The tackle was not pretty, but Notre Dame's Steve Quinn was still able to bring down Navy ball carrier Ricky Dobbs in the Irish 27–21, victory. Dobbs carried 13 times but was held to just 27 yards on the ground, and his passing numbers were little better, going just two-for-eight for 54 yards.

NAVY–TD, S White 24 YD RUN (M Harmon KICK) 13:21 4th Qtr

NAVY–TD, R Dobbs 1 YD RUN (M Harmon KICK) 13:39 4th Qtr

GAME STATISTICS

	NOTRE DAME	NAVY
First Downs	24	11
Yards Rushing	51–230	45–178
Yards Passing	110	64
Sacks—Yards Lost	1–5	1–3
Passing Efficiency	15–19–2	3–14–0
Punts	3–44	9–40.7
Fumbles—Lost	4–3	1–1
Penalties—Yards	6–72	5–44
Time of Possession	35:33	24:27

INDIVIDUAL STATISTICS - RUSHING
NOTRE DAME–James Aldridge 16–80, Robert Hughes 13–64, Armando Allen 8–60, Gary Gray 7–16, David Grimes 1–10, Jimmy Clausen 3–4, Evan Sharpley 1–0, Team 1–MINUS 1, Golden Tate 1–MINUS 3. NAVY–Eric Kettani 11–42, Jarod Bryant 10–41, Shun White 5–39, Ricky Dobbs 13–27, Cory Finnerty 1–22, Kevin Campbell 3–9, Greg Shinego 2–MINUS 2.

INDIVIDUAL STATISTICS - PASSING
NOTRE DAME–Jimmy Clausen 15–18–110– 2, Evan Sharpley 0–1–0– 0. NAVY–Ricky Dobbs 2–8–54– 0, Jarod Bryant 1–5–10– 0. Team 0–1–0– 0.

INDIVIDUAL STATISTICS - RECEIVING
NOTRE DAME–Armando Allen 7–60, David Grimes 3–22, Duval Kamara 1–13, Robby Parris 1–9, Kyle Rudolph 1–8, Robert Hughes 1–4, James Aldridge 1–MINUS 6. NAVY–Tyree Barnes 2–54, Mario Washington 1–10.

ATTENDANCE: 70,932

Game 11: Syracuse 24, Notre Dame 23

SOUTH BEND | Cameron Dantley, son of Notre Dame basketball legend Adrian, threw an 11-yard touchdown pass to Donte Davis with 42 seconds remaining to lead Syracuse days after Coach Greg Robinson was fired effective the end of the season.

Despite the seniors playing their last game at Notre Dame Stadium, the Fighting Irish turned four possessions inside the Syracuse 23-yard line (including three in the third quarter) into just six points.

For the first time in school history, Notre Dame fell to an eight-loss team. It was its fifth defeat of the season, after nine in 2007. The 14 combined losses were the most ever by Notre Dame during a two-season span. The Irish lost 13 games in 2003–04, 1960–61, and 1959–60.

	1st Qtr	2nd Qtr	3rd Qtr	4th Qtr	Final
SYRACUSE	3	7	0	14	24
NOTRE DAME	3	10	10	0	23

SCORING PLAYS

NOTRE DAME–FG, B Walker 34 YD 3:21 1st Qtr

SYRACUSE–FG, P Shadle 48 YD 15:00 1st Qtr

SYRACUSE–TD, C Brinkley 1 YD RUN (P Shadle KICK) 8:12 2nd Qtr

NOTRE DAME–FG, B Walker 45 YD 12:41 2nd Qtr

NOTRE DAME–TD, G Tate 35 YD PASS FROM J Clausen (B Walker KICK) 14:58 2nd Qtr

NOTRE DAME–TD, G Tate 36 YD PASS FROM J Clausen (B Walker KICK) 12:11 3rd Qtr

NOTRE DAME–FG, B Walker 23 YD 13:26 3rd Qtr

SYRACUSE–TD, A Bailey 26 YD RUN (P Shadle KICK) 2:30 4th Qtr

SYRACUSE–TD, D Davis 11 YD PASS FROM C Dantley (P Shadle KICK) 14:18 4th Qtr

GAME STATISTICS

	SYRACUSE	NOTRE DAME
First Downs	18	16
Yards Rushing	36–170	28–41
Yards Passing	147	291
Sacks—Yards Lost	2–7	2–23
Passing Efficiency	14–26–0	22–41–0
Punts	5–29	4–43
Fumbles—Lost	2–2	0–0
Penalties—Yards	7–50	5–50
Time of Possession	28:41	31:19

INDIVIDUAL STATISTICS - RUSHING

SYRACUSE–Antwon Bailey 16–126, Curtis Brinkley 17–44, Cameron Dantley 3–0. NOTRE DAME–Armando Allen 17–52, David Grimes 1–5, Golden Tate 1–5, James Aldridge 6–0, Jimmy Clausen 3–MINUS 21.

INDIVIDUAL STATISTICS - PASSING

SYRACUSE–Cameron Dantley 13–25–122– 0, Antwon Bailey 1–1–25– 0. NOTRE DAME–Jimmy Clausen 22–39–291– 0. – Team 0–2–0– 0.

INDIVIDUAL STATISTICS - RECEIVING

SYRACUSE–Donte Davis 2–34, Nick Provo 2–28, Dan Sheeran 1–25, Da'Mon Merkerson 2–19, Marcus Sales 2–18, Tony Fiammetta 2–17, Van Chew 1–5, Curtis Brinkley 1–1, Antwon Bailey 1–0. NOTRE DAME–Golden Tate 7–146, David Grimes 7–83, Kyle Rudolph 3–29, Duval Kamara 1–14, Armando Allen 3–13, James Aldridge 1–6.

ATTENDANCE: 80,795

Game 12: No. 5 Southern California 38, Notre Dame 3

LOS ANGELES | Southern California dominated to win its seventh straight against Notre Dame, the longest losing streak for the Fighting Irish against any single opponent since losing eight consecutive games to Michigan State from 1955 to 1963.

The Trojans finished with 22 first downs and 449 yards of total offense while Notre Dame had just four first downs and 91 yards. The Irish didn't get a first down until the last play of the third quarter on a 15-yard run by James Aldridge.

Coach Charlie Weis lost his eighth straight game against a ranked opponent, and 10th of 11.

The game was also marred by a brief skirmish roughly 45 minutes before kickoff after Notre Dame players came onto the field while Southern California was already warming up.

	1st Qtr	2nd Qtr	3rd Qtr	4th Qtr	Final
NOTRE DAME	0	0	0	3	3
USC (5)	7	17	7	7	38

SCORING PLAYS

USC–TD, S Johnson 2 YD RUN (D Buehler KICK) 10:54 1st Qtr

USC–TD, J McKNIGHT 55 YD RUN (D Buehler KICK) 5:55 2nd Qtr

USC–TD, D Williams 12 YD PASS FROM M Sanchez (D Buehler KICK) 10:22 2nd Qtr

USC–FG, D Buehler 35 YD 14:36 2nd Qtr

USC–TD, C Gable 1 YD RUN (D Buehler KICK) 9:57 3rd Qtr

NOTRE DAME–FG, B Walker 41 YD 3:15 4th Qtr

USC–TD, P Turner 17 YD PASS FROM M Sanchez (D Buehler KICK) 7:03 4th Qtr

GAME STATISTICS

	NOTRE DAME	USC (5)
First Downs	4	22
Yards Rushing	27–50	33–175
Yards Passing	41	274
Sacks—Yards Lost	4–29	2–15
Passing Efficiency	11–22–2	23–33–3
Punts	8–40.4	4–32.3
Fumbles—Lost	1–1	1–0
Penalties—Yards	2–22	8–80
Time of Possession	25:59	34:01

INDIVIDUAL STATISTICS - RUSHING

NOTRE DAME–James Aldridge 12–58, Robert Hughes 5–7, Armando Allen 4–7, Jimmy Clausen 6–MINUS 22. USC–Joe McKnight 4–63, Marc Tyler 7–58, C.J. Gable 10–27, Stafon Johnson 5–26, Mark Sanchez 5–2, Ronald Johnson 1–0, Team 1–MINUS 1.

INDIVIDUAL STATISTICS - PASSING

NOTRE DAME–Jimmy Clausen 11–22–41– 2. USC–Mark Sanchez 22–31–267– 2. Mitch Mustain 1–2–7– 1.

INDIVIDUAL STATISTICS - RECEIVING

NOTRE DAME–Golden Tate 2–15, Robert Hughes 3–9, Duval Kamara 1–7, Kyle Rudolph 1–4, Asaph Schwapp 1–3, Armando Allen 3–3. USC–Damian Williams 7–86, Patrick Turner 6–83, Stanley Havili 1–39, Anthony McCoy 2–26, Ronald Johnson 2–24, Stafon Johnson 1–9, Brandon Carswell 1–7, Joe McKnight 3–0.

ATTENDANCE: 90,689

Hawaii Bowl: Notre Dame 49, Hawaii 21

HONOLULU | Jimmy Clausen set Fighting Irish bowl records with 401 yards passing and five touchdowns to lead Notre Dame to its first postseason victory in 15 years.

"I told the team that's the only thing I wanted [for Christmas]. I just wanted to win a bowl game," Coach Charlie Weis said. "I heard it a hundred times in the locker room after the game and they wanted to know what I was giving them for Christmas. I told them 'a flight home.'"

Golden Tate had six catches for 177 yards and three touchdowns, including his backbreaking 69-yard score in the second quarter.

Incidentally, Notre Dame players wore names on their jersey backs for the first time since the 1988 Cotton Bowl vs. Texas A&M.

	1st Qtr	2nd Qtr	3rd Qtr	4th Qtr	Final
HAWAII	0	7	7	7	21
NOTRE DAME	7	21	21	0	49

SCORING PLAYS

NOTRE DAME–TD, R Hughes 2 YD RUN (B Walker KICK) 11:53 1st Qtr

NOTRE DAME–TD, D Grimes 14 YD PASS FROM J Clausen (B Walker KICK) 4:35 2nd Qtr

HAWAII–TD, A Bain 10 YD PASS FROM G Alexander (D Kelly KICK) 6:48 2nd Qtr

NOTRE DAME–TD, G Tate 69 YD PASS FROM J Clausen (B Walker KICK) 8:11 2nd Qtr

NOTRE DAME–TD, G Tate 18 YD PASS FROM J Clausen (B Walker KICK) 14:59 2nd Qtr

NOTRE DAME–TD, A Allen 18 YD PASS FROM J Clausen (B Walker KICK) 4:10 3rd Qtr

USC's Clay Matthews had a fistful of Jimmy Clausen's jersey on this play, but the Notre Dame pivot was still able to pitch the ball. The Notre Dame offense never got in gear on this day, managing just three points against Southern California's stingy defense.

NOTRE DAME–TD, G Tate 40 YD PASS FROM J Clausen (B Walker KICK) 7:38 3rd Qtr

HAWAII–TD, A Bain 21 YD PASS FROM G Alexander (D Kelly KICK) 10:35 3rd Qtr

NOTRE DAME–TD, A Allen 96 YD KICKOFF RETURN (B Walker KICK) 10:48 3rd Qtr

HAWAII–TD, M Washington 27 YD PASS FROM I Funaki (D Kelly KICK) 13:15 4th Qtr

GAME STATISTICS

	HAWAII	NOTRE DAME
First Downs	22	23
Yards Rushing	19–32	34–65
Yards Passing	326	413
Sacks—Yards Lost	8–55	2–8
Passing Efficiency	28–44–1	24–28–0
Punts	2–2	2–2.5
Fumbles—Lost	2–1	2–0
Penalties—Yards	8–69	5–60
Time of Possession	27:00	33:00

INDIVIDUAL STATISTICS - RUSHING

HAWAII–Kealoha Pilares 2–19, Inoke Funaki 1–15, Daniel Libre 1–12, David Farmer 1–1, Leon Wright–Jackson 1–1, Greg Alexander 13–MINUS 16. NOTRE DAME–Robert Hughes 17–55, Gary Gray 5–13, Armando Allen 4–9, Evan Sharpley 2–0, James Aldridge 1–0, Team 3–MINUS 6, Jimmy Clausen 2–MINUS 6.

INDIVIDUAL STATISTICS - PASSING

HAWAII–Greg Alexander 23–39–261– 1, Inoke Funaki 5–5–65– 0. NOTRE DAME–Jimmy Clausen 22–26–401– 0. Evan Sharpley 2–2–12– 0.

INDIVIDUAL STATISTICS - RECEIVING

HAWAII–Aaron Bain 8–109, Michael Washington 6–96, Greg Salas 7–76, Malcolm Lane 4–29, Kealoha Pilares 3–16. NOTRE DAME–Golden Tate 6–177, Kyle Rudolph 4–78, Armando Allen 2–59, David Grimes 4–34, Robert Hughes 3–27, Duval Kamara 3–21, Michael Floyd 2–17.

ATTENDANCE: 45,718

STARTING LINEUPS

OPENER (SAN DIEGO STATE)	LAST GAME (HAWAII)
OFFENSE	
WR 18 Duval Kamara	WR 23 Golden Tate
LT 77 Michael Turkovich	LT 77 Michael Turkovich
LG 55 Eric Olsen	LG 55 Eric Olsen
C 51 Dan Wenger	C 51 Dan Wenger
RG 59 Chris Stewart	RG 59 Chris Stewart
RT 74 Sam Young	RT 74 Sam Young
TE 9 Kyle Rudolph	TE 9 Kyle Rudolph
WR 11 David Grimes	WR 11 David Grimes
QB 7 Jimmy Clausen	QB 7 Jimmy Clausen
TE 84 Will Yeatman	WR 3 Michael Floyd
HB 33 Robert Hughes	HB 5 Armando Allen
DEFENSE	
DE 94 Justin Brown	DE 9 Ethan Johnson
NT 95 Ian Williams	DE/LB 48 Steve Quinn
DE 96 Pat Kuntz	DE 96 Pat Kuntz
ILB 58 Brian Smith	MLB 45 Darius Fleming
ILB 40 Maurice Crum Jr.	SLB 40 Maurice Crum Jr.
OLB 56 Kerry Neal	WLB 56 Kerry Neal
OLB 90 John Ryan	DB 31 Sergio Brown
CB 8 Raeshon McNeil	CB 8 Raeshon McNeil
FS 27 David Bruton	FS 27 David Bruton
SS 28 Kyle McCarthy	SS 28 Kyle McCarthy
CB 20 Terrail Lambert	CB 12 Robert Blanton

Notre Dame's leading rusher in 2008, Armando Allen, looks for daylight while trying to avoid the tackling attempt of Syracuse's Derrell Smith. In addition to his strong year on the ground, Allen set a Notre Dame bowl record with his 96-yard kick return against Hawaii.

FINAL STATISTICS

TEAM STATISTICS	ND	OPP
SCORING	321	288
Points Per Game	24.7	22.2
FIRST DOWNS	250	232
Rushing	91	93
Passing	133	122
Penalty	26	17
RUSHING YARDAGE	1,426	1,744
Yards Gained Rushing	1,764	2,058
Yards Lost Rushing	338	314
Rushing Attempts	436	430
Average Per Rush	3.3	4.1
Average Per Game	109.7	134.2
TDs Rushing	11	18
PASSING YARDAGE	3,190	2,544
Att-Comp-Int	447–271–17	422–228–14
Average Per Pass	7.1	6.0
Average Per Catch	11.8	11.2
Average Per Game	245.4	195.7
TDs Passing	25	15
TOTAL OFFENSE	4,616	4,288
Total Plays	883	852
Average Per Play	5.2	5.0
Average Per Game	355.1	329.8
KICK RETURNS:	52–1,121	59–972
PUNT RETURNS:	26–232	29–175
INT RETURNS:	14–236	17–134
KICK RETURN AVERAGE	21.6	16.5
PUNT RETURN AVERAGE	8.9	6.0
INT RETURN AVERAGE	16.9	7.9
FUMBLES-LOST	23–11	17–11
PENALTIES-Yards	70–649	95–834
Average Per Game	49.9	64.2
PUNTS-Yards	56–2,218	75–2,794
Average Per Punt	39.6	37.3

Net Punt Average	35.1	33.4
TIME OF POSSESSION	31:17	28:43
3rd-Down Conversions	63/180	57/174
3rd-Down Pct	35%	33%
4th-Down Conversions	11/30	5/13
4th-Down Pct	37%	38%
SACKS BY-Yards	26–195	22–185
TOUCHDOWNS SCORED	40	35
FIELD GOALS-ATTEMPTS	14–24	15–21
ONSIDE KICKS	0–0	2–3
RED-ZONE SCORES	31–44 70%	36–44 82%
RED-ZONE TOUCHDOWNS	23–44 52%	24–44 55%
PAT–ATTEMPTS	39–40 98%	33–34 97%
ATTENDANCE	484,770	388,210
Games/Avg Per Game	6/80,795	6/64,702

SCORE BY QUARTERS

	1st	2nd	3rd	4th	OT	Total
Notre Dame	69	103	90	50	9	321
Opponents	36	89	57	94	12	288

INDIVIDUAL STATISTICS

RUSHING

	GP	Att	Gain	Loss	Net	Avg	TD	Lg	Avg/G
ALLEN, Armando	13	134	621	36	585	4.4	3	21	45.0
HUGHES, Robert	12	112	412	30	382	3.4	4	18	31.8
ALDRIDGE, James	12	91	383	26	357	3.9	3	19	29.8
GRAY, Jonas	7	21	104	14	90	4.3	0	19	12.9
SMITH, Harrison	13	2	58	0	58	29.0	0	35	4.5
TATE, Golden	13	5	50	13	37	7.4	1	24	2.8
GRIMES, David	11	2	15	0	15	7.5	0	10	1.4

SCHWAPP, Asaph	13	1	2	0	2	2.0	0	2 0.	2
SHARPLEY, Evan	3	4	3	2	1	0.2	0	2	0.3
MAUST, Eric	13	1	0	8	-8	-8.0	0	0	-0.6
TEAM	10	9	0	20	-20	-2.2	0	0	-2.0
CLAUSEN, Jimmy	13	54	116	189	-73	-1.4	0	10	-5.6
Total	13	436	1,764	338	1,426	3.3	11	35	109.7
Opponents	13	430	2,058	314	1,744	4.1	18	63	134.2

PASSING

	GP	Eff	Comp-Att-Int	Pct	Yds	TD	Lg	Avg/G
CLAUSEN, Jimmy	13	132.49	268–440–17	60.9	3,172	25	69	244.0
SHARPLEY, Evan	3	90.24	3–5–0	60.0	18	0	6	6.0
TEAM	10	0.00	0–2–0	0.0	0	0	0	0.0
Total	13	131.42	271–447–17	60.6	3,190	25	69	245.4
Opponents	13	109.76	228–422–14	54.0	2,544	15	54	195.7

RECEIVING

	GP	No.	Yds	Avg	TD	Lg	Avg/G
TATE, Golden	13	58	1,080	18.6	10	69	83.1
ALLEN, Armando	13	50	355	7.1	2	41	27.3
FLOYD, Michael	11	48	719	15.0	7	51	65.4
GRIMES, David	11	35	321	9.2	3	31	29.2

Kyle Rudolph turns to head up field after making a catch against Stanford. Rudolph averaged nearly 12 yards per reception in 2008 and also caught a pair of touchdowns.

RUDOLPH, Kyle	13	29	340	11.7	2	29	26.2
KAMARA, Duval	13	20	206	10.3	1	28	15.8
HUGHES, Robert	12	14	93	6.6	0	15	7.8
PARRIS, Robby	7	9	50	5.6	0	12	7.1
ALDRIDGE, James	12	3	1	0.3	0	6	0.1
SCHWAPP, Asaph	13	2	13	6.5	0	10	1.0
YEATMAN, Will	3	2	6	3.0	0	4	2.0
WEST, George	5	1	6	6.0	0	6	1.2
Total	13	271	3,190	11.8	25	69	245.4
Opponents	13	228	2,544	11.2	15	54	195.7

PUNT RETURNS

	No.	Yds	Avg	TD	Lg
TATE, Golden	14	116	8.3	0	42
ALLEN, Armando	7	66	9.4	0	22
McNEIL, Raeshon	1	3	3.0	0	3
SMITH, Scott	1	6	6.0	0	6
GRIMES, David	1	-4	-4.0	0	0
WEST, George	1	3	3.0	0	3
ANELLO, Mike	1	28	28.	0	0
SMITH, Toryan	0	14	0.0	1	14
Total	26	232	8.9	1	42
Opponents	29	175	6.0	0	38

INTERCEPTIONS

	No.	Yds	Avg	TD	Lg
BRUTON, David	4	57	14.2	0	39
BLANTON, Robert	2	47	23.5	1	47
McCARTHY, Kyle	2	18	9.0	0	8
McNEIL, Raeshon	2	47	23.5	0	43
GRAY, Gary	2	65	32.5	0	41
NEAL, Kerry	1	2	2.0	0	2
KUNTZ, Pat	1	0	0.0	0	0
Total	14	236	16.9	1	47
Opponents	17	134	7.9	2	76

KICK RETURNS

	No.	Yds	Avg	TD	Lg
TATE, Golden	26	521	20.0	0	30
ALLEN, Armando	21	543	25.9	1	96
GRAY, Jonas	2	9	4.5	0	5
ALDRIDGE, James	1	15	15.0	0	15
WEST, George	1	33	33.0	0	33
TEAM	1	0	0.0	0	0
Total	52	1,121	21.6	1	96
Opponents	59	972	16.5	0	37

FUMBLE RETURNS

	Returns	Yds	Avg	TD	Lg
KUNTZ, Pat	1	2	2.0	0	2
SMITH, Brian	1	35	35.0	1	35
SMITH, Toryan	1	8	8.0	0	8
GRAY, Gary	0	20	0.0	0	20
Total	3	65	21.7	1	35
Opponents	0	0	0.0	0	0

Golden Tate makes a catch for a touchdown over San Diego State safety Vonnie Holmes in South Bend in September 2008.

Running back Robert Hughes breaks free from a tackler during the Hawaii Bowl. Hughes finished the season third on the team in total offense with 382 rushing yards.

TOTAL OFFENSE

	GP	Plays	Rush	Pass	Total	Avg/G
CLAUSEN, Jimmy	13	494	-73	3172	3,099	238.4
ALLEN, Armando	13	134	585	0	585	45.0
HUGHES, Robert	12	112	382	0	382	31.8
ALDRIDGE, James	12	91	357	0	357	29.8
GRAY, Jonas	7	21	90	0	90	12.9
SMITH, Harrison	13	2	58	0	58	4.5
TATE, Golden	13	5	37	0	37	2.8
SHARPLEY, Evan	3	9	1	18	19	6.3
GRIMES, David	11	2	15	0	15	1.4
SCHWAPP, Asaph	13	1	2	0	2	0.2
MAUST, Eric	13	1	-8	0	-8	-0.6
TEAM	10	11	-20	0	-20	-2.0
Total	13	883	1,426	3,190	4,616	355.1
Opponents	13	852	1,744	2,544	4,288	329.8

FIELD GOALS

	FG	Pct.	01-19	20-29	30-39	40-49	50-99	Lg	Blk
WALKER, Brandon	14-24	58.3	0-0	5-6	3-5	6-11	0-2	48	0

2008 Review

FG SEQUENCE	NOTRE DAME	OPPONENTS
San Diego State	47	–
Michigan	–	(23)
Michigan State	51,41	(45),(26),(23)
Purdue	31,(41)	28
Stanford	41,46	42
North Carolina	(42)	(41),(34),(42),52
Washington	(28),(42)	–
Pittsburgh	(39),(22),(26),(48),38	(35),(22),(32),(26),(22)
Boston College	–	34,(27),32
Navy	(28),(36)	–
Syracuse	(34),(45),26,(23),49,53	47,(48)
USC	(41)	(35)
Hawaii	–	–

Numbers in (parentheses) indicate field goal was made.

PUNTING

	No.	Yds	Avg	Lg	TB	FC	I20	50+	Blk
MAUST, Eric	54	2,218	41.1	54	4	10	16	8	2
TEAM	2	0	0.0	0	0	0	0	0	0
Total	56	2,218	39.6	54	4	10	16	8	2
Opponents	75	2,794	37.3	58	3	22	20	9	3

KICKOFFS

	No.	Yds	Avg	TB	OB	Retn	Net	Ydln
BURKHART, Ryan	62	3,789	61.1	1	2			
WALKER, Brandon	1	40	40.0	0	0			
Total	63	3,829	60.8	1	2	16.5	45.0	24
Opponents	56	3,620	64.6	5	0	21.6	42.8	27

ALL PURPOSE

	GP	Rush	Rec	PR	KR	IR	Total	Avg/G
TATE, Golden	13	37	1,080	116	521	0	1,754	134.9
ALLEN, Armand	13	585	355	66	543	0	1,549	119.2
FLOYD, Michael	11	0	719	0	0	0	719	65.4
HUGHES, Rober	12	382	93	0	0	0	475	39.6
ALDRIDGE, Jam	12	357	1	0	15	0	373	31.1
RUDOLPH, Kyle	13	0	340	0	0	0	340	26.2
GRIMES, David	11	15	321	-4	0	0	332	30.2
KAMARA, Duval	13	0	206	0	0	0	206	15.8
GRAY, Jonas	7	90	0	0	9	0	99	14.1
GRAY, Gary	9	0	0	0	0	65	65	7.2
SMITH, Harrison	13	58	0	0	0	0	58	4.5
BRUTON, David	13	0	0	0	0	57	57	4.4
PARRIS, Robby	7	0	50	0	0	0	50	7.1
McNEIL, Raesh	13	0	0	3	0	47	50	3.8
BLANTON, Rob	12	0	0	0	0	47	47	3.9
WEST, George	5	0	6	3	33	0	42	8.4
ANELLO, Mike	12	0	0	28	0	0	28	2.3
McCARTHY, Kyl	13	0	0	0	0	18	18	1.4

SCHWAPP, Asaph								
	13	2	13	0	0	0	15	1.2
SMITH, Toryan								
	10	0	0	14	0	0	14	1.4
SMITH, Scott								
	13	0	0	6	0	0	6	0.5
YEATMAN, Will								
	3	0	6	0	0	0	6	2.0
NEAL, Kerry								
	13	0	0	0	0	2	2	0.2
SHARPLEY, Ev								
	3	1	0	0	0	0	1	0.3
MAUST, Eric								
	13	-8	0	0	0	0	-8	-0.6
TEAM								
	10	-20	0	0	0	0	-20	-2.0
CLAUSEN, Jim								
	13	-73	0	0	0	0	-73	-5.6
Total								
	13	1,426	3,190	232	1,121	236	6,205	477.3
Opponents								
	13	1,744	2,544	175	972	134	5,569	428.4

DEFENSIVE STATISTICS

	GP	Solo	Ast	Total	TFL	Yds	Sacks	Yds
28 McCARTHY, Kyle								
	13	64	46	110	3.5	– 12	0	0
27 BRUTON, David								
	13	61	36	97	1.5	– 5	0	0
40 CRUM, Maurice								
	13	33	32	65	5.5	– 36	3.0	–24
22 SMITH, Harrison								
	13	39	18	57	8.5	– 39	3.5	–26
58 SMITH, Brian								
	11	33	21	54	4.0	– 33	2.0	–23
96 KUNTZ, Pat								
	13	19	23	42	8.0	– 38	3.5	– 26

8 McNEIL, Raeshon	13	28	13	41	0	0	0	0
95 WILLIAMS, Ian	13	18	22	40	2.0	-5	0	0
12 BLANTON, Robert	12	26	7	33	3	-14	0	0
20 LAMBERT, Terrail	11	20	13	33	0	0	0	0
31 BROWN, Sergio	13	21	7	28	2.0	- 15	1.0	-12
56 NEAL, Kerry	13	11	14	25	4.0	- 19	2.0	-15
94 BROWN, Justin	13	10	14	24	4.5	-5	0	0
45 FLEMING, Darius	13	13	11	24	2.5	-20	2.5	-20
37 ANELLO, Mike	12	15	8	23	0	0	0	0
9A JOHNSON, Ethan	13	9	9	18	5.0	-21	3.5	-17
49 SMITH, Toryan	10	11	7	18	0	0	0	0
6 HERRING, Ray	13	12	5	17	0.5	-2	0.5	-2
4 GRAY, Gary	9	15	0	15	0	0	0	0
48 QUINN, Steve	13	13	1	14	3.0	-22	3.0	-22
41 SMITH, Scott	13	9	3	12	1.0	-3	1.0	-3
53 RICHARDSON, Morrice	11	8	3	11	0.5	-5	0.5	-5
90 RYAN, John	12	2	5	7	0	0	0	0
24 GORDON, Leonard	13	3	2	5	0	0	0	0
TM TEAM	10	3	0	3	1.0	-1	0	0

91 NWANKWO, Emeka	7	2	0	2	0	0	0	0
43 MAUST, Eric	13	2	0	2	0	0	0	0
42 WASHINGTON, Kevin	5	0	1	1	0	0	0	0
23 TATE, Golden	13	1	0	1	0	0	0	0
3 FLOYD, Michael	11	1	0	1	0	0	0	0
18 KAMARA, Duval	13	1	0	1	0	0	0	0
35 BROOKS, Kevin	13	0	1	1	0	0	0	0
54 McDONALD, Anthony	1	1	0	1	0	0	0	0
46 FILER, Steve	11	1	0	1	0	0	0	0
4C LEONIS, John	2	1	0	1	0	0	0	0
55 OLSEN, Eric	13	1	0	1	0	0	0	0
11 GRIMES, David	11	1	0	1	0	0	0	0
93 MULLEN, Paddy	12	0	0	0	0	0	0	0
Total	13	508	322	830	60	–295	26	–195
Opponents	13	498	410	908	81	–343	22	–185

Notre Dame's leading tackler in 2008, Kyle McCarthy brings down Penn State wide receiver Terrell Golden. McCarthy finished the season with 110 total tackles, making him the only Irish defender to break the century mark.

THROUGH THE YEARS

1887

0–1

Nov. 23	Michigan	South Bend	L	8–0
Coach: None				0–8
Captain: Henry Luhn				

Notre Dame made arrangements to have the University of Michigan football team visit campus to teach a group of students the new game of "rugby football." The student newspaper, the *Scholastic*, wrote: "There is good material here for a fine team, and the boys will undoubtedly give the Michigan players a hard 'tussle.'" ... Brother Paul of the Cross, a prefect for the senior department who was born in Ireland, is credited with organizing the game.

1888

1–2

April 20	Michigan	South Bend	L	26–6
April 21	Michigan	South Bend	L	10–4
Dec. 6	Harvard Prep	South Bend	W	20–0
Coach: None				30–36
Captain: Edward Prudhomme				

Student newspaper the *Scholastic* announced two more games against Michigan: "We are pleased to note the interest taken by the students in the rugby football game. It is an interesting game, and affords exercise at those times of year when baseball and rowing cannot be enjoyed." ... Knute Rockne was born in Voss, Norway. Five years later his parents left for the United States and settled in Chicago. ... The second Michigan game resulted in a dispute between the teams, in part due to a call by referee Edward Sqrague, who was a Michigan player injured during the previous game.

1889

1–0

Nov. 14	Northwestern	Evanston	W	9–0
Coach: None				9–0
Captain: Edward Prudhomme				

1892

1–0–1

Oct. 19	South Bend H. S.	South Bend	W	56–0
Nov. 24	Hillsdale	South Bend	T	10–10
Coach: None				66–10
Captain: Pat Coady				

There was no team in 1890 or 1891.

1893

4–1

Oct. 25	Kalamazoo	South Bend	W	34–0
Nov. 11	Albion	South Bend	W	8–6
Nov. 23	De LaSalle	South Bend	W	28–0
Nov. 30	Hillsdale	South Bend	W	22–10
Jan. 1	Chicago	Chicago	L	8–0
Coach: None				92–24
Captain: Frank Keough				

1894

3–1–1

Oct. 13	Hillsdale	South Bend	W	14–0
Oct. 20	Albion	South Bend	T	6–6
Nov. 15	Wabash	South Bend	W	30–0
Nov. 22	Rush Medical	South Bend	W	18–6
Nov. 29	Albion	South Bend	L	19–12
Coach: James L. Morison				80–31
Captain: Frank Keough				

Notre Dame's first head coach, James Morrison, wrote an acquaintance after his first day on the job: "I arrived here this morning and found about as green a set of football players that ever donned

a uniform...They want to smoke, and when I told them that they would have to run and get up some wind, they thought I was rubbing it in on them. One big, strong cuss remarked that it was too much like work. Well, maybe you think I didn't give him hell! I bet you a hundred no one ever makes a remark like that again." ... Morrison had been hired for $40 plus expenses for two weeks. He won his first game against Hillsdale College of Michigan and a month later was hired to coach Hillsdale.

1895

3–1

Oct. 19	Northwestern Law	South Bend	W	20-0
Nov. 7	Illinois Cycling Club	South Bend	W	18-2
Nov. 22	Indianapolis Artillery	South Bend	L	18-0
Nov. 28	Chicago Physicians & Surgeons	South Bend	W	32-0
Coach: H.G. Hadden				70-20
Captain: Dan Casey				

1896

4–3

Oct. 8	Chicago Physicians & Surgeons	South Bend	L	4-0
Oct. 14	Chicago	South Bend	L	18-0
Oct. 27	South Bend Commercial Athletic Club	South Bend	W	46-0
Oct. 31	Albion	South Bend	W	24-0
Nov. 14	Purdue	South Bend	L	28-22
Nov. 20	Highland Views	South Bend	W	82-0
Nov. 26	Beloit	South Bend	W	8-0
Coach: Frank E. Hering				182-50
Captain: Frank E. Hering				

1897

4–1–1

Oct. 13	Rush Medical	South Bend	T	0–0
Oct. 23	DePauw	South Bend	W	4–0
Oct. 28	Chicago Dental Surgeons	South Bend	W	62–0
Nov. 6	Chicago	Chicago	L	34–5
Nov. 13	St. Viator	South Bend	W	60–0
Nov. 25	Michigan State	South Bend	W	34–6
Coach: Frank E. Hering				165–40
Captain: Jack Mullen				

1898

4–2

Oct. 8	Illinois	Champaign	W	5–0
Oct. 15	Michigan State	South Bend	W	53–0
Oct. 23	Michigan	Ann Arbor	L	23–0
Oct. 29	DePauw	South Bend	W	32–0
Nov. 5	Indiana	South Bend	L	11–5
Nov. 19	Albion	Albion	W	60–0
Coach: Frank E. Hering				155–34
Captain: Jack Mullen				

Coach Frank E. Hering (12–6–1) later came up with the idea for Americans to set aside one day a year for Mother's Day.

Between 1887 and 1899 Notre Dame compiled a record of 31 wins, 15 losses, and four ties against all opponents, including local Indiana high school teams and universities that they still play more than a century later.

Though the rivalry has not always been so lopsided, Notre Dame absolutely dominated Michigan State during the school's early meetings. Here, Arnaz Battle celebrates with Jeff Faine after his eventual game-winning touchdown with just minutes to go in the teams' 2002 meeting.

1899

6–3–1

Sept. 27	Englewood H. S.	South Bend	W	29–5
Sept. 30	Michigan State	South Bend	W	40–0
Oct. 4	Chicago	Chicago	L	23–6
Oct. 14	Lake Forest	South Bend	W	38–0
Oct. 18	Michigan	Ann Arbor	L	12–0
Oct. 23	Indiana	South Bend	W	17–0
Oct. 27	Northwestern	South Bend	W	12–0
Nov. 4	Rush Medical	South Bend	W	17–0
Nov. 18	Purdue	West Lafayette	T	10–10
Nov. 30	Chicago Physicians & Surgeons	South Bend	L	5–0
Coach: James McWeeney				169–55
Captain: Jack Mullen				

1900

6–3–1

Sept. 29	Goshen	South Bend	W	55–0
Oct. 6	Englewood H. S.	South Bend	W	68–0
Oct. 13	South Bend Howard Park	South Bend	W	64–0
Oct. 20	Cincinnati	South Bend	W	58–0
Oct. 25	Indiana	Bloomington	L	6–0
Nov. 3	Beloit	South Bend	T	6–6
Nov. 10	Wisconsin	Madison	L	54–0
Nov. 17	Michigan	Ann Arbor	L	7–0
Nov. 24	Rush Medical	South Bend	W	5–0
Nov. 29	Chicago Physicians & Surgeons	South Bend	W	5–0
Coach: Pat O'Dea				261–73
Captain: John Farley				

1901

8–1–1

Sept. 28	South Bend Athletic Club	South Bend	T	0–0
Oct. 5	Ohio Medical University	Columbus	W	6–0
Oct. 12	Northwestern	Evanston	L	2–0
Oct. 19	Chicago Medical College	South Bend	W	32–0
Oct. 26	Beloit	Beloit	W	5–0
Nov. 2	Lake Forest	South Bend	W	16–0
Nov. 9	Purdue	South Bend	W	12–6
Nov. 16	Indiana	South Bend	W	18–5
Nov. 23	Chicago Physicians & Surgeons	South Bend	W	34–0
Nov. 28	South Bend Athletic Club	South Bend	W	22–6
Coach: Pat O'Dea				145–19
Captain: Al Fortin				

1902

6–2–1

Sept. 27	Michigan State	South Bend	W	33–0
Oct. 11	Lake Forest	South Bend	W	28–0
Oct. 18	Michigan	Toledo	L	23–0
Oct. 25	Indiana	Bloomington	W	11–5
Nov. 1	Ohio Medical University	Columbus	W	6–5
Nov. 8	Knox College	Galesburg	L	12–5
Nov. 15	American Medical	South Bend	W	92–0
Nov. 22	DePauw	South Bend	W	22–0
Nov. 27	Purdue	West Lafayette	T	6–6
Coach: James F. Faragher				203–51
Captain: Louis "Red" Salmon				

Purdue and Notre Dame have had a fierce intrastate rivalry for over a century. In this 2002 meeting, the Notre Dame defense hounds Purdue's Kyle Orton into throwing the ball up for grabs. The Irish won, 24–17.

1903

8–0–1

Oct. 3	Michigan State	South Bend	W	12–0
Oct. 10	Lake Forest	South Bend	W	28–0
Oct. 17	DePauw	South Bend	W	56–0
Oct. 24	American Medical	South Bend	W	52–0
Oct. 29	Chicago Physicians & Surgeons	South Bend	W	46–0
Nov. 7	Missouri Osteopaths	South Bend	W	28–0
Nov. 14	Northwestern	South Side Park	T	0–0
Nov. 21	Ohio Medical University	South Bend	W	35–0
Nov. 26	Wabash	Crawfordsville	W	34–0
Coach: James F. Faragher				291–0
Captain: Louis "Red" Salmon				

Louis "Red" Salmon was considered the first great Notre Dame back. His 105 points scored as a senior and his 36 career touchdowns stood as school records until 1985. In four seasons he tallied 250 points, back when a touchdown was worth only five points. ... The defense didn't yield a single point.

1904

5–3

Oct. 1	Wabash	South Bend	W	12–4
Oct. 8	American Medical	South Bend	W	44–0
Oct. 15	Wisconsin	Milwaukee	L	58–0
Oct. 22	Ohio Medical University	Columbus	W	17–5
Oct. 27	Toledo Athletic Association	South Bend	W	6–0
Nov. 5	Kansas	Lawrence	L	24–5
Nov. 19	DePauw	South Bend	W	10–0
Nov. 24	Purdue	West Lafayette	L	36–0
Coach: Louis "Red" Salmon				94–127
Captain: Frank Shaughnessy				

1905

5–4

Sept. 30	Chicago North Division H.S.	South Bend	W	44–0
Oct. 7	Michigan State	South Bend	W	28–0
Oct. 14	Wisconsin	Milwaukee	L	21–0
Oct. 21	Wabash	South Bend	L	5–0
Oct. 28	American Medical	South Bend	W	142–0
Nov. 4	DePauw	South Bend	W	71–0
Nov. 11	Indiana	Bloomington	L	22–5
Nov. 18	Bennett Medical College	South Bend	W	22–0
Nov. 24	Purdue	West Lafayette	L	32–0
Coach: Henry J. McGlew				312–80
Captain: Pat Beacom				

After a 25-minute first half against American Medical, with Notre Dame leading 111–0, the second half was shortened to only eight minutes to permit the "doctors" time to eat before catching a train to Chicago. Notre Dame scored 27 touchdowns but missed 20 extra points. At the time, the scoring team was still able to receive the kickoff after scoring. ... Bennett Medical College was located in Chicago.

1906

6–1

Oct. 6	Franklin	South Bend	W	26–0
Oct. 13	Hillsdale	South Bend	W	17–0
Oct. 20	Chicago Physicians & Surgeons	South Bend	W	28–0
Oct. 27	Michigan State	South Bend	W	5–0
Nov. 3	Purdue	West Lafayette	W	2–0
Nov. 10	Indiana	Indianapolis	L	12–0
Nov. 24	Beloit	South Bend	W	29–0
Coach: Thomas A. Barry				107–12
Captain: Bob Bracken				

The forward pass was legalized but was mostly considered a gimmick and deemed too risky during the first few years.

1907

6–0–1

Oct. 12	Chicago Physicians & Surgeons	South Bend	W	32-0
Oct. 19	Franklin	South Bend	W	23-0
Oct. 26	Olivet	South Bend	W	22-4
Nov. 2	Indiana	South Bend	T	0-0
Nov. 9	Knox	South Bend	W	22-4
Nov. 23	Purdue	West Lafayette	W	17-0
Nov. 28	St. Vincent's	Chicago	W	21-12
Coach: Thomas A. Barry				137-20
Captain: Dom Callicrate				

1908

8–1

Oct. 3	Hillsdale	South Bend	W	39-0
Oct. 10	Franklin	South Bend	W	64-0
Oct. 17	Michigan	Ann Arbor	L	12-6
Oct. 24	Chicago Physicians & Surgeons	South Bend	W	88-0
Oct. 29	Ohio Northern	South Bend	W	58-4
Nov. 7	Indiana	Indianapolis	W	11-0
Nov. 13	Wabash	Crawfordsville	W	8-4
Nov. 18	St. Viator	South Bend	W	46-0
Nov. 26	Marquette	Milwaukee	W	6-0
Coach: Victor M. Place				326-20
Captain: Harry Miller				

1909

7–0–1

Oct. 9	Olivet	South Bend	W	58-0
Oct. 16	Rose Poly	South Bend	W	60-11
Oct. 23	Michigan State	South Bend	W	17-0
Oct. 30	Pittsburgh	Pittsburgh	W	6-0
Nov. 6	Michigan	Ann Arbor	W	11-3
Nov. 13	Miami (Ohio)	South Bend	W	46-0
Nov. 20	Wabash	South Bend	W	38-0
Nov. 25	Marquette	Milwaukee	T	0-0
Coach: Frank C. Longman				236-14
Captain: Howard Edwards				

The "Notre Dame Victory March" was introduced during Washington Day exercises. The song had been written the previous fall by brothers Michael J. and John E. Shea. It's considered the most recognized song in collegiate athletics. ... Notre Dame defeated Michigan for the first time. Coach Frank Longman had played for Fielding Yost at Michigan and lived in Ann Arbor during the off-season. ... The first reference to Notre Dame as the "Fighting Irish" was believed to be in a Nov. 6 *Detroit Free Press* article regarding the win at Michigan. Most of the Notre Dame starters were Irish.

1910

4–1–1

Oct. 8	Olivet	South Bend	W	48-0
Oct. 22	Butchel	South Bend	W	51-0
Oct. 29	Michigan State	East Lansing	L	17-0
Nov. 12	Rose Poly	Terre Haute	W	41-3
Nov. 19	Ohio Northern	South Bend	W	47-0
Nov. 24	Marquette	Milwaukee	T	5-5
Coach: Frank C. Longman				192-25
Captain: Ralph Dimmick				

Notre Dame celebrated its 100th victory against Ohio Northern. ... Butchel is located in Akron, Ohio.

1911

6–0–2

Oct. 7	Ohio Northern	South Bend	W	32-6
Oct. 14	St. Viator	South Bend	W	43-0
Oct. 21	Butler	South Bend	W	27-0
Oct. 28	Loyola	South Bend	W	80-0
Nov. 4	Pittsburgh	Pittsburgh	T	0-0
Nov. 11	St. Bonaventure	South Bend	W	34-0
Nov. 20	Wabash	Crawfordsville	W	6-3
Nov. 30	Marquette	Milwaukee	T	0-0
Coach: John L. Marks				222-9
Captain: Luke Kelly				

Alfred Bergman set the school record for longest kickoff return at a time when the field was 110 yards long. However, he didn't score on his 105-yard return from his own goal line against Loyola, Chicago. Art Smith had seven rushing touchdowns in the same game. ... Don Hamilton's 35-yard pass to end Lee Matthews was the first game-winning touchdown pass in program history.

1912

7–0

Oct. 5	St. Viator	South Bend	W	116-7
Oct. 12	Adrian	South Bend	W	74-7
Oct. 19	Morris Harvey	South Bend	W	39-0
Oct. 26	Wabash	South Bend	W	41-6
Nov. 2	Pittsburgh	Pittsburgh	W	3-0
Nov. 9	St. Louis	St. Louis	W	47-7
Nov. 28	Marquette	Comiskey Park	W	69-0
Coach: John L. Marks				389-27
Captain: Charles (Gus) Dorais				

Junior quarterback Gus Dorais led Notre Dame to the 116–7 rout of St. Viator in the season opener en route to an undefeated season.

Jesse Harper looks on from the athletics director's chair in 1931. After coaching Knute Rockne at Notre Dame, Harper retired his AD post to Rockne in 1918. Harper was sadly pressed back into service after Rockne's death in a plane crash.

1913

7–0

Oct. 4	Ohio Northern	South Bend	W	87–0
Oct. 18	South Dakota	South Bend	W	20–7
Oct. 25	Alma	South Bend	W	62–0
Nov. 1	Army	West Point	W	35–13
Nov. 7	Penn State	University Park	W	14–7
Nov. 22	Christian Brothers	St. Louis	W	20–7
Nov. 27	Texas	Austin	W	30–7
Coach: Jesse Harper				268–41
Captain: Knute Rockne				
All-American: Gus Dorais				

Under the direction of Jesse Harper, who played for Amos Alonzo Stagg on the 1905 national champion Chicago Maroons, Knute Rockne and Gus Dorais led the stunning victory against Army in a game that would popularize the forward pass. Dorais completed 14 of 17 passes for 243 yards, including a 40-yard completion to end Rockne. He completed his first 12 passes, three for touchdowns. On the Army bench that day was Dwight Eisenhower. ... Dorais was Notre Dame's only four-year starter at quarterback until Blair Kiel in 1980 and led the Fighting Irish to three consecutive undefeated seasons.

1914

6–2

Oct. 3	Alma	South Bend	W	56–0
Oct. 10	Rose Poly	South Bend	W	102–0
Oct. 17	Yale	New Haven	L	28–0
Oct. 24	South Dakota	Sioux Falls	W	33–0
Oct. 31	Haskell	South Bend	W	20–7
Nov. 7	Army	West Point	L	20–7
Nov. 14	Carlisle	Comiskey Park	W	48–6
Nov. 26	Syracuse	South Bend	W	20–0
Coach: Jesse Harper				286–61
Captain: Keith Jones				

Fullback Ray Eichenlaub concluded his career with 176 points. During the 1913 season alone he hammered out a dozen touchdowns in seven games. According to Notre Dame lore, Knute Rockne later gave Eichenlaub's cleats to a freshman named George Gipp.

1915

7–1

Oct. 2	Alma	South Bend	W	32–0
Oct. 9	Haskell	South Bend	W	34–0
Oct. 23	Nebraska	Lincoln	L	20–19
Oct. 30	South Dakota	South Bend	W	6–0
Nov. 6	Army	West Point	W	7–0
Nov. 13	Creighton	Omaha	W	41–0
Nov. 25	Texas	Austin	W	36–7
Nov. 27	Rice	Houston	W	55–2
Coach: Jesse Harper				230–29
Captain: Freeman Fitzgerald				

1916

8–1

Sept. 30	Case Tech	South Bend	W	48–0
Oct. 7	Western Reserve	Cleveland	W	48–0
Oct. 14	Haskell	South Bend	W	26–0
Oct. 28	Wabash	South Bend	W	60–0
Nov. 4	Army	West Point	L	30–10
Nov. 11	South Dakota	Sioux Falls	W	21–0
Nov. 18	Michigan State	East Lansing	W	14–0
Nov. 25	Alma	South Bend	W	46–0
Nov. 30	Nebraska	Lincoln	W	20–0
Coach: Jesse Harper				293–30
Captain: Stan Cofall				
All-American: Stan Cofall				

Coach Jesse Harper, who also doubled as athletics director, kept scheduling more national games because repeated attempts by the school to join the Big Ten were turned down. ... Assistant coach Knute Rockne referred to Army's Elmer Oliphant

as the "one-man team phenomenon. If anybody asks me who was the greatest player Army ever had, my vote goes to Oliphant." George Gipp, then a freshman, mimicked Oliphant during practices. "He gave a perfect imitation of Oliphant's veering style of ball carrying, which arched his body so that he could spin or pivot at any fraction of an instant. The only drawback was that in the actual game with Army Oliphant gave a perfect imitation of Gipp."

1917

6–1–1

Oct. 6	Kalamazoo	South Bend	W	55–0
Oct. 13	Wisconsin	Madison	T	0–0
Oct. 20	Nebraska	Lincoln	L	7–0
Oct. 27	South Dakota	South Bend	W	40–0
Nov. 3	Army	West Point	W	7–2
Nov. 10	Morningside	Sioux City	W	13–10
Nov. 17	Michigan State	East Lansing	W	23–0
Nov. 24	Washington & Jefferson	Washington	W	3–0
Coach: Jesse Harper				141–9
Captain: Jim Phelan				
All-American: Frank Rydzewski				

After five seasons, Jesse Harper resigned at age 33 to live on his 20,000-acre ranch in Sitka, Kansas. His record was 34–5–1 (.863). ... A key player for Notre Dame was center Frank Rydzewski, a consensus All-American.

1918

3–1–2

Sept. 28	Case Tech	Cleveland	W	26–6
Nov. 2	Wabash	Crawfordsville	W	67–7
Nov. 9	Great Lakes	South Bend	T	7–7
Nov. 16	Michigan State	East Lansing	L	13–7
Nov. 23	Purdue	West Lafayette	W	26–6
Nov. 28	Nebraska	Lincoln	T	0–0
Coach: Knute Rockne				133–39

George Gipp seen in a rare photo from his playing days. One of the most famous Notre Dame legends, Gipp could do it all on the field and was named an All-American posthumously. He had tragically passed away from strep throat in December 1920.

Captain: Leonard Bahan

Leaders: Rushing—George Gipp (541 yards, 98 carries); Passing—George Gipp (19 of 45, 293 yards); Receiving—Bernie Kirk (7 catches, 102 yards).

When Jesse Harper resigned after the 1917 season he was replaced by Knute Rockne, who had been an assistant coach since 1914. ... Notre Dame played only one home game but was fortunate to field a team during World War I.

1919

9-0

Oct. 4	Kalamazoo	South Bend	W	14-0
Oct. 11	Mount Union	South Bend	W	60-7
Oct. 18	Nebraska	Lincoln	W	14-9
Oct. 25	Western Michigan	South Bend	W	53-0
Nov. 1	Indiana	Indianapolis	W	16-3
Nov. 8	Army	West Point	W	12-9
Nov. 15	Michigan State	South Bend	W	13-0
Nov. 22	Purdue	West Lafayette	W	33-13
Nov. 27	Morningside	Sioux City	W	14-6

Coach: Knute Rockne 229-47

Captain: Leonard Bahan

Leaders: Rushing—George Gipp (729 yards, 106 carries); Passing—George Gipp (41 of 72, 727 yards); Receiving—Bernie Kirk (21 catches, 372 yards).

Eddie Anderson caught the pass from George Gipp to beat Army. ... The first year that Notre Dame kept complete attendance records the team attracted 56,500 fans. ... Notre Dame received its first consideration for the national championship, sharing the titles awarded by the National Championship Foundation and Parke Davis. However, most services preferred Harvard, if not Illinois or Texas A&M.

1920

9–0

Oct. 2	Kalamazoo	South Bend	W	39–0
Oct. 9	Western Michigan	South Bend	W	41–0
Oct. 16	Nebraska	Lincoln	W	16–7
Oct. 23	Valparaiso	South Bend	W	28–3
Oct. 30	Army	West Point	W	27–17
Nov. 6	Purdue	South Bend	W	28–0
Nov. 13	Indiana	Indianapolis	W	13–10
Nov. 20	Northwestern	Evanston	W	33–7
Nov. 25	Michigan State	East Lansing	W	25–0
Coach: Knute Rockne				250–44
Captain: Frank Coughlin				
All-American: George Gipp, Roger Kiley				
Leaders: Rushing—George Gipp (827 yards, 102 carries); Passing—George Gipp (30 of 62, 709 yards); Receiving—Eddie Anderson (17 catches, 293 yards).				

Northwestern was Gipp's last game. He contracted strep throat (filling in at quarterback, he completed five of six passes for 157 yards and two touchdowns) and died from complications of the disease on Dec. 14 at the age of 25. The day before, he supposedly made his impassioned plea to Knute Rockne, who later used it in his "Win One for the Gipper" speech. In four varsity years Gipp rushed for 2,341 yards, a school record until 1978. He also completed 93 passes for 1,769 yards, punted and returned kicks, and scored 156 points. His senior year he averaged 8.1 yards per carry. ... Notre Dame received consideration for the national championship, but California was the consensus choice. ... Purdue was the first homecoming game at Carter Field.

1921

10–1

Sept. 24	Kalamazoo	South Bend	W	56–0
Oct. 1	DePauw	South Bend	W	57–10
Oct. 8	Iowa	Iowa City	L	10–7
Oct. 15	Purdue	West Lafayette	W	33–0
Oct. 22	Nebraska	South Bend	W	7–0
Oct. 29	Indiana	Indianapolis	W	28–7
Nov. 5	Army	West Point	W	28–0
Nov. 8	Rutgers	Polo Grounds	W	48–0
Nov. 12	Haskell	South Bend	W	42–7
Nov. 19	Marquette	Milwaukee	W	21–7
Nov. 24	Michigan State	South Bend	W	48–0
Coach: Knute Rockne				375–41
Captain: Eddie Anderson				
All-American: Eddie Anderson, Hunk Anderson, Roger Kiley				
Leaders: Rushing—John Mohardt (781 yards, 136 carries); Passing—John Mohardt (53 of 98, 995 yards); Receiving—Eddie Anderson (26 catches, 394 yards).				

Hunk Anderson blocked two punts against Purdue and recovered them in the end zone. It was the first time in history a guard scored two touchdowns in a game. Grantland Rice wrote that "pound for pound Anderson was the toughest man I have ever known." ... Eddie Anderson went on to coach 39 years at Loras (1922–24), DePaul (1925–31), Holy Cross (1933–38), Iowa (1939–42 and 1946–49), and at Holy Cross again (1950–64). ... Notre Dame wore green for the first time against Iowa, which had dark jerseys that would have made it difficult to distinguish the players.

1922

8–1–1

Sept. 30	Kalamazoo	South Bend	W	46–0
Oct. 7	St. Louis	South Bend	W	26–0
Oct. 14	Purdue	West Lafayette	W	20–0
Oct. 21	DePauw	South Bend	W	34–7
Oct. 28	Georgia Tech	Atlanta	W	13–3
Nov. 4	Indiana	South Bend	W	27–0
Nov. 11	Army	West Point	T	0–0
Nov. 18	Butler	Indianapolis	W	31–3
Nov. 25	Carnegie Tech	Pittsburgh	W	19–0
Nov. 30	Nebraska	Lincoln	L	14–6
Coach: Knute Rockne				222–27

Captain: Glen Carberry

Leaders: Rushing—Jim Crowley (566 yards, 75 carries); Passing—Jim Crowley (10 of 21, 154 yards); Receiving—Don Miller (6 catches, 144 yards).

When Knute Rockne sized up 162-pound Jim Crowley he said, "Except for a nimble wit, Crowley shows me nothing" and even nicknamed him "Sleepy Jim." Crowley went on to lead the team in rushing and gain 1,841 yards during his three years as a member of the Four Horsemen backfield. Later, Rockne called him "the nerviest back I've ever known." ... Paul Castner set the school record for kickoff return yards in a single game with 253 on four attempts against Kalamazoo.

1923

9–1

Sept. 29	Kalamazoo	South Bend	W	74–0
Oct. 6	Lombard	South Bend	W	14–0
Oct. 13	Army	Ebbets Field	W	13–0
Oct. 20	Princeton	Princeton	W	25–2
Oct. 27	Georgia Tech	South Bend	W	35–7
Nov. 3	Purdue	South Bend	W	34–7
Nov. 10	Nebraska	Lincoln	L	14–7
Nov. 17	Butler	South Bend	W	34–7
Nov. 24	Carnegie Tech	Pittsburgh	W	26–0
Nov. 29	St. Louis	St. Louis	W	13–0

Knute Rockne, left, instructing players during practice in 1925.

Coach: Knute Rockne	275-37
Captain: Harvey Brown	
All-American: Don Miller	
Leaders: Rushing—Don Miller (698 yards, 89 carries); Passing—Jim Crowley (13 of 36, 154 yards); Receiving—Don Miller (9 catches, 149 yards).	

Don Miller, an unimposing 5-foot-11, 160-pound halfback, led the Fighting Irish in rushing for the first time. In 1924 he averaged 7.1 yards per carry and over his three-year career had a 6.8-yard average. Miller also led the team in receiving all three years. ... Incidentally, quarterback Harry Stuhldreher was just 5"-7, 151 pounds. ... Future coach Ara Parseghian was born in Akron, Ohio. He was named after an Armenian king of about the ninth century B.C., a legendary figure in Armenia's struggle for freedom. His father was an Armenian-born banker and his mother was born in France.

1924

10–0, National champions

Date	Opponent	Site	Result	Score
Oct. 4	Lombard	South Bend	W	40-0
Oct. 11	Wabash	South Bend	W	34-0
Oct. 18	Army	Polo Grounds	W	13-7
Oct. 25	Princeton	Princeton	W	12-0
Nov. 1	Georgia Tech	South Bend	W	34-3
Nov. 8	Wisconsin	Madison	W	38-3
Nov. 15	Nebraska	South Bend	W	34-6
Nov. 22	Northwestern	Soldier Field	W	13-6
Nov. 29	Carnegie Tech	Pittsburgh	W	40-19
Jan. 1	Stanford	Rose Bowl	W	27-10
Coach: Knute Rockne				285-54
Captain: Adam Walsh				
All-American: Jim Crowley, Elmer Layden, Harry Stuhldreher				
Leaders: Rushing—Don Miller (763 yards, 107 carries); Passing—Harry Stuhldreher (25 of 33, 471yards); Receiving—Don Miller (16 catches, 297 yards).				

Coach Knute Rockne said the 1924 team was his best and also his favorite. The first consensus

national champion in Notre Dame history was led by the Four Horsemen, behind the Seven Mules (led by center Adam Walsh) and the second-string Shock Troops. "At times, they caused me a certain amount of pain and exasperation, but mainly they brought me great joy," Rockne said. ... Notre Dame celebrated its 200th victory after defeating Georgia Tech. ... The Rose Bowl against Stanford, with Coach Pop Warner and quarterback Ernie Nevers, was Notre Dame's only postseason appearance until 1970. ... Walsh played most of the Army game with two broken hands and made an interception.

1925

7–2–1

Sept. 26	Baylor	South Bend	W	41–0
Oct. 3	Lombard	South Bend	W	69–0
Oct. 10	Beloit	South Bend	W	19–3
Oct. 17	Army	Yankee Stadium	L	27–0
Oct. 24	Minnesota	Minneapolis	W	19–7
Oct. 31	Georgia Tech	Atlanta	W	13–0
Nov. 7	Penn State	University Park	T	0–0
Nov. 14	Carnegie Tech	South Bend	W	26–0
Nov. 21	Northwestern	South Bend	W	13–10
Nov. 26	Nebraska	Lincoln	L	17–0
Coach: Knute Rockne				200–64
Captain: Clem Crowe				

Leaders: Rushing—Christie Flanagan (556 yards, 99 carries); Passing—Harry O'Boyle (7 of 21, 107 yards); Receiving—Gene Edwards (4 catches, 28 yards).

Future captain and All-American John "Clipper" Smith began his career at Notre Dame and would play fullback, halfback, center, and guard. The Irish went 23–4–2 during his career. ... After being "insulted" by Nebraska students on Thanksgiving Day, Notre Dame didn't play the Cornhuskers again until 1947. ... Knute Rockne agreed to become the head coach at Columbia but backed out when the story broke early.

1926

9–1

Oct. 2	Beloit	South Bend	W	77-0
Oct. 9	Minnesota	Minneapolis	W	20-7
Oct. 16	Penn State	South Bend	W	28-0
Oct. 23	Northwestern	Evanston	W	6-0
Oct. 30	Georgia Tech	South Bend	W	12-0
Nov. 6	Indiana	South Bend	W	26-0
Nov. 13	Army	Yankee Stadium	W	7-0
Nov. 20	Drake	South Bend	W	21-0
Nov. 27	Carnegie Tech	Pittsburgh	L	19-0
Dec. 4	Southern California	Los Angeles	W	13-12
Coach: Knute Rockne				210-38
Captains: Gene Edwards, Tom Hearden				
All-American: Bud Boeringer				
Leaders: Rushing—Christie Flanagan (535 yards, 68 carries); Passing—Christie Flanagan (12 of 29, 207 yards); Receiving—Ike Voedisch (6 catches, 95 yards).				

Notre Dame played Southern California for the first time, beginning one of college football's first nondivisional annual rivalries. It took Notre Dame four days on a series of trains to make the trip to Los Angeles. Behind 12–7 with four minutes to go, Knute Rockne inserted 160-pound quarterback Art Parasien, who hit "Butch" Niemiec with the crucial touchdown pass. ... The 77–0 victory against Beloit was the most lopsided game of the Rockne era.

1927

7–1–1

Oct. 1	Coe	South Bend	W	28-7
Oct. 8	Detroit	Detroit	W	20-0
Oct. 15	Navy	Baltimore	W	19-6
Oct. 22	Indiana	Bloomington	W	19-6
Oct. 29	Georgia Tech	South Bend	W	26-7
Nov. 5	Minnesota	Minneapolis	T	7-7
Nov. 12	Army	Yankee Stadium	L	18-0
Nov. 19	Drake	Des Moines	W	32-0

Nov. 26	Southern California	Soldier Field	W	7-6
Coach: Knute Rockne				158-57
Captain: John Smith				
All-American: Chrisie Flanagan, John Smith				
Leaders: Rushing—Christie Flanagan (731 yards, 118 carries); Passing—John Niemiec (14 of 33, 187 yards); Receiving—John Colrick (11 catches, 126 yards).				

Guard Jack Cannon played the first of three seasons at Notre Dame. Harry Stuhldreher, the quarterback in the Four Horsemen backfield, wrote of Cannon, who hated to use a helmet: "He was the apple of everybody's eye. Without a doubt, he was the best lineman Notre Dame ever turned out. He had the faculty of being able to diagnose opponents' plays and seemed to be at the point where the play developed every time." ... "Fighting Irish" became the official nickname, although it had been informally used for years, along with "Catholics" and "Ramblers". ... Paid attendance for the Southern California game at Soldier Field was 99,573 but announced as being 120,000

1928

5–4

Sept. 29	Loyola (New Orleans)	South Bend	W	12-6
Oct. 6	Wisconsin	Madison	L	22-6
Oct. 13	Navy	Soldier Field	W	7-0
Oct. 20	Georgia Tech	Atlanta	L	13-0
Oct. 27	Drake	South Bend	W	32-6
Nov. 3	Penn State	Philadelphia	W	9-0
Nov. 10	Army	Yankee Stadium	W	12-6
Nov. 17	Carnegie Tech	South Bend	L	27-7
Dec. 1	Southern California	Los Angeles	L	27-14
Coach: Knute Rockne				99-107
Captain: Fred Miller				
All-American: Fred Miller				
Leaders: Rushing—Jack Chevigny (539 yards, 120 carries); Passing—John Niemiec (37 of 108, 456 yards); Receiving—John Colrick (18 catches, 199 yards).				

The legendary Knute Rockne was one of the greatest college football coaches of all time. His 105 wins against just 12 losses still give him the best winning percentage of all coachs in Division 1-A history. He went out on top, winning the national championship in his final two seasons.

Knute Rockne made the "Win One for the Gipper" speech before playing heavily favored Army, eight years after Gipp died. ... Jack Chevigny, who scored the winning touchdown in the come-from-behind victory against Army, was killed on Iwo Jima near the end of World War II. ... Quarterback Frank Carideo scored the only touchdown in the shutout win against Penn State. ... The loss to Carnegie Tech, in the rain, was the first defeat at home since 1905. ... Paid attendance for the Navy game at Soldier Field was 103,081. The attendance was announced as 120,000.

1929

9–0, National champions

Oct. 5	Indiana	Bloomington	W	14–0
Oct. 12	Navy	Baltimore	W	14–7
Oct. 19	Wisconsin	Soldier Field	W	19–0
Oct. 26	Carnegie Tech	Pittsburgh	W	7–0
Nov. 2	Georgia Tech	Atlanta	W	26–6
Nov. 9	Drake	Soldier Field	W	19–7
Nov. 16	Southern California	Soldier Field	W	13–12
Nov. 23	Northwestern	Evanston	W	26–6
Nov. 30	Army	Yankee Stadium	W	7–0
Coach: Knute Rockne				145–38
Captain: John Law				
All-American: Jack Cannon, Frank Carideo				
Leaders: Rushing—Joe Savoldi (597 yards, 112 carries); Passing—Jack Elder (8 of 25, 187 yards); Receiving—John Colrick (4 catches, 90 yards).				

With Notre Dame Stadium under construction, the Fighting Irish didn't play any home games, with the closest to campus being Soldier Field in Chicago. ... Paid attendance against Southern California was 99,351 but announced at 112,912. ... Rockne struggled with phlebitis and doctors gave him a 50-50 chance of living. He coached some practices from his car, or a wheelchair, and didn't accompany the team to Baltimore to play Navy. When Rockne showed up for the Southern California game in Chicago he had a blood clot in one leg break free, go through his heart, and settle in his other leg. ... Guard Jack Cannon, the last player to play without a helmet, made the key block to spring Jack Elder on his 96-yard interception return for a touchdown to beat Army.

1930

10–0–0, National champions

Oct. 4	Southern Methodist	South Bend	W	20–14
Oct. 11	Navy	South Bend	W	26–2
Oct. 18	Carnegie Tech	South Bend	W	21–6
Oct. 25	Pittsburgh	Pittsburgh	W	35–19
Nov. 1	Indiana	South Bend	W	27–0
Nov. 8	Pennsylvania	Pittsburgh	W	60–20
Nov. 15	Drake	South Bend	W	28–7
Nov. 22	Northwestern	Evanston	W	14–0
Nov. 29	Army	Soldier Field	W	7–6
Dec. 6	Southern California	Los Angeles	W	27–0
Coach: Knute Rockne				265–74
Captain: Tom Conley				
All-American: Marty Brill, Frank Carideo, Bert Metzger, Marchy Schwartz				
Leaders: Rushing—Marchy Schwartz (927 yards, 124 carries); Passing—Marchy Schwartz (17 of 56, 319 yards); Receiving—Ed Kosky (4 catches, 76 yards).				

Notre Dame Stadium was dedicated with the Navy game. Attendance was listed as 40,593. ... The Army game filled Soldier Field to capacity (110,000) but paid attendance was 103,310. ... When injuries left the team with only one healthy fullback (Dan Hanley), Knute Rockne made backup halfback Bucky O'Connor his starting fullback but had Hanley and O'Connor trade jerseys. No one figured it out. ... Center Tommy Yarr made three interceptions in the fourth quarter against Southern Methodist. ... Against Northwestern, Frank Carideo punted four times in the fourth quarter and each was downed on the 1-yard line. ... All-American guard Bert Metzger weighed only 155 pounds. ... Schwartz posted three straight 100-yard rushing games against Pitt, Indiana, and Penn.

1931

6–2–1

Oct. 3	Indiana	Bloomington	W	25–0
Oct. 10	Northwestern	at Soldier Field	T	0–0
Oct. 17	Drake	South Bend	W	63–0
Oct. 24	Pittsburgh	South Bend	W	25–12
Oct. 31	Carnegie Tech	Pittsburgh	W	19–0
Nov. 7	Pennsylvania	South Bend	W	49–0
Nov. 14	Navy	Baltimore	W	20–0
Nov. 21	Southern California	South Bend	L	16–14
Nov. 28	Army	Yankee Stadium	L	12–0
Coach: Heartley "Hunk" Anderson				215–40
Captain: Tommy Yarr				
All-American: Nordy Hoffman, Joe Kurth, Marchy Schwartz, Tommy Yarr				
Leaders: Rushing—Marchy Schwartz (692 yards, 146 carries); Passing—Marchy Schwartz (9 of 51, 174 yards); Receiving—Paul Host (6 catches, 48 yards).				

Knute Rockne was killed in a plane crash on March 31 aboard Transcontinental-Western Flight 599 from Kansas City to Los Angeles, where he was to complete a football instructional movie. He was 43. His headstone simply reads: "Knute Rockne—Father." Rockne's teams went 105–12–5, for an amazing .881 winning percentage. "Notre Dame was Knute Rockne's address, but every gridiron in America was his home," Will Rogers said. ... The loss to Southern California was before the first capacity crowd (50,731) in Notre Dame Stadium. The Trojans rallied from a 14–0 deficit with six minutes to play to snap Notre Dame's string of 26 games without a loss. ... Against Army, Marchy Schwartz punted 15 times for 501 yards. He finished his career with 1,945 rushing yards and an average of 5.8 yards per carry.

1932

7–2–0

Oct. 8	Haskell	South Bend	W	73–0
Oct. 15	Drake	South Bend	W	62–0
Oct. 22	Carnegie Tech	South Bend	W	42–0
Oct. 29	Pittsburgh	Pittsburgh	L	12–0
Nov. 5	Kansas	Lawrence	W	24–6
Nov. 12	Northwestern	South Bend	W	21–0
Nov. 19	Navy	Cleveland	W	12–0
Nov. 26	Army	Yankee Stadium	W	21–0
Dec. 10	Southern California	Los Angeles	L	13–0

Coach: Heartley "Hunk" Anderson 255–31

Captain: Paul Host

All-American: Joe Kurth

Leaders: Rushing—George Melinkovich (503 yards, 88 carries); Passing—Nick Lukats (13 of 28, 252 yards); Receiving—George Melinkovich (7 catches, 106 yards).

Joe Kurth moved to right tackle. Against Northwestern, he tackled the punter for a big loss to set up a touchdown drive and blocked another punt to create another scoring opportunity. ... The 73 points against Haskell was a Notre Dame Stadium record.

1933

3–5–1

Oct. 7	Kansas	South Bend	T	0–0
Oct. 14	Indiana	Bloomington	W	12–2
Oct. 21	Carnegie Tech	Pittsburgh	L	7–0
Oct. 28	Pittsburgh	South Bend	L	14–0
Nov. 4	Navy	Baltimore	L	7–0
Nov. 11	Purdue	South Bend	L	19–0
Nov. 18	Northwestern	Evanston	W	7–0
Nov. 25	Southern California	South Bend	L	19–0
Dec. 2	Army	Yankee Stadium	W	13–12

Coach: Heartley "Hunk" Anderson 32–80

Captains: Hugh Devore, Tom Gorman

Leaders: Rushing—Nick Lukats (339 yards, 107 carries); Passing—Nick Lukats (21 of 67, 329 yards); Receiving—Steve Banas (6 catches, 59 yards).

Heartley "Hunk" Anderson went 16–9–2 during his three seasons. After Notre Dame he moved on to North Carolina State but in 1939 became the head coach of the Detroit Lions and later coached the Chicago Bears for 11 seasons. ... Wayne Millner's punt block, which he recovered for a touchdown, gave Notre Dame its season-ending 13–12 victory against Army. ... George Melinkovich missed the season due to a kidney ailment.

1934

6–3–0

Oct. 6	Texas	South Bend	L	7–6
Oct. 13	Purdue	South Bend	W	18–7
Oct. 20	Carnegie Tech	South Bend	W	13–0
Oct. 27	Wisconsin	South Bend	W	19–0
Nov. 3	Pittsburgh	Pittsburgh	L	19–0
Nov. 10	Navy	Cleveland	L	10–6
Nov. 17	Northwestern	Evanston	W	20–7
Nov. 24	Army	Yankee Stadium	W	12–6
Dec. 8	Southern California	Los Angeles	W	14–0
Coach: Elmer Layden				108–56
Captain: Dom Vairo				
All-American: Jack Robinson				
Leaders: Rushing—George Melinkovich (324 yards, 73 carries); Passing—Bill Shakespeare (9 of 29, 230 yards); Receiving—Dom Vairo (4 catches, 135 yards).				

Elmer Layden, one of the Four Horsemen, took over as both head coach and director of athletics. He resigned in 1940 and a year later became commissioner of the National Football League. ... After missing the 1933 season due to eye problems, center Jack Robinson made five interceptions.

1935

7-1-1

Sept. 28	Kansas	South Bend	W	28-7
Oct. 5	Carnegie Tech	Pittsburgh	W	14-3
Oct. 12	Wisconsin	Madison	W	27-0
Oct. 19	Pittsburgh	South Bend	W	9-6
Oct. 26	Navy	Baltimore	W	14-0
Nov. 2	Ohio State	Columbus	W	18-13
Nov. 9	Northwestern	South Bend	L	14-7
Nov. 16	Army	Yankee Stadium	T	6-6
Nov. 23	Southern California	South Bend	W	20-13
Coach: Elmer Layden				143-62
Captain: Joe Sullivan				
All-American: Wayne Millner, Bill Shakespeare				
Leaders: Rushing—Bill Shakespeare (374 yards, 104 carries); Passing—Bill Shakespeare (19 of 66, 267 yards); Receiving—Wally Fromhart (11 catches, 174 yards).				

Notre Dame called the victory against No. 1 Ohio State the "Game of the Century." It was dedicated to team captain Joe Sullivan, who died from complications of pneumonia in March. Andy Pilney was considered the star of the game, but he was being carried into the locker room (torn knee cartilage) when Bill Shakespeare threw the winning pass to Wayne Millner with 32 seconds remaining. ... Shakespeare punted 45 times for a 40-yard average, completed 19 passes, rushed for 374 yards, and scored four touchdowns. He set Notre Dame career punting records with 91 punts for a 40.7 average, and his longest punt was 86 yards against Pitt in 1935.

1936

6-2-1

Oct. 3	Carnegie Tech	South Bend	W	21-7
Oct. 10	Washington (St. Louis)	South Bend	W	14-6
Oct. 17	Wisconsin	South Bend	W	27-0
Oct. 24	Pittsburgh	Pittsburgh	L	26-0
Oct. 31	Ohio State	South Bend	W	7-2

Nov. 7	Navy	Baltimore	L	3–0
Nov. 14	Army	Yankee Stadium	W	20–6
Nov. 21	Northwestern	South Bend	W	26–6
Dec. 5	Southern California	Los Angeles	T	13–13
Coach: Elmer Layden				128–69

Captains: Bill Smith, John Lautar

Ranking (AP): First poll No. 7; Postseason No. 8

All-American: John Lautar

Leaders: Rushing—Bob Wilke (434 yards, 132 carries); Passing—Bob Wilke (19 of 52, 365 yards); Receiving—Joe O'Neill (8 catches, 140 yards).

Captain-elect Bill Smith resigned the position due to illness, with John Lautar named acting captain. ... Tackle Ed Beinor recovered a blocked kick in the 14–6 victory over Georgia Tech.

1937

6–2–1

Oct. 2	Drake	South Bend	W	21–0
Oct. 9	Illinois	Champaign	T	0–0
Oct. 16	Carnegie Tech	Pittsburgh	L	9–7
Oct. 23	Navy	South Bend	W	9–7
Oct. 30	Minnesota	Minneapolis	W	7–6
Nov. 6	Pittsburgh	South Bend	L	21–6
Nov. 13	Army	Yankee Stadium	W	7–0
Nov. 20	Northwestern	Evanston	W	7–0
Nov. 27	Southern California	South Bend	W	13–6
Coach: Elmer Layden				77–49

Captain: Joe Zwers

Ranking (AP): First poll NR; Postseason No. 9

All-American: Ed Beinor, Chuck Sweeney

Leaders: Rushing—Bunny McCormick (347 yards, 91 carries); Passing—Jack McCarthy (16 of 53, 225 yards); Receiving—Andy Puplis (5 catches, 86 yards).

End Chuck Sweeney stopped halfback Allen McFarland in the end zone to score the winning safety against Navy. ... Future coach Louis Leo Holtz was born on January 6 in Follansbee, West Virginia.

1938

8–1–0

Oct. 1	Kansas	South Bend	W	52–0
Oct. 8	Georgia Tech	Atlanta	W	14–6
Oct. 15	Illinois	South Bend	W	14–6
Oct. 22	Carnegie Tech	South Bend	W	7–0
Oct. 29	Army	Yankee Stadium	W	19–7
Nov. 5	Navy	Baltimore	W	15–0
Nov. 12	Minnesota	South Bend	W	19–0
Nov. 19	Northwestern	Evanston	W	9–7
Dec. 3	Southern California	Los Angeles	L	13–0
Coach: Elmer Layden				149–39

Captain: Jim McGoldrick

Ranking (AP): First poll No. 5; Postseason No. 5

All-American: Ed Beinor, Earl Brown

Leaders: Rushing—Bob Saggau (353 yards, 60 carries); Passing—Bob Saggau (8 of 28, 179 yards); Receiving—Earl Brown (6 catches, 192 yards).

The Minnesota game was Notre Dame's 300th victory.

1939

7–2–0

Sept. 30	Purdue	South Bend	W	3–0
Oct. 7	Georgia Tech	South Bend	W	17–14
Oct. 14	Southern Methodist	South Bend	W	20–19
Oct. 21	Navy	Cleveland	W	14–7
Oct. 28	Carnegie Tech	Pittsburgh	W	7–6
Nov. 4	Army	Yankee Stadium	W	14–0
Nov. 11	Iowa	Iowa City	L	7–6
Nov. 18	Northwestern	South Bend	W	7–0
Nov. 25	Southern California	South Bend	L	20–12
Coach: Elmer Layden				100–73

Captain: Johnny Kelly

Ranking (AP): First poll No. 2; Postseason No. 11

All-American: Bud Kerr

Leaders: Rushing—Milt Piepul (414 yards, 82 carries); Passing—Harry Stevenson (14 of 50, 236 yards); Receiving—Bud Kerr (6 catches, 129 yards).

1940

7–2–0

Oct. 5	Pacific	South Bend	W	25–7
Oct. 12	Georgia Tech	South Bend	W	26–20
Oct. 19	Carnegie Tech	South Bend	W	61–0
Oct. 26	Illinois	Champaign	W	26–0
Nov. 2	Army	Yankee Stadium	W	7–0
Nov. 9	Navy	Baltimore	W	13–7
Nov. 16	Iowa	South Bend	L	7–0
Nov. 23	Northwestern	Evanston	L	20–0
Dec. 7	Southern California	Los Angeles	W	10–6
Coach: Elmer Layden				168–67
Captain: Milt Piepul				
Ranking (AP): First poll No. 6; Postseason NR				
Leaders: Rushing—Steve Juzwik (407 yards, 71 carries); Passing—Bob Saggau (21 of 60, 483 yards); Receiving—Bob Hargrave (9 catches, 98 yards).				

End Bob Dove became the first sophomore to win a starting position since Wayne Millner in 1933. ... Elmer Layden was 47–13–3 during his seven seasons as head coach. ... The movie *Knute Rockne All American*, opened in South Bend.

1941

8–0–1

Sept. 27	Arizona	South Bend	W	38–7
Oct. 4	Indiana	South Bend	W	19–6
Oct. 11	Georgia Tech	Atlanta	W	20–0
Oct. 18	Carnegie Tech	Pittsburgh	W	16–0
Oct. 25	Illinois	South Bend	W	49–14
Nov. 1	Army	Yankee Stadium	T	0–0
Nov. 8	Navy	Baltimore	W	20–13
Nov. 15	Northwestern	Evanston	W	7–6
Nov. 22	Southern California	South Bend	W	20–18
Coach: Frank Leahy				189–64
Captain: Paul Lillis				
Ranking (AP): First poll No. 8; Postseason No. 3				
All-American: Bernie Crimmings, Bob Dove				
Leaders: Rushing—Fred Evans (490 yards, 141 carries);				

Passing—Angelo Bertelli (70 of 123, 1,027 yards); Receiving—Steve Juzwik (18 catches, 307 yards).

Former Notre Dame tackle Frank Leahy was hired as head coach. Between South Bend stints he was the line coach at Fordham with the famed Seven Blocks of Granite (which included Vince Lombardi) and as head coach led Boston College to a Sugar Bowl victory. ... Angelo Bertelli, as a tailback, finished second in Heisman Trophy voting.

1942

7-2-2

Sept. 26	Wisconsin	Madison	T	7-7
Oct. 3	Georgia Tech	South Bend	L	13-6
Oct. 10	Stanford	South Bend	W	27-0
Oct. 17	Iowa Pre-Flight	South Bend	W	28-0
Oct. 24	Illinois	Champaign	W	21-14
Oct. 31	Navy	Cleveland	W	9-0
Nov. 7	Army	Yankee Stadium	W	13-0
Nov. 14	Michigan	South Bend	L	32-20
Nov. 21	Northwestern	South Bend	W	27-20
Nov. 28	Southern California	Los Angeles	W	13-0
Dec. 5	Great Lakes	Soldier Field	T	13-13

Coach: Frank Leahy 184-99

Captain: George Murphy

Ranking (AP): First poll NR; Postseason No. 6

All-American: Angelo Bertelli, Bob Dove

Leaders: Rushing—Corwin Clatt (698 yards, 138 carries); Passing—Angelo Bertelli (72 of 159, 1,039 yards); Receiving—Bob Livingstone (17 catches, 272 yards).

Notre Dame switched to the T formation, with Angelo Bertelli moving from tailback to quarterback. Against Stanford he completed 10 consecutive passes and had four touchdowns en route to being named an All-American. He placed sixth in Heisman Trophy voting. ... The Washington Touchdown Club awarded Bob Dove its Rockne Trophy as the nation's best lineman. ... Creighton Miller rushed for 151 yards against Northwestern, a school record until 1974. ... The Great Lakes

Navy team of enlisted men and draftees was loaded with top players from around the country and had not allowed a point in the previous six games.

1943

9–1–0, National champions

Sept. 25	Pittsburgh	Pittsburgh	W	41–0
Oct. 2	Georgia Tech	South Bend	W	55–13
Oct. 9	Michigan	Ann Arbor	W	35–12
Oct. 16	Wisconsin	Madison	W	50–0
Oct. 23	Illinois	South Bend	W	47–0
Oct. 30	Navy	Cleveland	W	33–6
Nov. 6	Army	Yankee Stadium	W	26–0
Nov. 13	Northwestern	Evanston	W	25–6
Nov. 20	Iowa Pre-Flight	South Bend	W	14–13
Nov. 27	Great Lakes	Crestwood, Ill.	L	19–14
Coach: Frank Leahy				340–69

Captain: Pat Filley

Ranking (AP): First poll No. 1; Postseason No. 1

Major Awards: Angelo Bertelli, Heisman Trophy

All-American: Angelo Bertelli, Pat Filley, Creighton Miller, Jim White, John Yonakor

Leaders: Rushing—Creighton Miller (911 yards, 151 carries); Passing—Johnny Lujack (34 of 71, 525 yards); Receiving—John Yonakor (15 catches, 323 yards).

Notre Dame played seven teams ranked in the top 13 of the final Associated Press poll, played seven games on the road, and had only two returning starters. Nevertheless, Frank Leahy's T formation clicked under the direction of Angelo Bertelli, who moved from tailback to quarterback and won the Heisman Trophy despite being called into service with the Marine Corps (and serving as an officer at Iwo Jima and Guam) just prior to the seventh game of the season. Bertelli completed 69 percent of his passes for 10 touchdowns and the offense averaged 43 points a game. ... Creighton Miller averaged 16 yards per play against No. 2 Michigan and with 911 yards was the first player in Notre Dame history to lead the nation in rushing. ... The defense intercepted seven Wisconsin passes.

1944

8–2–0

Sept. 30	Pittsburgh	Pittsburgh	W	58–0
Oct. 7	Tulane	South Bend	W	26–0
Oct. 14	Dartmouth	Fenway Park	W	64–0
Oct. 21	Wisconsin	South Bend	W	28–13
Oct. 28	Illinois	Champaign	W	13–7
Nov. 4	Navy	Baltimore	L	32–13
Nov. 11	Army	Yankee Stadium	L	59–0
Nov. 18	Northwestern	South Bend	W	21–0
Nov. 25	Georgia Tech	Atlanta	W	21–0
Dec. 2	Great Lakes	South Bend	W	28–7
Coach: Ed McKeever				272–118

Captain: Pat Filley

Ranking (AP): First poll No. 1; Postseason No. 9

Leaders: Rushing—Bob Kelly (681 yards, 136 carries); Passing—Frank Dancewicz (68 of 163, 989 yards); Receiving—Bob Kelly (18 catches, 283 yards).

Coach Frank Leahy entered the Navy. He was later discharged as a lieutenant. Ed McKeever, who turned down the head coaching job at Boston College to follow Leahy to Notre Dame, handled the head coaching duties. However, he left in 1945 to be the head coach at Cornell. ... Able to essentially recruit players off college teams, Army won the national championship and defended the title in 1945.

1945

7–2–1

Sept. 29	Illinois	South Bend	W	7–0
Oct. 6	Georgia Tech	Atlanta	W	40–7
Oct. 13	Dartmouth	South Bend	W	34–0
Oct. 20	Pittsburgh	Pittsburgh	W	39–9
Oct. 27	Iowa	South Bend	W	56–0
Nov. 3	Navy	Cleveland	T	6–6
Nov. 10	Army	Yankee Stadium	L	48–0
Nov. 17	Northwestern	Evanston	W	34–7
Nov. 24	Tulane	New Orleans	W	32–6

Dec. 1	Great Lakes	Crestwood, Ill.	L	39-7
Coach: Hugh Devore				255-122
Captain: Frank Dancewicz				
Ranking (AP): First poll No. 3; Postseason No. 9				
All-American: John Mastrangelo				
Leaders: Rushing—Elmer Angsman (616 yards, 87 carries); Passing—Frank Dancewicz (30 of 90, 489 yards); Receiving—Bob Skoglund (9 catches, 100 yards).				

End coach Hugh Devore handled the team while Frank Leahy served in the military. When Leahy returned (he was discharged on Nov. 15 and quickly signed a 10-year contract), Devore became head coach at St. Bonaventure. ... Center Frank Szymanski was named captain but had to resign the position and his spot on his team after signing a professional contract with the Chicago Bears. ... Notre Dame attempted only one pass against Iowa in a 56–0 rout, and it was incomplete. ... A 78-yard run by halfback Phil Colella resulted in the only scoring against Illinois.

1946

8–0–1, National champions

Sept. 28	Illinois	Champaign	W	26-6
Oct. 5	Pittsburgh	South Bend	W	33-0
Oct. 12	Purdue	South Bend	W	49-6
Oct. 26	Iowa	Iowa City	W	41-6
Nov. 2	Navy	Baltimore	W	28-0
Nov. 9	Army	Yankee Stadium	T	0-0
Nov. 16	Northwestern	South Bend	W	27-0
Nov. 23	Tulane	New Orleans	W	41-0
Nov. 30	Southern California	South Bend	W	26-6
Coach: Frank Leahy				271-24
Captain: selected on a game-by-game basis				
Ranking (AP): First poll No. 3; Postseason No. 1				
Major Awards: George Connor, Outland Trophy				
All-American: George Connor, John Lujack, John Mastrangelo, George Strohmeyer				

Through the Years

Johnny Lujack, right, chats with Angelo Bertelli in 1943. Bertelli won the Heisman Trophy in 1943 despite playing in just six games before joining the U.S. Marines. Lujack followed him as a Heisman winner in 1947.

Leaders: Rushing—Emil Sitko (426 yards, 60 carries); Passing—Johnny Lujack (49 of 100, 778 yards); Receiving—Terry Brennan (10 catches, 154 yards).

The much-hyped No. 1 vs. No. 2 game against Army, which was riding a 25-game winning streak, at Yankee Stadium resulted in probably the most famous scoreless tie in football history. Although Johnny Lujack was known for his offensive prowess, his open-field tackle of Doc Blanchard saved the game. ... When Notre Dame outscored its final three opponents 94–6, it leapfrogged Army to No. 1 in the final poll. The Fighting Irish led the nation in total offense (441.3 yards), rushing (340.1), total defense (141.7), and scoring defense (2.7 points). The defense also allowed only 40 first downs all season. ... George Connor was the first recipient of the Outland Trophy, as the nation's best interior lineman. ... Coach Frank Leahy appeared on the cover of *Time* magazine with the quote: "Prayers work better when the players are bigger."

1947

9–0–0, National champions

Oct. 4	Pittsburgh	Pittsburgh	W	40-6
Oct. 11	Purdue	West Lafayette	W	22-7
Oct. 18	Nebraska	South Bend	W	31-0
Oct. 25	Iowa	South Bend	W	21-0
Nov. 1	Navy	Cleveland	W	27-0
Nov. 8	Army	South Bend	W	27-7
Nov. 15	Northwestern	Evanston	W	26-19
Nov. 22	Tulane	South Bend	W	59-6
Dec. 6	Southern California	Los Angeles	W	38-7
Coach: Frank Leahy				291-52

Captain: George Connor

Ranking (AP): First poll No. 1; Postseason No. 1

Major Awards: Johnny Lujack, Heisman Trophy

All-American: George Connoe, Ziggy Czarobski, Bill Fischer, Leon Hart, Johnny Lujack

Leaders: Rushing—Emil Sitko (426 yards, 60 carries); Passing—Johnny Lujack (61 of 109, 777 yards); Receiving—Terry Brennan (16 catches, 181 yards).

Michigan and Notre Dame traded the top spot in the polls through much of the season. Notre Dame was No. 1 and Michigan No. 2 in the final regular season Associated Press poll, but after the Wolverines crushed Southern California in the Rose Bowl the AP held an unprecedented postbowl poll, with voters reversing themselves. However, the final regular season poll was considered binding, making it one of the most controversial championships in history. Nearly every other poll had Michigan No. 1. ... Notre Dame never trailed and only one opponent, Northwestern, scored more than a touchdown. The roster included six players who would be elected into the Nationall Football Foundation Hall of Fame: Johnny Lujack, George Connor, Leon Hart, Bill Fisher, Emil Sitko, and Ziggy Czarobski. ... All-American guard Bill "Moose" Fischer played 300 minutes, which tied him for the team lead.

1948

9–0–1

Sept. 25	Purdue	South Bend	W	28–27
Oct. 2	Pittsburgh	Pittsburgh	W	40–0
Oct. 9	Michigan State	South Bend	W	26–7
Oct. 16	Nebraska	Lincoln	W	44–13
Oct. 23	Iowa	Iowa City	W	27–12
Oct. 30	Navy	Baltimore	W	41–7
Nov. 6	Indiana	Bloomington	W	42–6
Nov. 13	Northwestern	South Bend	W	12–7
Nov. 27	Washington	South Bend	W	46–0
Dec. 4	Southern California	Los Angeles	T	14–14
Coach: Frank Leahy				320–93

Captain: Bill Fischer

Ranking (AP): First poll No. 1; Postseason No. 2

Major Awards: Bill Fischer, Outland Trophy

All-American: Bill Fischer, Leon Hart, Emil Sitko, Marty Wendell

Leaders: Rushing—Emil Sitko (742 yards, 129 carries); Passing—Frank Tripuka (53 of 91, 660 yards); Receiving—Leon Hart (16 catches, 231 yards).

Not only was Bill Fisher the captain of the Fighting Irish, but he also captained the East team in the East-West Shrine Game. Additionally, he was named Most Valuable Player for his team in the 1949 College All-Star Game. ... According to Irish lore, Leon Hart took a 25-yard pass from Frank Tripucka and shook no fewer than eight Southern California tacklers on his way to a touchdown. Hart ran the ball 16 times that season on end-around plays and averaged 14 yards per attempt.

1949

10–0–0, National champions

Sept. 24	Indiana	South Bend	W	49–6
Oct. 1	Washington	Seattle	W	27–7
Oct. 8	Purdue	West Lafayette	W	35–12
Oct. 15	Tulane	South Bend	W	46–7
Oct. 29	Navy	Baltimore	W	40–0
Nov. 5	Michigan State	East Lansing	W	34–21
Nov. 12	North Carolina	Yankee Stadium	W	42–6
Nov. 19	Iowa	South Bend	W	28–7
Nov. 26	Southern California	South Bend	W	32–0
Dec. 3	Southern Methodist	Dallas	W	27–20
Coach: Frank Leahy				360–86

Captains: Leon Hart, Jim Martin

Ranking (AP): First poll No. 2; Postseason No. 1

Major Awards: Leon Hart, Heisman Trophy, Maxwell Award

All-American: Leon Hart, Jim Martin, Emil Sitko, Bob Williams

Leaders: Rushing—Emil Sitko (712 yards, 120 carries); Passing—Bob Williams (83 of 147, 1,374 yards); Receiving—Leon Hart (19 catches, 257 yards).

With Leon Hart at end, the emergence of quarterback Bobby Williams, who was only 19, keyed the title run during the second half of the season when only Southern Methodist challenged the Fighting Irish. ... Against SMU, center Jerry Groom intercepted two passes and blocked a kick to help clinch the national championship. ... Notre Dame finished off a four-year unbeaten run, 36–0–2. ... Hart was named the Associated Press Male Athlete of the Year. He and Larry Kelley of Yale

(1936) are the only linemen to win the Heisman Trophy. ... Jim Martin, who won a Bronze Star in the Marine Corps, was named an All-American after switching from end due to a Notre Dame shortage of tackles. ... Red Sitko led Notre Dame in rushing all four years of his career and never experienced a loss. He had a career average of 6.1 yards per carry and won the Walter Camp Trophy. ... Notre Dame ended the decade with a 38-game unbeaten streak.

1950

4–4–1

Sept. 30	North Carolina	South Bend	W	14–7
Oct. 7	Purdue	South Bend	L	28–14
Oct. 14	Tulane	New Orleans	W	13–9
Oct. 21	Indiana	Bloomington	L	20–7
Oct. 28	Michigan State	South Bend	L	36–33
Nov. 4	Navy	Cleveland	W	19–10
Nov. 11	Pittsburgh	South Bend	W	18–7
Nov. 18	Iowa	Iowa City	T	14–14
Dec. 2	Southern California	Los Angeles	L	9–7
Coach: Frank Leahy				139–140
Captain: Jerry Groom				
Ranking (AP): Preseason No. 1; Postseason NR				
All-American: Jerry Groom, Bob Williams				
Leaders: Rushing—Jack Landry (491 yards, 109 carries); Passing—Bob Williams (99 of 210, 1,035 yards); Receiving—Jim Mutscheller (35 catches, 426 yards).				

Notre Dame was voted No. 1 in the first preseason poll by the Associated Press but fell out of the top spot after its loss to Purdue. ... Center Jerry Groom played 465 career minutes, 86 percent of the total time possible. ... Bob Williams had 10 touchdown passes.

1951

7-2-1

Sept. 29	Indiana	South Bend	W	48-6
Oct. 5	Detroit	Briggs Stadium	W	40-6
Oct. 13	Southern Methodist	South Bend	L	27-20
Oct. 20	Pittsburgh	Pittsburgh	W	33-0
Oct. 27	Purdue	South Bend	W	30-9
Nov. 3	Navy	Baltimore	W	19-0
Nov. 10	Michigan State	East Lansing	L	35-0
Nov. 17	North Carolina	Chapel Hill	W	12-7
Nov. 24	Iowa	South Bend	T	20-20
Dec. 1	Southern California	Los Angeles	W	19-12
Coach: Frank Leahy				241-122
Captain: Jim Mutscheller				
Ranking (AP): Preseason No. 14; Postseason NR				
All-American: Bob Toneff				
Leaders: Rushing—Neil Worden (859 yards, 145 carries); Passing—John Mazur (48 of 110, 645 yards); Receiving—Jim Mutscheller (20 catches, 305 yards).				

Although Notre Dame didn't win the game, sophomore Johnny Lattner saved Notre Dame from a defeat against Iowa. On fourth-and-22 at the Irish 22 with less than 90 seconds remaining, Lattner, instead of punting, threw his first collegiate pass for a 23-yard gain. He subsequently ran 55 yards for a touchdown to salvage a tie. ... The North Carolina game was Notre Dame's 400th victory. ... Notre Dame wasn't ranked in the final Associated Press poll but was No. 13 in the final United Press coaches' poll.

Halfback John Lattner was one of the stars of the Notre Dame teams of the early 1950s. He won the Maxwell Award twice and the Heisman in 1953. He made the Pro Bowl with the Pittsburgh Steelers in his rookie NFL season, but he joined the Air Force in 1954 and a knee injury prevented him from ever returning to the NFL.

1952

7-2-1

Sept. 27	Pennsylvania	Philadelphia	T	7-7
Oct. 4	Texas	Austin	W	14-3
Oct. 11	Pittsburgh	South Bend	L	22-19
Oct. 18	Purdue	West Lafayette	W	26-14
Oct. 25	North Carolina	South Bend	W	34-14
Nov. 1	Navy	Cleveland	W	17-6
Nov. 8	Oklahoma	South Bend	W	27-21
Nov. 15	Michigan State	East Lansing	L	21-3
Nov. 22	Iowa	Iowa City	W	27-0
Nov. 29	Southern California	South Bend	W	9-0

Coach: Frank Leahy 183-108

Captain: Jack Alessandrini

Ranking (AP): Preseason No. 10; Postseason No. 3

Major Awards: John Lattner, Maxwell Award

All-American: John Lattner

Leaders: Rushing—John Lattner (732 yards, 148 carries); Passing—Ralph Guglielmi (62 of 143, 725 yards); Receiving—Joe Heap (29 catches, 437 yards).

Oklahoma was riding a 13-game unbeaten streak and averaging 42 points per game before losing at South Bend. Cleveland scribe Jack Clowser described it as "a duel between a bulldog and a wolfhound." ... Oklahoma was Notre Dame's first game broadcasted live on national television. ... Neil "Bull" Worden led the team in scoring with 60 points.

1953

9-0-1

Sept. 26	Oklahoma	Norman	W	28-21
Oct. 3	Purdue	West Lafayette	W	37-7
Oct. 17	Pittsburgh	South Bend	W	23-14
Oct. 24	Georgia Tech	South Bend	W	27-14
Oct. 31	Navy	South Bend	W	38-7
Nov. 7	Pennsylvania	Philadelphia	W	28-20
Nov. 14	North Carolina	Chapel Hill	W	34-14
Nov. 21	Iowa	South Bend	T	14-14
Nov. 28	Southern California	Los Angeles	W	48-14

Dec. 5	Southern Methodist	South Bend	W	40–14

Coach: Frank Leahy 317–139

Captain: Don Penza

Ranking (AP): Preseason No. 1; Postseason No. 2

Major Awards: John Lattner, Heisman Trophy, Maxwell Award

All-American: Art Hunter, John Lattner

Leaders: Rushing—Neil Worden (859 yards, 145 carries); Passing—Ralph Guglielmi (52 of 113, 792 yards); Receiving—Joe Heap (22 catches, 335 yards).

Notre Dame's 323–131 edge in rushing yardage was the key in ending Georgia Tech's 31-game unbeaten streak. Coach Frank Leahy fainted due to a lower chest muscle spasm while walking into the locker room at halftime. ... In 11 seasons, Leahy compiled a record of 87–11–9 (.855 winning percentage). ... Despite not leading his team in rushing, passing, receiving, or scoring, Lattner won the Heisman Trophy in the second closest balloting ever, to edge Minnesota's Paul Giel. ... Although numerous services named Notre Dame its national champion, both the Associated Press and coaches' polls had Maryland No. 1. ... Against Southern Methodist, Don Schaefer appeared at three backfield positions: quarterback, left halfback, and right halfback.

1954

9–1–0

Sept. 25	Texas	South Bend	W	21–0
Oct. 2	Purdue	South Bend	L	27–14
Oct. 9	Pittsburgh	Pittsburgh	W	33–0
Oct. 16	Michigan State	South Bend	W	20–19
Oct. 30	Navy	Baltimore	W	6–0
Nov. 6	Pennsylvania	Philadelphia	W	42–7
Nov. 13	North Carolina	South Bend	W	42–13
Nov. 20	Iowa	Iowa City	W	34–18
Nov. 27	Southern California	South Bend	W	23–17
Dec. 4	Southern Methodist	Dallas	W	26–14

Coach: Terry Brennan 261–115

Captains: Paul Matz, Dan Shannon

Ranking (AP): Preseason No. 1; Postseason No. 4

All-American: Ralph Guglielmi, Frank Varrichione

Leaders: Rushing—Don Schaefer (766 yards, 141 carries); Passing—Ralph Guglielmi (68 of 127, 1,162 yards); Receiving—Joe Heap (18 catches, 369 yards).

Quarterback Ralph Guglielmi finished his career with 13 rushing touchdowns and 18 passing. He completed 209 passes for 3,117 yards, made 10 interceptions as a defensive back, and returned two kickoffs for 15 yards. ... Former Notre Dame halfback Terry Brennan returned to South Bend in 1953 to coach the freshman squad and succeeded Frank Leahy as head coach.

1955

8–2–0

Sept. 24	Southern Methodist	South Bend	W	17–0
Oct. 1	Indiana	South Bend	W	19–0
Oct. 7	Miami (Fla.)	Miami	W	14–0
Oct. 15	Michigan State	East Lansing	L	21–7
Oct. 22	Purdue	West Lafayette	W	22–7
Oct. 29	Navy	South Bend	W	21–7
Nov. 5	Pennsylvania	Philadelphia	W	46–14
Nov. 12	North Carolina	Chapel Hill	W	27–7
Nov. 19	Iowa	South Bend	W	17–14
Nov. 26	Southern California	Los Angeles	L	42–20
Coach: Terry Brennan				210–112

Captain: Ray Lemek

Ranking (AP): Preseason No. 6; Postseason No. 9

All-American: Pat Bisceglia, Paul Hornung, Don Schaefer

Leaders: Rushing—Don Schaefer (638 yards, 145 carries); Passing—Paul Hornung (46 of 103, 743 yards); Receiving—Jim Morse (17 catches, 424 yards).

Paul Hornung's legendary status began to take shape with his 57-yard touchdown run against Southern Methodist. ... Down 14–7 in the fourth quarter to Iowa, Hornung made a 23-yard run, followed by a 40-yard touchdown pass to Jim Morse, and then kicked the extra point to tie the game. He topped it off with 26-yard field goal for the victory.

1956

2–8–0

Sept. 22	Southern Methodist	Dallas	L	19–13
Oct. 6	Indiana	South Bend	W	20–6
Oct. 13	Purdue	South Bend	L	28–14
Oct. 20	Michigan State	South Bend	L	47–14
Oct. 27	Oklahoma	South Bend	L	40–0
Nov. 3	Navy	Baltimore	L	33–7
Nov. 10	Pittsburgh	Pittsburgh	L	26–13
Nov. 17	North Carolina	South Bend	W	21–14
Nov. 24	Iowa	Iowa City	L	48–8
Dec. 1	Southern California	Los Angles	L	28–20

Coach: Terry Brennan 130–289

Captain: Jim Morse

Ranking (AP): Preseason No. 3; Postseason NR

Major Awards: Paul Hornung, Heisman Trophy

All-American: Paul Hornung

Leaders: Rushing—Paul Hornung (420 yards, 94 carries); Passing—Paul Hornung (59 of 111, 917 yards); Receiving—Jim Morse (20 catches, 442 yards).

Paul Hornung was second in the nation in total offense, second in kickoff returns, 15th in passing, and 16th in scoring. Consequently, he became the only player on a losing team to ever win the Heisman Trophy, beating out Tommy McDonald and Jerry Tubbs, Oklahoma; Johnny Majors, Tennessee; Jim Brown, Syracuse; John Brodie, Stanford; Jim Parker, Ohio State; and Joe Walton, Pittsburgh. ... After going 25–0–3, Notre Dame lost its first game ever in September, to Southern Methodist.

1957

7–3–0

Sept. 28	Purdue	West Lafayette	W	12–0
Oct. 5	Indiana	South Bend	W	26–0
Oct. 12	Army	Philadelphia	W	23–21
Oct. 26	Pittsburgh	South Bend	W	13–7
Nov. 2	Navy	South Bend	L	20–6
Nov. 9	Michigan State	East Lansing	L	34–6

Nov. 16	Oklahoma	Norman	W	7–0
Nov. 23	Iowa	South Bend	L	21–13
Nov. 30	Southern California	South Bend	W	40–12
Dec. 7	Southern Methodist	Dallas	W	54–21
Coach: Terry Brennan				200–136

Captains: Dick Prendergast, Ed Sullivan

Ranking (AP): Preseason No. 18; Postseason No. 10

All-American: Al Ecuyer

Leaders: Rushing—Nick Pietrosante (449 yards, 90 carries); Passing—Bob Williams (53 of 106, 565 yards); Receiving—Dick Lynch (13 catches, 128 yards).

Notre Dame's 7–0 victory against Oklahoma, with Dick Lynch scoring the lone touchdown, snapped the Sooners' 47-game unbeaten streak, the longest in college football history. Oklahoma won the previous meeting in 1956, 40–0, but the Fighting Irish had also been the last team to defeat the Sooners prior to the streak in 1953. ... Guard Al Ecuyer made 17 tackles against Iowa.

1958

6–4–0

Sept. 27	Indiana	South Bend	W	18–0
Oct. 4	Southern Methodist	Dallas	W	14–6
Oct. 11	Army	South Bend	L	14–2
Oct. 18	Duke	South Bend	W	9–7
Oct. 25	Purdue	South Bend	L	29–22
Nov. 1	Navy	Baltimore	W	40–20
Nov. 8	Pittsburgh	Pittsburgh	L	29–26
Nov. 15	North Carolina	South Bend	W	34–24
Nov. 22	Iowa	Iowa City	L	31–21
Nov. 29	Southern California	Los Angeles	W	20–13
Coach: Terry Brennan				206–173

Captains: Al Ecuyer, Chuck Puntillo

Ranking (AP): Preseason No. 3; Postseason No. 17

All-American: Al Ecuyer, Nick Pietrosante, Monty Stickles

Leaders: Rushing—Nick Pietrosante (549 yards, 117 carries); Passing—George Izo (68 of 118, 1,067 yards); Receiving—Monty Stickles (20 catches, 328 yards).

Head coach Terry Brennan chats with tackle Bronko Nagurski Jr. in 1958. Nagurski is the son of former Minnesota All-American and NFL Hall of Famer Bronko Nagurski. It was Brennan's last season at the helm of the Irish.

End Monty Stickles led the team in minutes, scored 60 points, and made 31 tackles. He also topped the Irish in receiving. ... Terry Brennan went 32–18–0 in five seasons.

1959

5–5–0

Sept. 26	North Carolina	South Bend	W	28-8
Oct. 3	Purdue	West Lafayette	L	28-7
Oct. 10	California	Berkeley	W	28-6
Oct. 17	Michigan State	East Lansing	L	19-0
Oct. 24	Northwestern	South Bend	L	30-24
Oct. 31	Navy	South Bend	W	25-22
Nov. 7	Georgia Tech	South Bend	L	14-10
Nov. 14	Pittsburgh	Pittsburgh	L	28-13
Nov. 21	Iowa	Iowa City	W	20-19
Nov. 28	Southern California	South Bend	W	16-6
Coach: Joe Kuharich				171-180
Captain: Ken Adamson				
Ranking (AP): Preseason No. 16; Postseason No. 17				
All-American: Monty Stickles				
Leaders: Rushing—Gerry Gray (256 yards, 50 carries); Passing—George Izo (44 of 95, 661 yards); Receiving—Bob Scarpitto (15 catches, 297 yards).				

New coach Joe Kuharich enjoyed one of the few highlights during his brief run at Notre Dame, the season-opening 28–8 victory against North Carolina. ... Notre Dame added a green shamrock to its gold helmets, which lasted through 1962.

1960

2–8–0

Sept. 24	California	South Bend	W	21-7
Oct. 1	Purdue	South Bend	L	51-19
Oct. 8	North Carolina	Chapel Hill	L	12-7
Oct. 15	Michigan State	South Bend	L	21-0
Oct. 22	Northwestern	Evanston	L	7-6
Oct. 29	Navy	Philadelphia	L	14-7
Nov. 5	Pittsburgh	South Bend	L	20-13

Nov. 12	Miami (Fla.)	Miami	L	28-21
Nov. 19	Iowa	South Bend	L	28-0
Nov. 26	Southern California	Los Angeles	W	17-0

Coach: Joe Kuharich 111-188

Captain: Myron Pottios

Ranking (AP): Preseason No. 17; Postseason NR

Leaders: Rushing—Angelo Dabiero (325 yards, 80 carries); Passing—George Haffner (30 of 108, 548 yards); Receiving—Les Traver (14 catches, 225 yards).

Iowa suddenly dropped Notre Dame from its schedule beginning after the 1964 season. Michigan State agreed to fill the hole, with the 1966 meeting one of the most famous games in college football history.

1961

5-5-0

Sept. 30	Oklahoma	South Bend	W	19-6
Oct. 7	Purdue	West Lafayette	W	22-20
Oct. 14	Southern California	South Bend	W	30-0
Oct. 21	Michigan State	East Lansing	L	17-7
Oct. 28	Northwestern	South Bend	L	12-10
Nov. 4	Navy	South Bend	L	13-10
Nov. 11	Pittsburgh	Pittsburgh	W	26-20
Nov. 18	Syracuse	South Bend	W	17-15
Nov. 25	Iowa	Iowa City	L	42-21
Dec. 2	Duke	Durham	L	37-13

Coach: Joe Kuharich 175-182

Captains: Norb Roy, Nick Buoniconti

Leaders: Rushing—Angelo Dabiero (637 yards, 92 carries); Passing—Frank Budka (40 of 95, 636 yards); Receiving—Les Traver (17 catches, 349 yards).

Tom McDonald recorded the first of 15 career interceptions, which was a school record for players with only three years of eligibility.

1962

5-5-0

Sept. 29	Oklahoma	Norman	W	13-7
Oct. 6	Purdue	South Bend	L	24-6
Oct. 13	Wisconsin	Madison	L	17-8
Oct. 20	Michigan State	South Bend	L	31-7
Oct. 27	Northwestern	Evanston	L	35-6
Nov. 3	Navy	Philadelphia	W	20-12
Nov. 10	Pittsburgh	South Bend	W	43-22
Nov. 17	North Carolina	South Bend	W	21-7
Nov. 24	Iowa	South Bend	W	35-12
Dec. 1	Southern California	Los Angeles	L	25-0
Coach: Joe Kuharich				159-192
Captain: Mike Lind				
Leaders: Rushing—Don Hogan (454 yards, 90 carries); Passing—Daryle Lamonica (64 of 128, 821 yards); Receiving—Jim Kelly (41 catches, 523 yards).				

The 61,296 on hand for the Purdue game set a Notre Dame Stadium record that would last until the stadium expansion in 1997. ... Joe Kuharich's teams went 17–23 over four seasons. After leaving South Bend, he became supervisor of officials for the NFL and from 1964 to 19 was head coach and general manager of the Philadelphia Eagles. ... Daryle Lamonica went on to have a much more successful NFL career. During his 12 years, he completed 1,288 of 2,601 passes for 19,154 yards.

1963

2-7-0

Sept. 28	Wisconsin	South Bend	L	14-9
Oct. 5	Purdue	West Lafayette	L	7-6
Oct. 12	Southern California	South Bend	W	17-14
Oct. 19	UCLA	South Bend	W	27-12
Oct. 26	Stanford	Stanford	L	24-14
Nov. 2	Navy	South Bend	L	35-14
Nov. 9	Pittsburgh	South Bend	L	27-7
Nov. 16	Michigan State	East Lansing	L	12-7

Nov. 23	Iowa	Iowa City	Canceled	
Nov. 28	Syracuse	Yankee Stadium	L	14-7

Coach: Hugh Devore 108-159

Captain: Bob Lehmann

All-American: Jim Kelly

Leaders: Rushing—Joe Kantor (330 yards, 88 carries); Passing—Frank Budka (21 of 40, 239 yards); Receiving—Jim Kelly (18 catches, 264 yards).

The Iowa game was canceled due to the death of President John F. Kennedy. ... The gold helmets had the players' numbers in white. ... Five straight losing seasons led to the hiring of Ara Parseghian away from Northwestern.

1964

9-1-0

Sept. 26	Wisconsin	Madison	W	31-7
Oct. 3	Purdue	South Bend	W	34-15
Oct. 10	Air Force	Colorado Springs	W	34-7
Oct. 17	UCLA	South Bend	W	24-0
Oct. 24	Stanford	South Bend	W	28-6
Oct. 31	Navy	Philadelphia	W	40-0
Nov. 7	Pittsburgh	South Bend	W	17-15
Nov. 14	Michigan State	South Bend	W	34-7
Nov. 21	Iowa	South Bend	W	28-0
Nov. 28	Southern California	Los Angeles	L	20-17

Coach: Ara Parseghian 287-77

Captain: Jim Carroll

Ranking (AP): Preseason NR; Postseason No. 3

All-American: Jim Carroll, John Huarte, Jack Snow

Major Awards: John Huarte, Heisman Trophy

Leaders: Rushing—Bill Wolski (657 yards, 136 carries); Passing—John Huarte (114 of 205, 2,062 yards); Receiving—Jack Snow (60 catches, 1,114 yards).

Quarterback John Huarte was coming off an injury-plagued sophomore year and limited junior year but broke virtually every Notre Dame single-season passing record and won the Heisman Trophy. ... Notre Dame squandered a 17–0 lead in the first

half against Southern California, with Craig Fertig completing a 15-yard touchdown pass with 1:33 remaining to cost the Fishing Irish the national championship. "I like to think our record in 1964 was 9 and ¾ and ¼," Parseghian later said. ... End Alan Page blocked a punt, recovered the ball, and ran 67 yards for a touchdown against Purdue. ... Jack Snow had 217 receiving yards in the opener against Wisconsin. ... Air Force managed just 37 rushing yards in the first meeting between the schools.

1965

7–2–1

Sept. 18	California	Berkley	W	48–6
Sept. 25	Purdue	West Lafayette	L	25–21
Oct. 2	Northwestern	South Bend	W	38–7
Oct. 9	Army	Shea Stadium	W	17–0
Oct. 23	Southern California	South Bend	W	28–7
Oct. 30	Navy	South Bend	W	29–3
Nov. 6	Pittsburgh	Pittsburgh	W	69–13
Nov. 13	North Carolina	South Bend	W	17–0
Nov. 20	Michigan State	South Bend	L	12–3
Nov. 27	Miami (Fla.)	Miami	T	0–0
Coach: Ara Parseghian				270–73

Captain: Phil Sheridan

Ranking (AP): Preseason No. 3; Postseason No. 9

All-American: Dick Aarrington, Nick Rassas

Leaders: Rushing—Nick Eddy (582 yards, 115 carries); Passing—Bill Zloch (36 of 88, 558 yards); Receiving—Nick Eddy (13 catches, 233 yards).

Notre Dame adopted the leprechaun as its mascot. Previously, it had been a series of Irish terrier dogs, beginning with one named Brick Top Shaum-Rhu in 1930. Most of the succeeding dogs were named Clashmore Mike. ... All-American defensive back Nick Rassas, who began his career as a walk-on, returned three punts for touchdowns. He set the school single-season record with a 19.1 yard average in punt returns. ... The defense held eventual Heisman Trophy winner Mike Garrett to 43 yards on 16 carries.

Linebacker Jim Lynch was one of the finest players in college football, and Ara Parseghian said he was one of the best he had ever coached. Lynch was inducted into the College Football Hall of Fame in 1992.

1966

9–0–1, National champions

Sept. 24	Purdue	South Bend	W	26–14
Oct. 1	Northwestern	Evanston	W	35–7
Oct. 8	Army	South Bend	W	35–0
Oct. 15	North Carolina	South Bend	W	32–0
Oct. 22	Oklahoma	Norman	W	38–0
Oct. 29	Navy	Philadelphia	W	31–7
Nov. 5	Pittsburgh	South Bend	W	40–0
Nov. 12	Duke	South Bend	W	64–0
Nov. 19	Michigan State	East Lansing	T	10–10
Nov. 26	Southern California	Los Angeles	W	51–0
Coach: Ara Parseghian				362–38
Captain: Jim Lynch				
Ranking (AP): Preseason No. 6; Postseason No. 1				
Major Awards: Jim Lynch, Maxwell Award				
All-American: Pete Duranko, Nick Eddy, Jim Lynch, Alan Page, Tom Regner				
Leaders: Rushing—Nick Eddy (553 yards, 78 carries); Passing—Terry Hanratty (78 of 147, 1,247 yards); Receiving—Jim Seymour (48 catches, 862 yards).				

The tie against No. 2 Michigan State arguably gave No. 1 Notre Dame the most controversial national championship in college football history. In addition to Ara Parseghian's decision not to go for the victory, two-time defending national champion Alabama finished with a perfect record only to be snubbed by the polls. ... Halfback Nick Eddy slipped and aggravated a shoulder injury while disembarking the train prior to the Michigan State game. He didn't play. ... Against Purdue, which went on to play in the Rose Bowl, Terry Hanratty and end Jim Seymour connected 13 times for 276 yards and three touchdowns. ... "I am often asked who was the best player to coach, and Jim Lynch always comes to mind," Parseghian said of the linebacker. "He was All-America in every sense: talented, hard-nosed, and honest." ... As a defensive end, Alan Page made 63 tackles. After a very successful pro career, he became an attorney and was appointed as a justice to the Minnesota Supreme Court in 1992.

1967

8-2-0

Sept. 23	California	South Bend	W	41-8
Sept. 30	Purdue	West Lafayette	L	28-21
Oct. 7	Iowa	South Bend	W	56-6
Oct. 14	Southern California	South Bend	L	24-7
Oct. 21	Illinois	Champaign	W	47-7
Oct. 28	Michigan State	South Bend	W	24-12
Nov. 4	Navy	South Bend	W	43-14
Nov. 11	Pittsburgh	Pittsburgh	W	38-0
Nov. 18	Georgia Tech	Atlanta	W	36-3
Nov. 24	Miami (Fla.)	Miami	W	24-22

Coach: Ara Parseghian 337-124

Captain: Bob "Rocky" Bleier

Ranking (AP): Preseason No. 1; Postseason No. 5

All-American: Kevin Hardy, Tom Schoen, Jim Seymour

Leaders: Rushing—Jeff Zimmerman (591 yards, 133 carries); Passing—Terry Hanratty (110 of 206, 1,439 yards); Receiving—Jim Seymour (37 catches, 515 yards).

The Georgia Tech game was Notre Dame's 500th victory. ... Defensive back Tom Schoen, who had seven interceptions and two touchdowns for the 1966 title team, set numerous school records, including most punt returns per game (nine vs. Pitt for 167 yards), and most punt returns per season (42 for 447 yards). He finished his career with 11 interceptions for 226 return yards, three for touchdowns. ... The defense set long-standing NCAA records for lowest completion percentage allowed (.333) and fewest yards per pass attempt (3.78). ... Rocky Bleier was the team captain and considered the steal of the subsequent NFL Draft when he went in the 16th round to the Pittsburgh Steelers. After his rookie season, he was drafted into military service and was seriously wounded in Vietnam. Although doctors said he would be lucky to walk again, by 1974 he was the Steelers starting halfback. He won four Super Bowls and retired with 3,864 yards rushing on 928 carries and 136 receptions for 675 yards. He also scored 23 touchdowns.

1968

7–2–1

Sept. 21	Oklahoma	South Bend	W	45–21
Sept. 28	Purdue	South Bend	L	37–22
Oct. 5	Iowa	Iowa City	W	51–28
Oct. 12	Northwestern	South Bend	W	27–7
Oct. 19	Illinois	South Bend	W	58–8
Oct. 26	Michigan State	East Lansing	L	21–17
Nov. 2	Navy	Philadelphia	W	45–14
Nov. 9	Pittsburgh	South Bend	W	56–7
Nov. 16	Georgia Tech	South Bend	W	34–6
Nov. 30	Southern California	Los Angeles	T	21–21

Coach: Ara Parseghian 376–170

Captains: George Kunz, Bob Olson

Ranking (AP): Preseason No. 3; Postseason No. 5

All-American: Terry Hanratty, George Kunz, Jim Seymour

Leaders: Rushing—Bob Gladieux (713 yards, 152 carries); Passing—Terry Hanratty (116 of 197, 1,466 yards); Receiving—Jim Seymour (53 catches, 736 yards).

An assistant coach remarked that 5-foot-10, 147-pound Joe Theismann looked more like the team's water boy than a quarterback. He took over late in the season after Terry Hanratty was lost to an injury and in three games led the Irish to two wins and a tie as Notre Dame finished the season ranked fifth. ... For his career, Hanratty passed for 4,152 yards and 27 touchdowns, to go with 181 carries and 586 rushing yards.

1969

8–2–1

Sept. 20	Northwestern	South Bend	W	35–10
Sept. 27	Purdue	West Lafayette	L	28–14
Oct. 4	Michigan State	South Bend	W	42–28
Oct. 11	Army	Yankee Stadium	W	45–0
Oct. 18	Southern California	South Bend	T	14–14
Oct. 25	Tulane	New Orleans	W	37–0
Nov. 1	Navy	South Bend	W	47–0
Nov. 8	Pittsburgh	Pittsburgh	W	49–7
Nov. 15	Georgia Tech	Atlanta	W	38–20
Nov. 22	Air Force	South Bend	W	13–6
Jan. 1	Texas	Cotton Bowl	L	21–17

Coach: Ara Parseghian 351–134

Captains: Bob Olson, Mike Oriard

Ranking (AP): Preseason No. 11; Postseason No. 5

All-American: Larry DiNardi, Mike McCoy, Jim Reilly

Leaders: Rushing—Denny Allan (612 yards, 148 carries); Passing—Joe Theismann (108 of 192, 1,531 yards); Receiving—Tom Gatewood (47 catches, 743 yards).

After a 45-year self-imposed absence, Notre Dame played in a bowl game. ... Texas entered the Cotton Bowl ranked No. 1 and won the national championship with the victory. The game came down to a late 76-yard drive by the Longhorns. Joe Theismann set Cotton Bowl records with 231 passing yards and 267 yards of total offense. ... Safety Clarence Ellis set the school record for passes broken up in a second season with 13. He went on to set the career record of 32. ... Notre Dame began a 14-game winning streak against teams from the Big Ten conference. ... Against Navy, Notre Dame had 91 rushing attempts for 597 yards. ... Georgia Tech was a rare night game.

1970

10-1-0

Sept. 19	Northwestern	Evanston	W	35-14
Sept. 26	Purdue	South Bend	W	48-0
Oct. 3	Michigan State	East Lansing	W	29-0
Oct. 10	Army	South Bend	W	51-10
Oct. 17	Missouri	Columbia	W	24-7
Oct. 31	Navy	Philadelphia	W	56-7
Nov. 7	Pittsburgh	South Bend	W	46-14
Nov. 14	Georgia Tech	South Bend	W	10-7
Nov. 21	LSU	South Bend	W	3-0
Nov. 28	Southern California	Los Angeles	L	38-28
Jan. 1	Texas	Cotton Bowl	W	24-11

Coach: Ara Parseghian 354-108

Captains: Larry DiNardo, Tim Kelly

Ranking (AP): Preseason No. 6; Postseason No. 2

All-American: Larry DiNardo, Clarence Ellis, Tom Gatewood, Joe Theismann

Leaders: Rushing—Ed Gulyas (534 yards, 118 carries); Passing—Joe Theismann (155 of 268, 2,429 yards); Receiving—Tom Gatewood (77 catches, 1,123 yards).

Joe Theismann came up short in his bid to win the Heisman Trophy (to Stanford's Jim Plunkett), but he threw for 526 yards in a driving rain storm in the loss to Southern California and threw three touchdown passes in the first 16 minutes of the Cotton Bowl to end Texas' 30-game winning streak. Led by Walt Patulski and Mike Kadish, the defense forced nine fumbles and recovered five. ... As a starting quarterback, Theismann compiled a 20-3-2 record while throwing for 4,411 yards and 31 touchdowns. He set school records for passing yards in a game (526), yards in a season (2,429), and single-season touchdowns (16). ... Tom Gatewood's 77 receptions for 1,123 yards set school records. ... The offense averaged 510.5 yards per game. ... Notre Dame played its first game on artificial turf at Michigan State.

1971

8-2-0

Sept. 18	Northwestern	South Bend	W	50-7
Sept. 25	Purdue	West Lafayette	W	8-7
Oct. 2	Michigan State	South Bend	W	14-2
Oct. 9	Miami (Fla.)	Miami	W	17-0
Oct. 16	North Carolina	South Bend	W	16-0
Oct. 23	Southern California	South Bend	L	28-14
Oct. 30	Navy	South Bend	W	21-0
Nov. 6	Pittsburgh	Pittsburgh	W	56-7
Nov. 13	Tulane	South Bend	W	21-7
Nov. 20	LSU	Baton Rouge	L	28-8
Coach: Ara Parseghian				225-86

Captains: Walt Patulski, Tom Gatewood

Ranking (AP): Preseason No. 1; Postseason No. 13

Major Awards: Walt Patulski, Lombardi Award

All-American: Clarence Ellis, Walt Patulski

Leaders: Rushing—Bob Minnix (337 yards, 78 carries); Passing—Cliff Brown (56 of 111, 669 yards); Receiving—Tom Gatewood (33 catches, 417 yards).

Cornerback Clarence Ellis finished his career with 13 interceptions for 157 yards and one touchdown. ... Receiver Tom Gatewood had 157 career receptions for 2,283 yards and set numerous Notre Dame receiving records. ... Defensive end Walt Patulski started every game of his collegiate career and tallied 186 tackles (40 for a loss), broke up 10 passes, and recovered five fumbles. However, he arrived on campus as a fullback. "One practice they had me try defensive end, and on my first play there I stopped a sweep cold," he said. "(The freshman coach) went crazy. It was my first play there and I stuck out. From that moment on I was a defensive end."

1972

8–3–0

Sept. 23	Northwestern	Evanston	W	37-0
Sept. 30	Purdue	South Bend	W	35-14
Oct. 7	Michigan State	East Lansing	W	16-0
Oct. 14	Pittsburgh	South Bend	W	42-16
Oct. 21	Missouri	South Bend	L	30-26
Oct. 28	Texas Christian	South Bend	W	21-0
Nov. 4	Navy	Philadelphia	W	42-23
Nov. 11	Air Force	Colorado Springs	W	21-7
Nov. 18	Miami (Fla.)	South Bend	W	20-17
Dec. 2	Southern California	Los Angeles	L	45-23
Jan. 1	Nebraska	Orange Bowl	L	40-6
Coach: Ara Parseghian				289-192
Captains: John Dampeer, Greg Marx				
Ranking (AP): Preseason No. 13; Postseason No. 14				
All-American: Greg Marx				
Leaders: Rushing—Eric Penick (726 yards, 124 carries); Passing—Tom Clements (83 of 162, 1,163 yards); Receiving—Willie Townsend (25 catches, 369 yards).				

Heisman Trophy winner Johnny Rodgers scored four touchdowns and passed for another to lead Nebraska in the Orange Bowl. The final game for Cornhuskers coach Bob Devaney, it was the worst defeat for the Irish since Ara Parseghian took over. ... Defensive tackle Greg Marx made 263 career tackles and broke up six passes. ... Defensive back Mike Townsend made 10 interceptions to lead the nation.

1973

11–0–0, National champions

Sept. 22	Northwestern	South Bend	W	44-0
Sept. 29	Purdue	West Lafayette	W	20-7
Oct. 6	Michigan State	South Bend	W	14-10
Oct. 13	Rice	Houston	W	28-0
Oct. 20	Army	West Point	W	62-3
Oct. 27	Southern California	South Bend	W	23-14
Nov. 3	Navy	South Bend	W	44-7

Nov. 10	Pittsburgh	Pittsburgh	W	31–10
Nov. 22	Air Force	South Bend	W	48–15
Dec. 1	Miami (Fla.)	Miami	W	44–0
Dec. 31	Alabama	Sugar Bowl	W	24–23

Coach: Ara Parseghian 382–89

Captains: Dave Casper, Frank Pomerico, Mike Townsend

Ranking (AP): Preseason No. 8; Postseason No. 1

All-American: Dave Casper, Mike Townsend

Leaders: Rushing—Wayne Bullock (752 yards, 162 carries); Passing—Tom Clements (60 of 113, 882 yards); Receiving—Pete Demmerle (26 catches, 404 yards).

The national championship was on the line against Alabama in the Sugar Bowl, a game that saw six lead changes and was decided by Bob Thomas' 19-yard field goal with 4:26 remaining. ... The Thanksgiving Day game against Air Force was the only nonsellout at Notre Dame since 1966. With students on break, the crowd was estimated to be 1,800 short of capacity. ... Eric Penick's 85-yard run helped end Southern California's 23-game unbeaten streak. ... Notre Dame had four backs with 300-plus rushing yards: Wayne Bullock (752), Art Best (700), Eric Penick (586) and Tom Clements (360). ... The offense set a school record with 3,502 rushing yards.

1974

10–2–0

Sept. 9	Georgia Tech	Atlanta	W	31–7
Sept. 21	Northwestern	Evanston	W	49–3
Sept. 28	Purdue	South Bend	L	31–20
Oct. 5	Michigan State	East Lansing	W	19–14
Oct. 12	Rice	South Bend	W	10–3
Oct. 19	Army	South Bend	W	48–0
Oct. 26	Miami (Fla.)	South Bend	W	38–7
Nov. 2	Navy	Philadelphia	W	14–6
Nov. 16	Pittsburgh	South Bend	W	14–10
Nov. 23	Air Force	South Bend	W	38–0
Nov. 30	Southern California	Los Angeles	L	55–24
Jan. 1	Alabama	Orange Bowl	W	13–11

Coach: Ara Parseghian	318–147
Captains: Tom Clements, Greg Collins	
Ranking (AP): Preseason No. 3; Postseason No. 6	
All-American: Tom Clements, Greg Collins, Pete Demmerle, Mike Fanning, Gerry DiNardo	
Leaders: Rushing—Wayne Bullock (855 yards, 203 carries); Passing—Tom Clements (122 of 215, 1,549 yards); Receiving—Pete Demmerle (43 catches, 667 yards).	

Notre Dame built a 24–0 lead in the second quarter against Southern California when the Trojans scored 55 unanswered points, 49 of which came in a span of 16:44. "We turned into madmen," USC's Anthony Davis said. ... In Ara Parseghian's final game, the Fighting Irish knocked off No. 1 Alabama in the Orange Bowl. He resigned after 11 seasons due to health reasons and finished with a 95–17–4 (.836) record. His worst season was 7–2–1. ... Defensive tackle Steve Niehaus made 95 tackles (13 for a loss) and recovered a fumble. ... Joe Montana was one of seven quarterbacks to arrive on campus after turning down a basketball scholarship with North Carolina State.

1975

8–3–0

Date	Opponent	Site	Result	Score
Sept. 15	Boston College	Foxboro Stadium	W	17–3
Sept. 20	Purdue	West Lafayette	W	17–0
Sept. 27	Northwestern	South Bend	W	31–7
Oct. 4	Michigan State	South Bend	L	10–3
Oct. 11	North Carolina	Chapel Hill	W	21–14
Oct. 18	Air Force	Colorado Springs	W	31–30
Oct. 25	Southern California	South Bend	L	24–17
Nov. 1	Navy	South Bend	W	31–10
Nov. 8	Georgia Tech	South Bend	W	24–3
Nov. 15	Pittsburgh	Pittsburgh	L	34–20
Nov. 22	Miami (Fla.)	Miami	W	32–9
Coach: Dan Devine				244–144
Captains: Ed Bauer, Jim Stock				
Ranking (AP): Preseason No. 10; Postseason NR				

All-American: Ken MacAfee, Steve Niehaus

Leaders: Rushing—Jerome Heavens (756 yards, 129 carries); Passing—Rick Slager (66 of 139, 686 yards); Receiving—Ken MacAfee (26 catches, 333 yards).

Prior to Notre Dame, Dan Devine had been the head coach at Arizona State, Missouri, and the Green Bay Packers. ... Ross Browner blocked a Navy punt and recovered it in the end zone to score his only collegiate touchdown. When he left school after the 1977 season his career numbers were 340 tackles (a school record), ten deflected passes, two blocked kicks, and two safeties. ... Luther Bradley returned an interception 99 yards for a touchdown against Purdue. ... The legend of Daniel "Rudy" Ruettiger, the walk-on whose story became a feature movie, came to fruition when he sacked the Georgia Tech quarterback on the final play of the game and was carried off the field by teammates.

1976

9-3-0

Sept. 11	Pittsburgh	South Bend	L	31-10
Sept. 18	Purdue	South Bend	W	23-0
Sept. 25	Northwestern	Evanston	W	48-0
Oct. 2	Michigan State	East Lansing	W	24-6
Oct. 16	Oregon	South Bend	W	41-0
Oct. 23	South Carolina	Columbia	W	13-6
Oct. 30	Navy	Cleveland	W	27-21
Nov. 6	Georgia Tech	Atlanta	L	23-14
Nov. 13	Alabama	South Bend	W	21-18
Nov. 20	Miami (Fla.)	South Bend	W	40-27
Nov. 27	Southern California	Los Angeles	L	17-13
Dec. 27	Penn State	Gator Bowl	W	20-9
Coach: Dan Devine				294-158

Captains: Mark McLane, Willie Fry

Ranking (AP): Preseason No. 11; Postseason No. 12

Major Awards: Ross Browner, Outland Trophy

All-American: Ross Browner, Ken MacAfee

Leaders: Rushing—Al Hunter (1,058 yards, 233 carries); Passing—Rick Slager (86 of 172, 1,281 yards); Receiving—Ken MacAfee (34 catches, 483 yards).

Al Hunter became the first Notre Dame back to rush for more than 1,000 yards in a single season. ... Led by linebackers Bob Golic, Doug Becker, and Steve Heimkreiter, as well as strong safety Jim Browner, Notre Dame's defense didn't allow Penn State past its own 32-yard line in the first half after its initial possession. Hunter was named MVP of the Gator Bowl for scoring two first-half touchdowns and accumulating 102 rushing yards. ... Dave Reeve set the school record for longest field goal by kicking a 53-yarder against Pittsburgh. ... Joe Montana missed the entire season with a separated shoulder.

1977

11–1–0, National champions

Sept. 10	Pittsburgh	Pittsburgh	W	19–9
Sept. 17	Ole Miss	Jackson	L	20–13
Sept. 24	Purdue	West Lafayette	W	31–24
Oct. 1	Michigan State	South Bend	W	16–6
Oct. 15	Army	Giants Stadium	W	24–0
Oct. 22	Southern California	South Bend	W	49–19
Oct. 29	Navy	South Bend	W	43–10
Nov. 5	Georgia Tech	South Bend	W	69–14
Nov. 12	Clemson	Clemson	W	21–17
Nov. 19	Air Force	South Bend	W	49–0
Dec. 3	Miami (Fla.)	Miami	W	48–10
Jan. 2	Texas	Cotton Bowl	W	38–10

Coach: Dan Devine 420–139

Captains: Ross Browner, Terry Eurick, Willie Fry, Steve Orsini

Ranking (AP): Preseason No. 3; Postseason No. 1

Major Awards: Ross Browner, Lombardi Award, Maxwell Award; Ken MacAfee, Walter Camp Player of the Year

All-American: Luther Bradley, Ross Browner, Ken MacAfee

Leaders: Rushing—Jerome Heavens (994 yards, 229 carries); Passing—Joe Montana (99 of 189, 1,604 yards); Receiving—Ken MacAfee (54 catches, 797 yards).

After defeating No. 1 Texas in the Cotton Bowl, Notre Dame vaulted from No. 5 to the top of the rankings. The Fighting Irish forced six turnovers in the game. Backs Jerome Heavens and Vagas Ferguson both reached 100 rushing yards, with Ferguson adding three touchdowns. ... Dan Devine surprised his players and everyone else at Notre Dame Stadium by having the Irish wear green against Southern California. The Fighting Irish won in a rout, 49–19. ... Quarterback Joe Montana earned the nickname "The Comeback Kid" with late rallies against Purdue and Clemson. ... Tight end Ken MacAfee was an academic All-American, won the Walter Camp Player of the Year Award, and was third in voting for the Heisman Trophy. He was the first lineman to win the Walter Camp and caught 128 career passes for 1,759 yards. ... Safety Luther Bradley finished his career with 17 interceptions.

1978

9–3–0

Sept. 9	Missouri	South Bend	L	3–0
Sept. 23	Michigan	South Bend	L	28–14
Sept. 30	Purdue	South Bend	W	10–6
Oct. 7	Michigan State	East Lansing	W	29–25
Oct. 14	Pittsburgh	South Bend	W	26–17
Oct. 21	Air Force	Colorado Springs	W	38–15
Oct. 28	Miami (Fla.)	South Bend	W	20–0
Nov. 4	Navy	Cleveland	W	27–7
Nov. 11	Tennessee	South Bend	W	31–14
Nov. 18	Georgia Tech	Atlanta	W	38–21
Nov. 25	Southern California	Los Angeles	L	27–25
Jan. 1	Houston	Cotton Bowl	W	35–34

Coach: Dan Devine 293–197

Captains: Bob Golic, Jerome Heavens, Joe Montana

Ranking (AP): Preseason No. 5; Postseason No. 7

All-American: Bob Golic, Dave Huffman

Leaders: Rushing—Vagas Ferguson (1,192 yards, 211 carries); Passing—Joe Montana (141 of 260, 2,010 yards); Receiving—Kris Haines (32 catches, 699 yards).

Joe Montana calls the signals on October 22, 1977, against USC at Notre Dame Stadium. The Fighting Irish, ranked 11th, upset the fifth ranked Trojans 49–19 while wearing the green jerseys for the first time in 14 years.

Joe Montana, who had four interceptions and missed most of the third quarter with below-normal body temperature, led Notre Dame back from a 34–12 halftime deficit in the Cotton Bowl and connected with Kris Haines on the winning touchdown pass as time expired. The Fighting Irish scored 23 points in the final 7:37. ... Jerome Heavens broke George Gipp's career rushing record of 2,341 yards, which had stood for 58 years. ... Linebacker Bob Golic made 152 tackles during his senior season and finished with 479 for his career to go with six interceptions. He made 26 tackles in the first game against Michigan in 35 years.

1979

7-4-0

Sept. 15	Michigan	Ann Arbor	W	12-10
Sept. 22	Purdue	West Lafayette	L	28-22
Sept. 29	Michigan State	South Bend	W	27-3
Oct. 6	Georgia Tech	South Bend	W	21-13
Oct. 13	Air Force	Colorado Springs	W	38-13
Oct. 20	Southern California	South Bend	L	42-23
Oct. 27	South Carolina	South Bend	W	18-17
Nov. 3	Navy	South Bend	W	14-0
Nov. 10	Tennessee	Knoxville	L	40-18
Nov. 17	Clemson	South Bend	L	16-10
Nov. 24	Miami (Fla.)	Tokyo, Japan	W	40-15
Coach: Dan Devine				243-197

Captains: Vagas Ferguson, Tim Foley, Dave Waymer

Ranking (AP): Preseason No. 9; Postseason NR

All-American: Vagas Ferguson, Tim Foley

Leaders: Rushing—Vagas Ferguson (1,437 yards, 301 carries); Passing—Rusty Lisch (108 of 208, 1,781 yards); Receiving—Dean Masztak (28 catches, 428 yards).

The Miami game was played at National Olympic Stadium in Tokyo. ... Vagas Ferguson set school records of 1,437 rushing yards on 301 carries and finished his career as Notre Dame's all-time leader with 3,472 rushing yards and 32 touchdowns. ... Linebacker Bob Crable made 26 tackles versus Clemson and finished the season with 187.

1980

9–2–1

Sept. 6	Purdue	South Bend	W	31–10
Sept. 20	Michigan	South Bend	W	29–27
Oct. 4	Michigan State	East Lansing	W	26–21
Oct. 11	Miami	South Bend	W	32–14
Oct. 18	Army	South Bend	W	30–3
Oct. 25	Arizona	Tucson	W	20–3
Nov. 1	Navy	Giants Stadium	W	33–0
Nov. 8	Georgia Tech	Atlanta	T	3–3
Nov. 15	Alabama	Birmingham	W	7–0
Nov. 22	Air Force	South Bend	W	24–10
Dec. 6	Southern California	Los Angeles	L	20–3
Jan. 1	Georgia	Sugar Bowl	L	17–10
Coach: Dan Devine				248–128

Captains: Bob Crable, Tom Gibbons, John Scully

Ranking (AP): Preseason No. 11; Postseason No. 9

All-American: Bob Crable, Scott Zettek, John Scully

Leaders: Rushing—Jim Stone (908 yards, 192 carries); Passing—Blair Kiel (48 of 124, 531 yards); Receiving—Tony Hunter (23 catches, 303 yards).

Led by Herschel Walker, Georgia won its first national championship with the Sugar Bowl victory. Although Notre Dame outgained the Bulldogs 328–127, four turnovers and other miscues helped put the Fighting Irish into a hole they couldn't escape. ... Dan Devine's record over six seasons was 53–16–1 (.764). ... Notre Dame defeated Michigan on a 51-yard field goal by Harry Oliver as time expired. ... Phil Carter became the first Notre Dame running back to have 40 carries in a single game, finishing with 254 yards at Michigan State.

Georgia's Herschel Walker (34) goes up and over for a touchdown against Notre Dame in the Sugar Bowl on January 1, 1981, in New Orleans.

1981

5-6-0

Sept. 12	LSU	South Bend	W	27-9
Sept. 19	Michigan	Ann Arbor	L	25-7
Sept. 26	Purdue	West Lafayette	L	15-14
Oct. 3	Michigan State	South Bend	W	20-7
Oct. 10	Florida State	South Bend	L	19-13
Oct. 24	Southern California	South Bend	L	14-7
Oct. 31	Navy	South Bend	W	38-0
Nov. 7	Georgia Tech	South Bend	W	35-3
Nov. 14	Air Force	Colorado Springs	W	35-7
Nov. 21	Penn State	University Park	L	24-21
Nov. 27	Miami	Miami	L	37-15

Coach: Gerry Faust 232-160

Captains: Bob Crable, Phil Carter

Ranking (AP): Preseason No. 3; Postseason NR

All-American: Bob Crable

Leaders: Rushing—Phil Carter (727 yards, 165 carries); Passing—Blair Kiel (67 of 151, 936 yards); Receiving—Tony Hunter (28 catches, 387 yards).

Before Notre Dame, former Dayton quarterback Gerry Faust compiled a 174–17–2 record at Moeller High School in Cincinnati. ... Linebacker Bob Crable finished his career with 521 tackles.

1982

6-4-1

Sept. 18	Michigan	South Bend	W	23-17
Sept. 25	Purdue	South Bend	W	28-14
Oct. 2	Michigan State	East Lansing	W	11-3
Oct. 9	Miami	South Bend	W	16-14
Oct. 16	Arizona	South Bend	L	16-13
Oct. 23	Oregon	Eugene	T	13-13
Oct. 30	Navy	Giants Stadium	W	27-10
Nov. 6	Pittsburgh	Pittsburgh	W	31-16
Nov. 13	Penn State	South Bend	L	24-14
Nov. 20	Air Force	Colorado Springs	L	30-17
Nov. 27	Southern California	Los Angeles	L	17-13

Coach: Gerry Faust 206-174

Captains: Phil Carter, Dave Duerson, Mark Zavagnin
Ranking (AP): Preseason No. 18; Postseason NR
All-American: Dave Duerson
Leaders: Rushing—Phil Carter (715 yards, 179 carries); Passing—Blair Kiel (118 of 219, 1,273 yards); Receiving—Tony Hunter (42 catches, 507 yards).

Joe Howard's 96-yard touchdown reception from Blair Keil against Georgia Tech set a Notre Dame record. ... The season opener against Michigan was the first night game at Notre Dame Stadium. The Wolverines managed just 41 rushing yards, their lowest output in 12 years. ... After leading the team in receiving for two years, Tony Hunter moved to tight end. He finished his career with 120 receptions for 1,897 yards. ... Injuries led to Tom Thayer starting three games at one guard position, four at another, and four at center. ... Mike Johnston's 32-yard field goal with 11 seconds remaining beat No. 17 Miami.

1983

7-5-0

Sept. 10	Purdue	West Lafayette	W	52-6
Sept. 17	Michigan State	South Bend	L	28-23
Sept. 24	Miami	Miami	L	20-0
Oct. 1	Colorado	Boulder	W	27-3
Oct. 8	South Carolina	Columbia	W	30-6
Oct. 15	Army	Giants Stadium	W	42-0
Oct. 22	Southern California	South Bend	W	27-6
Oct. 29	Navy	South Bend	W	28-12
Nov. 5	Pittsburgh	South Bend	L	21-16
Nov. 12	Penn State	University Park	L	34-30
Nov. 19	Air Force	South Bend	L	23-22
Dec. 29	Boston College	Liberty Bowl	W	19-18
Coach: Gerry Faust				316-177
Captains: Blair Kiel, Stacey Toran				
Ranking (AP): Preseason No. 6; Postseason NR				
Leaders: Rushing—Allen Pinkett (1,394 yards, 252 carries); Passing—Steve Beuerlein (75 of 145, 1,061 yards); Receiving—Allen Pinkett (28 catches, 288 yards).				

After losing last-second games against Penn State and Air Force, the defense kept Doug Flutie from pulling off any late heroics in the Liberty Bowl. While not using its usual I formation, tailback Allen Pinkett had 111 rushing yards on 28 carries and two touchdowns, and fullback Chris Smith had 104 yards on 18 carries.

1984

7-5-0

Sept. 8	Purdue	Hoosier Dome	L	23-21
Sept. 15	Michigan State	East Lansing	W	24-20
Sept. 22	Colorado	South Bend	W	55-14
Sept. 29	Missouri	Columbia	W	16-14
Oct. 6	Miami	South Bend	L	31-13
Oct. 13	Air Force	South Bend	L	21-7
Oct. 20	South Carolina	South Bend	L	36-32
Oct. 27	LSU	Baton Rouge	W	30-22
Nov. 3	Navy	Giants Stadium	W	18-17
Nov. 17	Penn State	South Bend	W	44-7
Nov. 24	Southern California	Los Angeles	W	19-7
Dec. 29	Southern Methodist	Aloha Bowl	L	27-20
Coach: Gerry Faust				299-239

Captains: Mike Golic, Joe Johnson, Larry Williams

Ranking (AP): Preseason No. 8; Postseason No. NR

All-American: Mark Bravaro

Leaders: Rushing—Allen Pinkett (1,105 yards, 275 carries); Passing—Steve Beuerlein (140 of 232, 1,920 yards); Receiving—Mark Bavaro (32 catches, 395 yards).

Steve Beuerlein barely missed Mile Jackson in the end zone as Notre Dame's comeback against Southern Methodist came up just short in the Aloha Bowl.

1985

5–6–0

Sept. 14	Michigan	Ann Arbor	L	20–12
Sept. 21	Michigan State	South Bend	W	27–10
Sept. 28	Purdue	West Lafayette	L	35–17
Oct. 5	Air Force	Colorado Springs	L	21–15
Oct. 19	Army	South Bend	W	24–10
Oct. 26	Southern California	South Bend	W	37–3
Nov. 2	Navy	South Bend	W	41–17
Nov. 9	Ole Miss	South Bend	W	37–14
Nov. 16	Penn State	University Park	L	36–6
Nov. 23	LSU	South Bend	L	10–7
Nov. 30	Miami	Miami	L	58–7
Coach: Gerry Faust				230–234

Captains: Tony Furjanic, Mike Larkin, Allen Pinkett, Tim Scannell

Ranking (AP): Preseason No. 14; Postseason NR

Leaders: Rushing—Allen Pinkett (1,100 yards, 255 carries); Passing—Steve Beuerlein (107 of 214, 1,335 yards); Receiving—Tim Brown (45 catches, 910 yards).

Gerry Faust compiled a 30–26–1 record (.535) over five seasons. ... Allen Pinkett set numerous school rushing records, including career yards with 4,131 yards.

1986

5–6–0

Sept. 13	Michigan	South Bend	L	24–23
Sept. 20	Michigan State	East Lansing	L	20–15
Sept. 27	Purdue	South Bend	W	41–9
Oct. 4	Alabama	Birmingham	L	28–10
Oct. 11	Pittsburgh	South Bend	L	10–9
Oct. 18	Air Force	South Bend	W	31–3
Nov. 1	Navy	Memorial Stadium	W	33–14
Nov. 8	Southern Methodist	South Bend	W	61–29
Nov. 15	Penn State	South Bend	L	24–19
Nov. 22	LSU	Baton Rouge	L	21–19
Nov. 29	Southern California	Los Angeles	W	38–37
Coach: Lou Holtz				299–219

Gerry Faust shouts orders during his final game as head coach of Notre Dame, against Miami in 1985. Faust would have liked to have gone out on a high note, but the Hurricanes dominated the Fighting Irish in a 58–7 drubbing.

Captain: Mike Kovaleski

All-American: Tim Brown

Leaders: Rushing—Mark Green (406 yards, 96 carries); Passing—Steve Beuerlein (151 of 259, 2,211 yards); Receiving—Tim Brown (39 catches, 846 yards).

Lou Holtz was hired away from Minnesota and had also coached at Arkansas, North Carolina State, and William & Mary. In his first game, against No. 3 Michigan, Notre Dame accumulated 455 yards, 27 first downs, and converted 8 of 12 third-down situations, but missed a game-winning 45-yard field goal with 13 seconds remaining. ... After starting 11 games at fullback in 1985, Frank Stams switched to defensive end where he would become an All-American. ... Steve Beuerlein set school career passing records for attempts (850), completions (6,527), and total offense (6,459).

1987

8–4–0

Sept. 12	Michigan	Ann Arbor	W	26-7
Sept. 19	Michigan State	South Bend	W	31-8
Sept. 26	Purdue	West Lafayette	W	44-20
Oct. 10	Pittsburgh	Pittsburgh	L	30-22
Oct. 17	Air Force	Colorado Springs	W	35-14
Oct. 24	Southern California	South Bend	W	26-15
Oct. 31	Navy	South Bend	W	56-13
Nov. 7	Boston College	South Bend	W	32-25
Nov. 14	Alabama	South Bend	W	37-6
Nov. 21	Penn State	University Park	L	21-20
Nov. 28	Miami	Miami	L	24-0
Jan. 1	Texas A&M	Cotton Bowl	L	35-10

Coach: Lou Holtz 339-218

Captains: Chuck Lanza, Byron Spruell

Ranking (AP): Preseason No. 18; Postseason No. 17

Major Awards: Tim Brown, Heisman Trophy, Walter Camp Player of the Year

All-American: Tim Brown

Leaders: Rushing—Mark Green (861 yards, 146 carries); Passing—Tony Rice (35 of 82, 663 yards); Receiving—Tim Brown (39 catches, 846 yards).

Tim Brown returned two punts for touchdowns to lead the victory against Michigan State and solidify his Heisman bid. He finished his career as Notre Dame's all-time receiving leader with 2,493 yards and also returned six kicks for touchdowns. ... Brown set career school records for receiving yardage (2,493), kickoff return yards (1,613), combined kickoff and punt return yards (2,089), and kickoffs and punts returned for touchdowns (6). He was third in pass receptions (137). ... Notre Dame played in its first New Year's Day bowl in seven years. ... An interception in the end zone turned the momentum Texas A&M's way, and the Fighting Irish only accumulated 76 yards in the second half.

1988

12–0–0, National champions

Sept. 10	Michigan	South Bend	W	19–17
Sept. 17	Michigan State	East Lansing	W	20–3
Sept. 24	Purdue	South Bend	W	52–7
Oct. 1	Stanford	South Bend	W	42–14
Oct. 8	Pittsburgh	Pittsburgh	W	30–20
Oct. 15	Miami	South Bend	W	31–30
Oct. 22	Air Force	South Bend	W	41–13
Oct. 29	Navy	Memorial Stadium	W	22–7
Nov. 5	Rice	South Bend	W	54–11
Nov. 19	Penn State	South Bend	W	21–3
Nov. 26	Southern California	Los Angeles	W	27–10
Jan. 2	West Virginia	Fiesta Bowl	W	34–21
Coach: Lou Holtz				393–156

Captains: Ned Bolcar, Mark Green, Andy Heck

Ranking (AP): Preseason No. 13; Postseason No. 1

All-American: Andy Heck, Frank Stams, Mike Stonebreaker

Leaders: Rushing—Tony Rice (700 yards, 121 carries); Passing—Tony Rice (70 of 138, 1,176 yards); Receiving—Ricky Watters (15 catches, 286 yards).

Notre Dame snapped No. 1 Miami's 36-game regular-season winning streak and 20-game road winning streak. The Hurricanes had also outscored the Fighting Irish 133–20 in the previous

four meetings. The game came down to a two-point conversion pass by quarterback Steve Walsh that was knocked away by Pat Terrell. Walsh passed for 424 yards, but Notre Dame forced seven turnovers. ... Notre Dame ran the ball on 16 of its first 17 plays against West Virginia and quarterback Tony Rice was named the Fiesta Bowl's offensive MVP despite attempting only 11 passes. Frank Stams was defensive MVP. ... Ricky Watters returned a punt 81 yards for a touchdown as Notre Dame defeated Michigan without scoring an offensive touchdown.

1989

12-1-0

Aug. 31	Virginia	Giants Stadium	W	36-13
Sept. 16	Michigan	Ann Arbor	W	24-19
Sept. 23	Michigan State	South Bend	W	21-13
Sept. 30	Purdue	West Lafayette	W	40-7
Oct. 7	Stanford	Stanford	W	27-17
Oct. 14	Air Force	Colorado Springs	W	41-27
Oct. 21	Southern California	South Bend	W	28-24
Oct. 28	Pittsburgh	South Bend	W	45-7
Nov. 4	Navy	South Bend	W	41-0
Nov. 11	Southern Methodist	South Bend	W	59-6
Nov. 18	Penn State	University Park	W	34-23
Nov. 25	Miami	Miami	L	27-10
Jan. 1	Colorado	Orange Bowl	W	21-6
Coach: Lou Holtz				427-179

Captains: Ned Bolcar, Anthony Johnson, Tony Rice

Ranking (AP): Preseason No. 2; Postseason No. 2

Major Awards: Tony Rice, Johnny Unitas Golden Arm Award

All-American: Raghib Ismail, Todd Lyght, Chris Zorich

Leaders: Rushing—Tony Rice (884 yards, 174 carries); Passing—Tony Rice (68 of 137, 1,122 yards); Receiving—Raghib Ismail (27 catches, 535 yards).

Raghib Ismail returned two kickoffs for touchdowns to lead the victory against No. 2 Michigan. ... Colorado was No. 1 heading into the Orange Bowl, with the Fighting Irish preventing the

Buffaloes from winning the national title. Despite averaging 34 points and 473 offensive yards per game, Colorado mustered only six points and 282 yards and was stymied by a key goal-line stand. ... Cornerback Todd Lyght made 47 tackles, broke up 6.5 passes, and made 8 interceptions for 42 return yards and one touchdown. ... Quarterback Tony Rice broke his own school record for rushing yards by a quarterback with 884. ... Behind offensive lineman Tom Grunhard, Notre Dame averaged 287.7 rushing yards per game. ... Ricky Watters returned a punt 97 yards for a touchdown to break a 90-year school record. ... Miami snapped the 23-game Irish winning streak.

1990

9-3-0

Sept. 15	Michigan	South Bend	W	28–24
Sept. 22	Michigan State	East Lansing	W	20–19
Sept. 29	Purdue	South Bend	W	37–11
Oct. 6	Stanford	South Bend	L	36–31
Oct. 13	Air Force	South Bend	W	57–27
Oct. 20	Miami	South Bend	W	29–20
Oct. 27	Pittsburgh	Pittsburgh	W	31–22
Nov. 3	Navy	Giants Stadium	W	52–31
Nov. 10	Tennessee	Knoxville	W	34–29
Nov. 17	Penn State	South Bend	L	24–21
Nov. 24	Southern California	Los Angeles	W	10–6
Jan. 1	Colorado	Orange Bowl	L	10–9

Coach: Lou Holtz 359–259

Captains: Mike Heldt, Todd Lyght, Ricky Watters, Chris Zorich

Ranking (AP): Preseason No. 2; Postseason No. 6

Major Awards: Chris Zorich, Lombardi Award; Raghib Ismail, Walter Camp Player of the Year

All-American: Raghib Ismail, Todd Lynch, Mike Stonebreaker, Chris Zorich

Leaders: Rushing—Rodney Culver (710 yards, 150 carries); Passing—Rick Mirer (110 of 200, 1,824 yards); Receiving—Raghib Ismail (32 catches, 699 yards).

For the second straight year, Colorado came into the Orange Bowl ranked No. 1, but this time the team was able to secure at least a share of the national title. Notre Dame lost five turnovers, had a point-after attempt blocked, and saw a 50-yard field goal attempt clang off the upright. Raghib Ismail's 91-yard punt return appeared to give Notre Dame the last-minute lead, but the play was nullified by a clipping penalty. ... Nose guard Chris Zorich was named defensive MVP of the Orange Bowl in his final collegiate game. ... Ismail's career totals included 273 all-purpose attempts for 4,187 yards and 15 touchdowns, and he averaged 15.3 yards every time he touched the ball. ... Cornerback Todd Lyght finished his career with 11 interceptions. ... Craig Hentrick made five field goals against No. 2 Miami. ... Adrian Jarrell made dramatic catches to beat Michigan and Michigan State.

1991

Record: 10–3–0

Sept. 7	Indiana	South Bend	W	49–27
Sept. 14	Michigan	Ann Arbor	L	24–14
Sept. 21	Michigan State	South Bend	W	49–10
Sept. 28	Purdue	West Lafayette	W	45–20
Oct. 5	Stanford	Stanford	W	42–26
Oct. 12	Pittsburgh	South Bend	W	42–7
Oct. 19	Air Force	Colorado Springs	W	28–15
Oct. 26	Southern California	South Bend	W	24–20
Nov. 2	Navy	South Bend	W	38–0
Nov. 9	Tennessee	South Bend	L	35–34
Nov. 16	Penn State	University Park	L	35–13
Nov. 30	Hawaii	Honolulu	W	48–42
Jan. 1	Florida	Sugar Bowl	W	39–28

Coach: Lou Holtz 474–289

Captain: Rodney Culver

Ranking (AP): Preseason No. 6; Postseason No. 13

All-American: Derek Brown, Mirko Jurkovic

Leaders: Rushing—Jerome Bettis (972 yards, 168 carries); Passing—Rick Mirer (132 of 234, 1,876 yards); Receiving—Tony Smith (42 catches, 789 yards).

Raghib Ismail has teammates piling on him in celebration after his apparent punt return touchdown in the Orange Bowl. The celebration was short-lived, however, when a clipping penalty wiped out the play.

The Tennessee game was the 300th played at Notre Dame Stadium. ... After being down 16–7, and outgained 288–142 by Florida in the first half, the Fighting Irish pounded out 32 points led by three Jerome Bettis touchdowns. Although Gators quarterback Shane Matthews finished 28 of 58 for 370 yards, he had just 11 second-half completions. ... Notre Dame signed a lucrative exclusive television contract with NBC. ... Desmond Howard's diving touchdown catch on a fourth-and-inches pass from Elvis Grbac keyed Michigan's early-season victory.

1992

10–1–1

Sept. 5	Northwestern	Soldier Field	W	42–7
Sept. 12	Michigan	South Bend	T	17–17
Sept. 19	Michigan State	East Lansing	W	52–31
Sept. 26	Purdue	South Bend	W	48–0
Oct. 3	Stanford	South Bend	L	33–16
Oct. 10	Pittsburgh	Pittsburgh	W	52–21
Oct. 24	Brigham Young	South Bend	W	42–16
Oct. 31	Navy	Giants Stadium	W	38–7
Nov. 7	Boston College	South Bend	W	54–7
Nov. 14	Penn State	South Bend	W	17–16
Nov. 28	Southern California	Los Angeles	W	31–23
Jan. 1	Texas A&M	Cotton Bowl	W	28–3
Coach: Lou Holtz				437–181

Captains: Demetrius DuBose, Rick Mirer

Ranking (AP): Preseason No. 3; Postseason No. 4

All-American: Aaron Taylor

Leaders: Rushing—Reggie Brooks (1,343 yards, 167 carries); Passing—Rick Mirer (120 of 234, 1,876 yards); Receiving—Lake Dawson (25 catches, 462 yards).

With the "Thunder and Lightning" running attack of Jerome Bettis and Reggie Brooks, Notre Dame tallied 290 rushing yards against undefeated Texas A&M. During one second-half stretch the Fighting Irish ran the ball on 34 consecutive plays. Nevertheless, quarterback Rick Mirer was

named the Cotton Bowl's offensive MVP, while Devon McDonald earned the defensive honor. ... Rick Mirer's two-point conversion pass in the snow meant victory against Penn State. ... Craig Hentrich set numerous school records including punting average (44.1 yards), extra points (177), and extra-point percentage (.983). With 294 career points, he finished second in all-time scoring. ... Brooks' 8.0 yards per carry just missed George Gipp's school record of 8.1 set in 1920.

1993

11–1–0

Sept. 4	Northwestern	South Bend	W	27–12
Sept. 11	Michigan	Ann Arbor	W	27–23
Sept. 18	Michigan State	South Bend	W	36–14
Sept. 25	Purdue	West Lafayette	W	17–0
Oct. 2	Stanford	Stanford	W	48–20
Oct. 9	Pittsburgh	South Bend	W	44–0
Oct. 16	Brigham Young	Provo	W	45–20
Oct. 23	Southern California	South Bend	W	31–13
Oct. 30	Navy	Veterans Stadium	W	58–27
Nov. 13	Florida State	South Bend	W	31–24
Nov. 20	Boston College	South Bend	L	41–39
Jan. 1	Texas A&M	Cotton Bowl	W	24–21
Coach: Lou Holtz				427–215

Captains: Jeff Burris, Tim Ruddy, Aaron Taylor, Bryant Young

Ranking (AP): Preseason No. 7; Postseason No. 2

Major Awards: Aaron Taylor, Lombardi Award

All-American: Jeff Burris, Aaron Taylor, Bobby Taylor, Bryant Young

Leaders: Rushing—Lee Becton (1,044 yards, 164 carries); Passing—Kevin McDougal (98 of 159, 1,541 yards); Receiving—Lake Dawson (25 catches, 395 yards).

The game at No. 3 Michigan drew 106,851 fans, the largest regular-season attendance in NCAA history at the time. ... Both Notre Dame and Florida State had 16-game winning streaks when they met in a high-profile game hyped as the battle for No. 1. ... Texas A&M was again undefeated

Ron Powlus rolls out of the pocket and looks downfield to pass against Purdue. Today, Powlus is Notre Dame's quarterbacks coach.

heading into the Cotton Bowl but had its fourth-quarter comeback come up short. ... Safety Jeff Burris finished his career with 10 interceptions and 10 touchdowns as the goal-line tailback. ... Center Tim Ruddy had a 4.0 GPA and played 298 minutes, 57 seconds, despite missing a start with a pulled abdominal muscle.

1994

6–5–1

Sept. 3	Northwestern	Soldier Field	W	42–15
Sept. 10	Michigan	South Bend	L	26–24
Sept. 17	Michigan State	East Lansing	W	21–20
Sept. 24	Purdue	South Bend	W	39–21
Oct. 1	Stanford	South Bend	W	34–15
Oct. 8	Boston College	Boston	L	30–11
Oct. 15	Brigham Young	South Bend	L	21–14
Oct. 29	Navy	South Bend	W	58–21
Nov. 12	Florida State	Orlando	L	23–16
Nov. 19	Air Force	South Bend	W	42–30
Nov. 26	Southern California	Los Angeles	T	17–17
Jan. 2	Colorado	Fiesta Bowl	L	41–24
Coach: Lou Holtz				342–280

Captains: Lee Becton, Justin Goheen, Brian Hamilton, Ryan Leahy

Ranking (AP): Preseason No. 2; Postseason NR

All-American: Bobby Taylor

Leaders: Rushing—Randy Kinder (702 yards, 119 carries); Passing—Ron Powlus (119 of 222, 1,729 yards); Receiving—Derrick Mayes (47 catches, 847 yards).

Although Colorado running back and Heisman Trophy winner Rashaan Salaam was limited to 83 rushing yards on 27 carries, he scored three touchdowns in the Fiesta Bowl. Meanwhile, quarterback Kordell Stewart carved up the Fighting Irish with 226 passing yards and 143 rushing. ... Cornerback Bobby Taylor was named Defensive Back of the Year by the Columbus (Ohio) Touchdown Club. ... The Board of Trustees approved the first plan to expand Notre Dame Stadium since its construction in 1930. An expansion of the rectangular bowl raised the stadium's capacity by 21,150 seats to 80,225 in 1997. ... Quarterback Ron Powlus had four touchdown passes against Northwestern in his first career start.

1995

9–3–0

Sept. 2	Northwestern	South Bend	L	17-15
Sept. 9	Purdue	West Lafayette	W	35-28
Sept. 16	Vanderbilt	South Bend	W	41-0
Sept. 23	Texas	South Bend	W	55-27
Sept. 30	Ohio State	Columbus	L	45-26
Oct. 7	Washington	Seattle	W	29-21
Oct. 14	Army	Giants Stadium	W	28-27
Oct. 21	Southern California	South Bend	W	38-10
Oct. 28	Boston College	South Bend	W	20-10
Nov. 4	Navy	South Bend	W	35-17
Nov. 18	Air Force	Colorado Springs	W	44-14
Jan. 1	Florida State	Orange Bowl	L	31-26
Coach: Lou Holtz				392-247

Captains: Paul Grasmanis, Ryan Leahy, Derrick Mayes, Shawn Wooden, Dusty Zeigler

Ranking (AP): Preseason No. 9; Postseason No. 11

Leaders: Rushing—Randy Kinder (809 yards, 143 carries); Passing—Ron Powlus (133 of 232, 1,942 yards); Receiving—Derrick Mayes (48 catches, 881 yards).

The game against Florida State was the final Orange Bowl game played at the Orange Bowl before moving to Joe Robbie Stadium. Without quarterback Ron Powlus and leading rusher Randy Kinder, Notre Dame managed to take a 26–14 lead with less than 12 minutes remaining, but Florida scored 17 points in the fourth quarter to win. ... Notre Dame kept its unbeaten streak, which dated back to 1983, alive against Southern California. Five of the wins during that span were by more than two touchdowns. ... Northwestern, coached by Gary Barnett, shocked Notre Dame in the season opener.

1996

8–3

Sept. 5	Vanderbilt	Nashville	W	14–7
Sept. 14	Purdue	South Bend	W	35–0
Sept. 21	Texas	Austin	W	27–24
Sept. 28	Ohio State	Columbus	L	29–16
Oct. 12	Washington	South Bend	W	54–20
Oct. 19	Air Force	South Bend	L OT	20–17
Nov. 2	Navy	Dublin, Ireland	W	54–27
Nov. 9	Boston College	Chestnut Hill	W	48–21
Nov. 16	Pittsburgh	South Bend	W	60–6
Nov. 23	Rutgers	South Bend	W	62–0
Nov. 30	Southern California	Los Angeles	L OT	27–20

Coach: Lou Holtz 407–181

Captains: Lyron Cobbins, Marc Edwards, Ron Powlus

Ranking (AP): Preseason No. 6; Postseason No. 19

Leaders: Rushing—Autry Denson (1,179 yards, 202 carries); Passing—Ron Powlus (133 of 232, 1,942 yards); Receiving—Pete Chryplewicz (27 catches, 331 yards).

In 11 seasons at Notre Dame, Lou Holtz was 100–30–2, and he set the school record for games coached (132). ... The victory against Vanderbilt was Notre Dame's 1,000th game. ... Notre Dame played Navy at Croke Park, in Dublin, Ireland. ... No. 9 Notre Dame stormed back in the fourth quarter to upset No. 6 Texas, with freshman Jim Sanson making the game-winning 39-yard field goal as time expired. ... Notre Dame turned down an invitation to play in the Independence Bowl.

1997

7–6

Sept. 6	Georgia Tech	South Bend	W	17–13
Sept. 13	Purdue	West Lafayette	L	28–17
Sept. 20	Michigan State	South Bend	L	23–7
Sept. 27	Michigan	Ann Arbor	L	21–14
Oct. 4	Stanford	Stanford	L	33–15
Oct. 11	Pittsburgh	Pittsburgh	W	45–21
Oct. 18	Southern California	South Bend	L	20–17

Oct. 25	Boston College	South Bend	W	52-20
Nov. 1	Navy	South Bend	W	21-17
Nov. 15	LSU	Baton Rouge	W	24-6
Nov. 22	West Virginia	South Bend	W	21-14
Nov. 29	Hawaii	Honolulu	W	23-22
Dec. 28	LSU	Independence Bowl	L	27-9
Coach: Bob Davie				282-265

Captains: Melvin Dansby, Ron Powlus, Allen Rossum

Ranking (AP): Preseason No. 11; Postseason NR

Leaders: Rushing—Autry Denson (1,268 yards, 264 carries); Passing—Ron Powlus (182 of 298, 2,078 yards); Receiving—Bobby Brown (45 catches, 543 yards).

After serving as Lou Holtz's defensive coordinator for three years, Bob Davie was promoted to replace him. Davie became the first Notre Dame coach to take the Fighting Irish to a bowl game during his first season. ... The season opener against Georgia Tech featured the rededication of Notre Dame Stadium. ... The Fighting Irish lost their regular-season rematch with LSU in the Independence Bowl, with Tigers running back Rondell Mealey accumulating 222 rushing yards, all but 37 of which were in the second half.

1998

9–3

Sept. 5	Michigan	South Bend	W	36-20
Sept. 12	Michigan State	East Lansing	L	45-23
Sept. 26	Purdue	South Bend	W	31-30
Oct. 3	Stanford	South Bend	W	35-17
Oct. 10	Arizona State	Tempe	W	28-9
Oct. 24	Army	South Bend	W	20-17
Oct. 31	Baylor	South Bend	W	27-3
Nov. 7	Boston College	Chestnut Hill	W	31-26
Nov. 14	Navy	Baltimore	W	30-0
Nov. 21	LSU	South Bend	W	39-36
Nov. 28	Southern California	Los Angeles	L	10-0
Jan. 1	Georgia Tech	Gator Bowl	L	35-28
Coach: Bob Davie				328-248

Captains: Bobbie Howard, Kory Minor, Mike Rosenthal

Ranking (AP): Preseason No. 22; Postseason No. 22

All-American: Mike Rosenthal

Leaders: Rushing—Autry Denson (1,176 yards, 251 carries); Passing—Jarious Jackson (104 of 188, 1,740 yards); Receiving—Malcolm Johnson (43 catches, 642 yards).

Despite Jarious Jackson playing hurt and Autry Denson's 130 rushing yards on 26 carries, Notre Dame couldn't stop Georgia Tech's offense, led by quarterback Joe Hamilton's 237 passing yards and touchdown receptions of 44 and 55 by Dez White in the second half.

1999

5–7

Aug. 28	Kansas	South Bend	W	48–13
Sept. 4	Michigan	Ann Arbor	L	26–22
Sept. 11	Purdue	West Lafayette	L	28–23
Sept. 18	Michigan State	South Bend	L	23–13
Oct. 2	Oklahoma	South Bend	W	34–30
Oct. 9	Arizona State	South Bend	W	48–17
Oct. 16	Southern California	South Bend	W	25–24
Oct. 30	Navy	South Bend	W	28–24
Nov. 6	Tennessee	Knoxville	L	38–14
Nov. 13	Pittsburgh	Pittsburgh	L	37–27
Nov. 20	Boston College	South Bend	L	31–29
Nov. 27	Stanford	Stanford	L	40–37
Coach: Bob Davie				348–331

Captain: Jarious Jackson

Ranking (AP): Preseason No. 18; Postseason NR

Leaders: Rushing—Tony Fisher (783 yards, 156 carries); Passing—Jarious Jackson (184 of 316, 2,753 yards); Receiving—Bobby Brown (36 catches, 608 yards).

Notre Dame opened the season against Kansas in the State of Indiana Eddie Robinson Classic. ... The Michigan game drew 111,523, the largest regular-season attendance in NCAA history at the time. ... Jarious Jackson set school records with 184 completions in 316 attempts for 2,753

yards. ... For the first time in its history Notre Dame was placed on probation by the NCAA, for two years and one scholarship each year. The issue primarily revolved around booster Kimberly Dunbar, who gave gifts to football players with money she later pled guilty to embezzling.

2000

9–3

Sept. 2	Texas A&M	South Bend	W	24–10
Sept. 9	Nebraska	South Bend	L OT	27–24
Sept. 16	Purdue	South Bend	W	23–21
Sept. 23	Michigan State	East Lansing	L	27–21
Oct. 7	Stanford	South Bend	W	20–14
Oct. 14	Navy	Orlando	W	45–14
Oct. 21	West Virginia	Morgantown	W	42–28
Oct. 28	Air Force	South Bend	W OT	34–31
Nov. 11	Boston College	South Bend	W	28–16
Nov. 18	Rutgers	Piscataway	W	45–17
Nov. 25	Southern California	Los Angeles	W	38–21
Jan. 1	Oregon State	Fiesta Bowl	L	41–9
Coach: Bob Davie				353–267

Captains: Anthony Denman, Jabari Holloway, Grant Irons, Dan O'Leary

Ranking (AP): Preseason NR; Postseason No. 15

Leaders: Rushing—Julius Jones (657 yards, 162 carries); Passing—Matt LoVecchio (73 of 125, 980 yards); Receiving—David Givens (25 catches, 310 yards).

Four third-quarter touchdowns by Oregon State did in Notre Dame in the first meeting between the schools. It was also the fifth straight bowl loss for the Fighting Irish and the program's worst defeat since a 58–7 loss at Miami in 1985. Notre Dame was limited to 155 yards of total offense and 17 rushing yards, both season lows. ... The Navy game was at the Citrus Bowl in Orlando.

2001

5–6

Sept. 8	Nebraska	Lincoln	L	27–10
Sept. 22	Michigan State	South Bend	L	17–10
Sept. 29	Texas A&M	College Station	L	24–3
Oct. 6	Pittsburgh	South Bend	W	24–7
Oct. 13	West Virginia	South Bend	W	34–24
Oct. 20	Southern California	South Bend	W	27–16
Oct. 27	Boston College	Chestnut Hill	L	21–17
Nov. 3	Tennessee	South Bend	L	28–18
Nov. 17	Navy	South Bend	W	34–16
Nov. 24	Stanford	Stanford	L	17–13
Dec. 1	Purdue	West Lafayette	W	24–18
Coach: Bob Davie				214–215

Captains: Rocky Boiman, David Givens, Grant Irons, Anthony Weaver

Ranking (AP): Preseason No. 18; Postseason NR

Leaders: Rushing—Julius Jones (718 yards, 168 carries); Passing—Carlyle Holiday (73 of 144, 784 yards); Receiving—Javin Hunter (37 catches, 387 yards).

George O'Leary resigned as Notre Dame football coach five days after being hired, admitting he lied about his academic and athletic background. O'Leary claimed to have a master's degree in education from New York University and to have played college football for three years at New Hampshire, but checks into his background showed it wasn't true. O'Leary was 52–33 in seven seasons at Georgia Tech when hired.

2002

10–3

Aug. 31	Maryland	Giants Stadium	W	22–0
Sept. 7	Purdue	South Bend	W	24–17
Sept. 14	Michigan	South Bend	W	25–23
Sept. 21	Michigan State	East Lansing	W	21–17
Oct. 5	Stanford	South Bend	W	31–7
Oct. 12	Pittsburgh	South Bend	W	14–6
Oct. 19	Air Force	Colorado Springs	W	21–14
Oct. 26	Florida State	Tallahassee	W	34–24
Nov. 2	Boston College	South Bend	L	14–7
Nov. 9	Navy	Ravens Stadium	W	30–23
Nov. 23	Rutgers	South Bend	W	42–0
Nov. 30	Southern California	Los Angeles	L	44–13
Jan. 1	North Carolina State	Alltel Stadium	L	28–6
Coach: Tyrone Willingham				296–235

Captains: Arnaz Battle, Sean Mahan, Gerome Sapp, Shane Walton

Ranking (AP): Preseason NR; Postseason No. 17

All-American: Jeff Faine, Shane Walton

Leaders: Rushing—Ryan Grant (1,085 yards, 261 carries); Passing—Carlyle Holiday (129 of 257, 1,788 yards); Receiving—Arnaz Battle (58 catches, 786 yards).

In wake of the George O'Leary resignation, Notre Dame hired Tyrone Willingham, the first black head coach in any sport for the Fighting Irish. ... Three costly interceptions nullified a sizable time-of-possession advantage against North Carolina State, which saw quarterback Phillip Rivers engineer two long touchdown drives. ... The season opener against Maryland was the Kickoff Classic in East Rutherford, N.J. ... Notre Dame topped one million in attendance for the first time with 1,008,693. ... Cornerback Shane Walton tied a single-game school record with three interceptions. ... Former coach Dan Devine died on May 9.

2003

5–7

Sept. 6	Washington State	South Bend	W OT	29–26
Sept. 13	Michigan	Ann Arbor	L	38–0
Sept. 20	Michigan State	South Bend	L	22–16
Sept. 27	Purdue	West Lafayette	L	23–10
Oct. 11	Pittsburgh	Pittsburgh	W	20–14
Oct. 18	Southern California	South Bend	L	45–14
Oct. 25	Boston College	Chestnut Hill	L	27–25
Nov. 1	Florida State	South Bend	L	37–0
Nov. 8	Navy	South Bend	W	27–24
Nov. 15	Brigham Young	South Bend	W	33–14
Nov. 29	Stanford	Stanford	W	57–7
Dec. 6	Syracuse	Syracuse	L	38–12
Coach: Tyrone Willingham				243–315

Captains: Darrell Campbell, Vontez Duff, Omar Jenkins, Jim Molinaro

Ranking (AP): Preseason No. 20; Postseason NR

Leaders: Rushing—Julius Jones (1,341 yards, 229 carries); Passing—Brady Quinn (195 of 411, 2,149 yards); Receiving—Rhema McKnight (47 catches, 600 yards).

Syracuse won the first meeting between the schools in 40 years and handed Notre Dame its third losing season in five years—a first for the Fighting Irish. ... Running back Julius Jones averaged 200 rushing yards per game during the late-season three-game winning streak. ... No. 5 Michigan's 38–0 victory was the most lopsided in series history and the first shutout since 1902. Nine of the previous 11 meetings were decided by seven points or fewer. ... No. 1 Southern California beat Notre Dame by 31 points for the second straight year.

2004

6–6

Sept. 4	Brigham Young	Provo	L	20–17
Sept. 11	Michigan	South Bend	W	28–20
Sept. 18	Michigan State	East Lansing	W	31–24
Sept. 25	Washington	South Bend	W	38–3
Oct. 2	Purdue	West Lafayette	L	41–16
Oct. 9	Stanford	Stanford	W	23–15
Oct. 16	Navy	Giants Stadium	W	27–9
Oct. 23	Boston College	South Bend	L	24–23
Nov. 6	Tennessee	Knoxville	W	17–14
Nov. 13	Pittsburgh	South Bend	L	41–38
Nov. 27	Southern California	Los Angeles	L	41–10
Dec. 28	Oregon State	Insight Bowl	L	38–21

Coach: Tyrone Willingham (Kent Baer interim) 310–327

Captains: Mike Goolsby, Ryan Grant, Carlyle Holiday, Justin Tuck

Leaders: Rushing—Darius Walker (786 yards, 185 carries); Passing—Brady Quinn (191 of 353, 2,586 yards); Receiving—Rhema McKnight (42 catches, 610 yards).

Tyrone Willingham (21–15) was fired at the end of the regular season, just three years into a five-year deal. "We simply have not made the progress on the field that we need to make," athletics director Kevin White said. "Nor have we been able to create the positive momentum necessary in our efforts to return the Notre Dame program to the elite level of the college football world." Defensive coordinator Kent Baer served as interim head coach for the Insight Bowl, where Sammie Stroughter's 52-yard punt return and Derrick Doggett's blocked punt helped Oregon State to an early 21–0 lead. ... After Notre Dame produced just 11 rushing yards against BYU, Darius Walker became the first freshman to have a 100-yard performance since Julius Jones had 146 yards against Navy in 1999, to lead the upset of No. 7 Michigan. He had 115 yards on 31 carries and scored two fourth-quarter touchdowns.

2005

9–3

Sept. 3	Pittsburgh	Pittsburgh	W	42-21
Sept. 10	Michigan	Ann Arbor	W	17-10
Sept. 17	Michigan State	South Bend	L OT	44-41
Sept. 24	Washington	Seattle	W	36-17
Oct. 1	Purdue	West Lafayette	W	49-28
Oct. 15	Southern California	South Bend	L	34-31
Oct. 22	Brigham Young	South Bend	W	49-23
Nov. 5	Tennessee	South Bend	W	41-21
Nov. 12	Navy	South Bend	W	42-21
Nov. 19	Syracuse	South Bend	W	34-10
Nov. 26	Stanford	Stanford	W	38-31
Jan. 2	Ohio State	Fiesta Bowl	L	34-20
Coach: Charlie Weis				460-328

Captains: Brady Quinn, Brandon Hoyte

Ranking (AP): Preseason NR; Postseason No. 9

All-American: Jeff Samardzija

Leaders: Rushing—Darius Walker (1,196 yards, 253 carries); Passing—Brady Quinn (292 of 450, 3,919 yards); Receiving—Jeff Samardzija (77 catches, 1,249 yards).

Charlie Weis, offensive coordinator for the New England Patriots, was hired as head coach and signed a 10-year contract. During his first season Notre Dame set a school record for points scored. The offense was also the most improved in the nation, upping its tally 131.8 yards per game for a 477.33 average. ... Notre Dame snapped Michgan's 16-game winning streak at Michigan Stadium and handed the Wolverines their first loss against a nonconference team at home since 1998. ... Brady Quinn passed for a school-record five touchdowns and a career-high 487 yards as Notre Dame came from 21 points down in the third quarter, only to lose to Michigan State in overtime. ... Troy Smith completed 19 of 28 passes for a career-high 342 yards and ran for 66 more to lead Ohio State in the Fiesta Bowl.

2006

10–3

Sept. 2	Georgia Tech	Atlanta	W	14–10
Sept. 9	Penn State	South Bend	W	41–17
Sept. 16	Michigan	South Bend	L	47–21
Sept. 23	Michigan State	East Lansing	W	40–37
Sept. 30	Purdue	South Bend	W	35–21
Oct. 7	Stanford	South Bend	W	31–10
Oct. 21	UCLA	South Bend	W	20–17
Oct. 28	Navy	M&T Bank Stadium	W	38–14
Nov. 4	North Carolina	South Bend	W	45–26
Nov. 11	Air Force	Colorado Springs	W	39–17
Nov. 18	Army	South Bend	W	41–9
Nov. 25	Southern California	Los Angeles	L	44–24
Jan. 3	LSU	Sugar Bowl	L	41–14
Coach: Charlie Weis				417–351

Captains: Brady Quinn, Tom Zbikowski, Travis Thomas

Ranking (AP): Preseason No. 2; Postseason No. 17

Major Award: Brady Quinn, Johnny Unitas Golden Arm Award

All-American: Jeff Samardzija

Leaders: Rushing—Darius Walker (1,267 yards, 255 carries); Passing—Brady Quinn (289 of 467, 3,426 yards); Receiving—Jeff Samardzija (78 catches, 1,017 yards).

The 264.1 passing yards per game was the second-best mark in school history, trailing only the 330.3 mark set in 2005. The 19 wins by Charlie Weis were the most by a Notre Dame coach during his first two seasons. ... With LSU tallying 245 rushing yards, the Tigers were able to control the clock and hand Notre Dame its ninth consecutive bowl loss, a string dating back to the 1994 Cotton Bowl. ... Brady Quinn's 10-yard touchdown pass to Jeff Samardzija in the second quarter of the Sugar Bowl was the 95th of his career, tying him for seventh on the NCAA all-time list with former North Carolina State quarterback Philip Rivers.

2007

3–9

Sept. 1	Georgia Tech	South Bend	L	33–3
Sept. 8	Penn State	University Park	L	31–10
Sept. 15	Michigan	Ann Arbor	L	38–0
Sept. 22	Michigan State	South Bend	L	31–14
Sept. 29	Purdue	West Lafayette	L	33–19
Oct. 6	UCLA	Pasadena	W	20–6
Oct. 13	Boston College	South Bend	L	27–14
Oct. 20	Southern California	South Bend	L	38–0
Nov. 3	Navy	South Bend	L (3OT)	46–44
Nov. 10	Air Force	South Bend	L	41–24
Nov. 17	Duke	South Bend	W	28–7
Nov. 24	Stanford	Stanford	W	21–14
Coach: Charlie Weis				197–345

Captains: John Carlson, Maurice Crum Jr., John Sullivan, Travis Thomas, Tom Zbikowski

Leaders: Rushing—James Aldridge (463 yards, 121 carries); Passing—Jimmy Clausen (138 of 245, 1,254yards); Receiving—John Carlson (40 catches, 372 yards).

The offense scored just one touchdown during the first three games. Notre Dame opened with a five-game losing streak and lost nine of its first 10 games. ... The team had its 43-game winning streak against Navy snapped in triple overtime. It was the longest active streak by one team against a single opponent in the NCAA. The game was also a school-record fifth straight home loss. ... Robert Hughes (whose brother was fatally shot the week of the Navy game) had 136 rushing yards and scored the go-ahead touchdown against Stanford as the Fighting Irish ended the season with consecutive wins for the first time in 15 years.

2008

7–6

Sept. 6	San Diego State	South Bend	W	21-13
Sept. 13	Michigan	South Bend	W	35-17
Sept. 20	at Michigan State	East Lansing	L	23-17
Sept. 27	Purdue	South Bend	W	38-21
Oct. 4	Stanford	South Bend	W	28-21
Oct. 11	at North Carolina	Chapel Hill	L	29-24
Oct. 25	at Washington	Seattle	W	33-7
Nov. 1	Pittsburgh	South Bend	L (4OT)	36-33
Nov. 8	at Boston College	Chestnut Hill	L	17-0
Nov. 15	at Navy	M&T Bank Stadium	W	27-21
Nov. 22	Syracuse	South Bend	L	24-23
Nov. 29	Southern California	Los Angeles	L	38-3
Dec. 24	Hawaii	Hawaii Bowl	W	49-21
Coach: Charlie Weis				379-309
Captains: David Bruton, Maurice Crum Jr., David Grimes				
Leaders: Rushing—Armando Allen Jr. (585 yards, 134 carries); Passing—Jimmy Clausen (268 of 440, 3,172 yards); Receiving—Golden Tate (58 catches, 1,080 yards).				

For the first time in school history Notre Dame was defeated by an eight-loss team, Syracuse. ... The combined 15 losses were the most ever by Notre Dame in a two-season span. ... Jimmy Clausen set school bowl records with 401 yards passing and five touchdowns while leading Notre Dame to its first postseason victory in 15 years. Wide receiver Golden Tate had six catches for 177 yards and three touchdowns, including his backbreaking 69-yard score in the second quarter of the Hawaii Bowl. ... Coach Charlie Weis tore ligaments in his right knee after being hit along the sideline during the second quarter of the Michigan game.

Future Schedules

2009

(All games tentative after 2009)

Sept. 5	Nevada	South Bend
Sept. 12	Michigan	Ann Arbor
Sept. 19	Michigan State	South Bend
Sept. 26	Purdue	West Lafayette
Oct. 3	Washington	South Bend
Oct. 17	Southern California	Notre Dame
Oct. 24	Boston College	South Bend
Oct. 31	Washington State	San Antonio
Nov. 7	Navy	Notre Dame
Nov. 14	Pittsburgh	Pittsburgh
Nov. 21	Connecticut	South Bend
Nov. 28	Stanford	Stanford

2010

Sept. 4	Purdue	South Bend
Sept. 11	Michigan	South Bend
Sept. 18	Michigan State	East Lansing
Sept. 25	Stanford	South Bend
Oct. 2	Boston College	Chestnut Hill
Oct. 9	Pittsburgh	South Bend
Oct. 16	Army	Chicago
Oct. 23	Navy	Baltimore
Nov. 6	TBA	
Nov. 13	Utah	South Bend
Nov. 20	TBA	
Nov. 27	Southern California	Los Angeles

Through the Years

2011

Sept. 3	Purdue	West Lafayette
Sept. 10	Michigan	Ann Arbor
Sept. 17	Michigan State	South Bend
Sept. 24	Pittsburgh	Pittsburgh
Oct. 1	South Florida	South Bend
Oct. 8	TBA	
Oct. 15	Army	Orlando
Oct. 22	Southern California	South Bend
Oct. 29	Navy	South Bend
Nov. 5	Connecticut	South Bend
Nov. 12	TBA	
Nov. 26	Stanford	Stanford

2012

Sept. 1	Navy	Dublin, Ireland
Sept. 8	Purdue	South Bend
Sept. 15	Michigan State	East Lansing
Sept. 22	Michigan	South Bend
Oct. 6	Baylor	New Orleans
Oct. 13	TBA	
Oct. 20	Pittsburgh	South Bend
Oct. 27	Oklahoma	Norman
Nov. 3	TBA	
Nov. 10	TBA	
Nov. 17	Wake Forest	South Bend
Nov. 24	Southern California	Los Angeles

2013

Aug. 31	TBA	
Sept. 7	Michigan	Ann Arbor
Sept. 14	Purdue	West Lafayette
Sept. 21	Michigan State	East Lansing
Sept. 28	Oklahoma	South Bend
Oct. 5	Arizona State	Arlington
Oct. 19	Southern California	South Bend
Oct. 26	Connecticut	Foxboro
Nov. 2	Navy	South Bend
Nov. 9	TBA	
Nov. 16	Rutgers	Piscataway
Nov. 23	TBA	

2014

Aug. 30	TBA	
Sept. 6	Navy	TBD
Sept. 13	Purdue	South Bend
Sept. 20	Michigan	South Bend
Oct. 4	TBA	
Oct. 11	Army	Orlando
Oct. 18	Connecticut	South Bend
Oct. 25	Arizona State	Tempe
Nov. 8	Pittsburgh	South Bend
Nov. 15	TBA	
Nov. 22	TBA	
Nov. 29	Southern California	Los Angeles

2015

Sept. 5	Missouri	South Bend
Sept. 12	Michigan	Ann Arbor
Sept. 19	Purdue	West Lafayette
Sept. 26	TBA	
Oct. 3	TBA	
Oct. 10	Navy	South Bend
Oct. 17	Southern California	South Bend
Oct. 24	Connecticut	East Rutherford
Nov. 2	TBA	
Nov. 7	TBA	
Nov. 14	Pittsburgh	Pittsburgh
Nov. 21	TBA	

2016

Sept. 3	TBA	
Sept. 10	Michigan	South Bend
Sept. 17	Stanford	South Bend
Sept. 24	Michigan State	East Lansing
Oct. 1	TBA	
Oct. 8	TBA	
Oct. 15	Navy	TBD
Oct. 29	Pittsburgh	South Bend
Nov. 5	TBA	
Nov. 12	Connecticut	South Bend
Nov. 19	Army	TBD
Nov. 26	South California	Los Angeles

Notre Dame Bowl Games

Won 14, Lost 15

Season	Bowl	Opponent	W/L	Score
Jan. 1, 1925	Rose	Stanford	W	27–10
Jan. 1, 1970	Cotton	Texas	L	21–17
Jan. 1, 1971	Cotton	Texas	W	24–11
Jan. 1, 1973	Orange	Nebraska	L	40–6
Dec. 31, 1973	Sugar	Alabama	W	24–23
Jan. 1, 1975	Orange	Alabama	W	13–11
Dec. 27, 1976	Gator	Penn State	W	20– 9
Jan. 2, 1978	Cotton	Texas	W	38–10
Jan. 1, 1979	Cotton	Houston	W	35–34
Jan. 1, 1981	Sugar	Georgia	L	17–10
Dec. 29, 1983	Liberty	Boston College	W	19–18
Dec. 29, 1984	Aloha	S. Methodist	L	27–20
Jan. 1, 1988	Cotton	Texas A&M	L	35–10
Jan. 2, 1989	Fiesta	West Virginia	W	34–21
Jan. 1, 1990	Orange	Colorado	W	21–6
Jan. 1, 1991	Orange	Colorado	L	10–9
Jan. 1, 1992	Sugar	Florida	W	39–28
Jan. 1, 1993	Cotton	Texas A&M	W	28–3
Jan. 1, 1994	Cotton	Texas A&M	W	24–21
Jan. 2, 1995	Fiesta	Colorado	L	41–24
Jan. 1, 1996	Orange	Florida State	L	31–26
Dec. 28, 1997	Independence	LSU	L	27–9
Jan. 1, 1999	Gator	Georgia Tech	L	35–28
Jan. 1, 2001	Fiesta	Oregon State	L	41–9
Jan. 1, 2003	Gator	N. Carolina State	L	28–6
Dec. 28, 2004	Insight	Oregon State	L	38–21
Jan. 2, 2006	Fiesta	Ohio State	L	34–20
Jan. 3, 2007	Sugar	LSU	L	41–14
Dec. 24, 2008	Hawaii	Hawaii Bowl	W	49–21

Notre Dame vs. No. 1 Teams in Bowl Games

Season	Bowl	Result (AP rankings)	ND Final
1969	Cotton	No. 1 Texas 21 No. 9 Notre Dame 17	5
1970	Cotton	No. 5 Notre Dame 24 No. 1 Texas 11	2
1972	Orange	No. 9 Nebraska 40 No. 12 Notre Dame 6	14
1973	Sugar	No. 3 Notre Dame 24 No. 1 Alabama 23	1
1974	Orange	No. 9 Notre Dame 13 No. 2-x Alabama 11	6
1976	Gator	No. 15 Notre Dame 20 No. 20 Penn State 9	12
1977	Cotton	No. 5 Notre Dame 38 No. 1 Texas 10	1
1978	Cotton	No. 10 Notre Dame 35 No. 9 Houston 34	7
1980	Sugar	No. 1 Georgia 17 No. 7 Notre Dame 10	9

x–Ranked No. 1 by coaches.

All-Time Record vs. Opponents

Opponent	First	Last	W L T
Adrian	1912	1912	1–0–0
Air Force	1964	2007	22–6–0
Akron	1910	1910	1–0–0
Alabama	1973	1987	5–1–0
Albion	1893	1898	3–1–1
Alma	1913	1916	4–0–0
American Medical College	1901	1905	5–0–0
Arizona	1941	1982	2–1–0
Arizona State	1998	1999	2–0–0
Army	1913	2006	37–8–4
Baylor	1925	1998	2–0–0
Beloit	1896	1926	5–0–1
Bennett Medical College	1905	1905	1–0–0
Boston College	1975	2008	9–9–0

BYU	1992	2005	4-2-0
Butler	1911	1923	3-0-0
California	1959	1967	4-0-0
Carlisle	1914	1914	1-0-0
Carnegie Tech	1922	1941	15-4-0
Case Tech	1916	1918	2-0-0
Chicago	1894	1899	0-4-0
Chicago Dental	1897	1897	1-0-0
Chicago Physicians & Surgeons	1895	1908	7-2-0
Christian Brothers	1913	1913	1-0-0
Cincinnati	1900	1900	1-0-0
Clemson	1977	1979	1-1-0
Coe	1927	1927	1-0-0
Colorado	1983	1994	3-2-0
Creighton	1915	1915	1-0-0
Dartmouth	1944	1945	2-0-0
DeLaSalle	1893	1893	1-0-0
DePauw	1897	1922	8-0-0
Detroit	1927	1951	2-0-0
Drake	1926	1937	8-0-0
Duke	1958	2007	3-1-0
Englewood (Chicago) High School	1899	1900	2-0-0
Florida	1991	1991	1-0-0
Florida State	1981	2003	2-4-0
Franklin	1906	1908	3-0-0
Georgia	1980	1980	0-1-0
Georgia Tech	1922	2007	27-6-1
Goshen	1900	1900	1-0-0
Great Lakes	1918	1945	1-2-2
Harvard (Chicago) Prep	1888	1888	1-0-0
Haskell	1914	1932	5-0-0
Hawaii	1991	2008	3-0-0
Highland Views	1896	1896	1-0-0
Hillsdale	1892	1908	4-0-1
Houston	1978	1978	1-0-0
Illinois	1898	1968	11-0-1
Illinois Cycling Club	1895	1895	1-0-0
Indiana	1898	1991	23-5-1
Indianapolis Artillery	1895	1895	0-1-0
Iowa	1921	1968	13-8-3

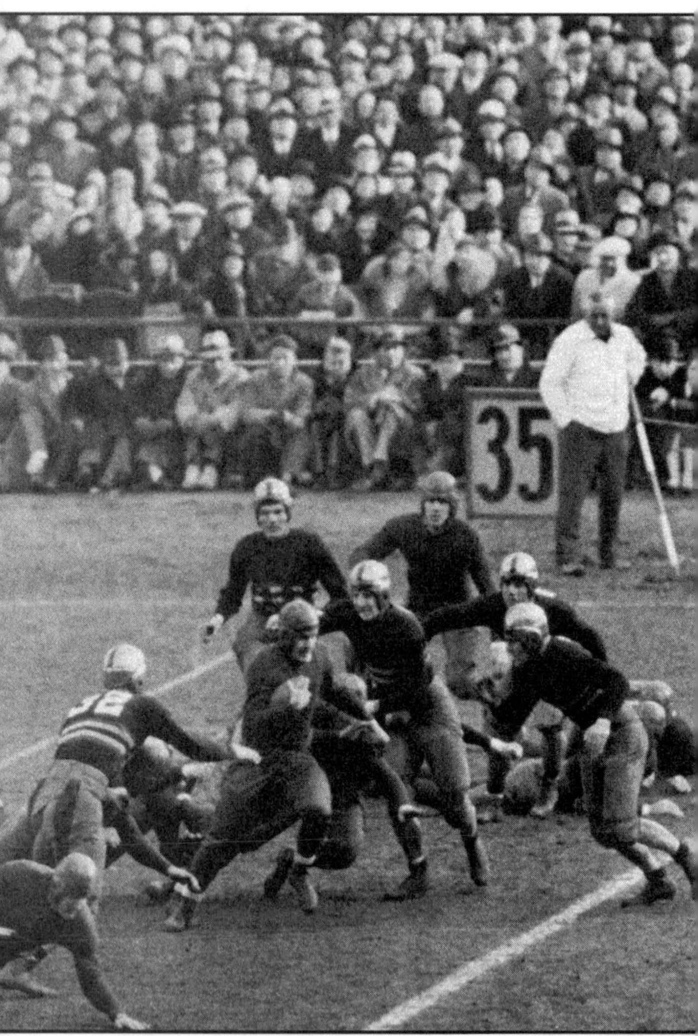

Notre Dame's rivalries with the service academies are well-established but today mostly one-sided. Army and Navy were once two of the top teams in the country. More than 80,000 turned out at Yankee Stadium to watch the Irish take on Army in 1932.

Iowa Pre-Flight	1942	1943	2-0-0
Kalamazoo	1893	1923	7-0-0
Kansas	1904	1999	4-1-1
Knox	1902	1907	1-1-0
Lake Forest	1899	1903	4-0-0
Lombard	1923	1925	3-0-0
LSU	1970	1998	5-4-0
Loyola (Chicago)	1911	1911	1-0-0
Loyola (New Orleans)	1928	1928	1-0-0
Marquette	1908	1921	3-0-3
Maryland	2002	2002	1-0-0
Miami (Florida)	1955	1990	15-7-1
Miami (Ohio)	1909	1909	1-0-0
Michigan	1887	2008	15-20-1
Michigan State	1897	2008	44-27-1
Minnesota	1925	1938	4-0-1
Mississippi	1977	1985	1-1-0
Missouri	1970	1984	2-2-0
Missouri Osteopaths	1903	1903	1-0-0
Morningside	1917	1919	2-0-0
Morris Harvey	1912	1912	1-0-0
Mount Union	1919	1919	1-0-0
Navy	1927	2008	71-10-1
Nebraska	1915	2001	7-8-1
North Carolina	1949	2008	16-2-0
North Carolina State	2002	2002	0-1-0
North Division High School	1905	1905	1-0-0
Northwestern	1889	1995	37-8-2
Northwestern Law	1895	1895	1-0-0
Ohio Medical University	1901	1904	4-0-0
Ohio Northern	1908	1913	4-0-0
Ohio State	1935	1996	2-2-0
Oklahoma	1952	1999	8-1-0
Olivet	1907	1910	3-0-0
Oregon	1976	1982	1-0-1
Oregon State	2000	2004	0-2-0
Pacific	1940	1940	1-0-0
Penn State	1913	2007	9-9-1
Pennsylvania	1930	1955	5-0-1
Pittsburgh	1909	2008	44-19-1
Princeton	1923	1924	2-0-0

Purdue	1896	2008	52-26-2
Rice	1915	1988	4-0-0
Rose Poly	1909	1914	3-0-0
Rush Medical	1894	1900	3-0-1
Rutgers	1921	2002	4-0-0
St. Bonaventure	1911	1911	1-0-0
Saint Louis	1912	1923	3-0-0
St. Viator	1897	1912	4-0-0
St. Vincent's (Chicago)	1907	1907	1-0-0
San Diego State	2008	2008	1-0-0
South Bend Athletic Club	1901	1901	1-0-1
South Bend Commercial Athletic Club	1896	1896	1-0-0
South Bend High School	1892	1892	1-0-0
South Bend Howard Park	1900	1900	1-0-0
South Carolina	1976	1984	3-1-0
South Dakota	1913	1917	5-0-0
Southern California	1926	2008	42-33-5
Southern Methodist	1930	1989	10-3-0
Stanford	1924	2008	17-6-0
Syracuse	1914	2008	3-3-0
Tennessee	1978	2005	4-4-0
Texas	1913	1996	8-2-0
Texas A&M	1987	2001	3-2-0
Texas Christian	1972	1972	1-0-0
Toledo Athletic Association	1904	1904	1-0-0
Tulane	1944	1971	8-0-0
UCLA	1963	2007	4-0-0
Valparaiso	1920	1920	1-0-0
Vanderbilt	1995	1996	2-0-0
Virginia	1989	1989	1-0-0
Wabash	1894	1924	10-1-0
Washington	1948	2008	7-0-0
Washington & Jefferson	1917	1917	1-0-0
Washington (St. Louis)	1936	1936	1-0-0
Washington State	2003	2003	1-0-0
Western Michigan	1919	1920	2-0-0
Western Reserve	1916	1916	1-0-0
West Virginia	1988	2001	4-0-0
Wisconsin	1900	1964	8-6-2
Yale	1914	1914	0-1-0
Totals			821-269-42

One of the finest kickers to ever play at Notre Dame, Nick Setta celebrates a 47-yard field goal against Purdue. The Fighting Irish have dominated of their in-state rivals, winning twice as many games as they have lost to the Boilermakers.

THE GREATEST PLAYERS

MAJOR AWARDS

Heisman Trophies: Angelo Bertelli, QB, 1943; John Lujack, QB, 1947; Leon Hart, E, 1949; John Lattner, HB, 1953; Paul Hornung, QB, 1956; John Huarte, QB, 1964; Tim Brown, FL, 1987

Rotary Lombardi Award (outstanding lineman): Walt Patulski, DE, 1971; Ross Browner, DE, 1977; Chris Zorich, DT, 1990; Aaron Taylor, OL, 1993

Outland Trophy (interior lineman): George Connor, T, 1946; Bill Fischer, G, 1948; Ross Browner, DE, 1976

Walter Camp Player of the Year: Ken MacAfee, TE, 1977; Tim Brown, FL, 1987; Raghib Ismail, FL, 1990

Maxwell Award (player of the year): Leon Hart, TE, 1949; John Lattner, HB, 1952–53; Jim Lynch, LB, 1966; Ross Browner. DE, 1977; Brady Quinn, QB, 2006

Johnny Unitas Golden Arm Award (top quarterback): Tony Rice, QB, 1989; Brady Quinn, QB, 2006

HEISMAN TROPHY WINNERS

ANGELO BERTELLI
QUARTERBACK
1943 HEISMAN TROPHY

Angelo Bertelli, Also known as the Springfield Rifle, was inducted into the College Football Hall of Fame in 1972, 30 years after he eased Notre Dame's transition from the single wing to the T formation under Frank Leahy. In 1941, Leahy's first year as head coach at his alma mater, Bertelli threw for more than 1,000 yards as a single-wing tailback and led the Irish to an 8–0–1 record and No. 3 final national ranking. He finished second to Minnesota's Bruce Smith in the Heisman voting that fall and sixth in 1942 after transforming into a T formation quarterback. As a senior in 1943, with America embroiled in World War II, Bertelli answered the call of the Marine Corps and reported for service after six games. Before leaving the team, Bertelli had completed 69 percent of his passes, throwing for 10 scores. He sparked the Irish to a 6–0 record and 43.5 points per game, propelling the team to the national championship. He was awarded the Heisman Trophy while at boot camp.

JOHNNY LUJACK
QUARTERBACK
1947 HEISMAN TROPHY

Johnny Lujack, a 1960 Hall of Fame inductee, took over as Notre Dame's quarterback six games into the 1943 season when Angelo Bertelli left to join the marines. In his first collegiate start, versus Army in 1943, Lujack threw for two touchdowns, ran for another, and intercepted a pass. He spent the next two years in the navy, returning to Notre Dame after World War II ended. He was one of the keys to establishing the school's total dominance of the game in the post war years of 1946 to 1949. With Lujack as the starting quarterback in 1946 and 1947, the Fighting Irish won two national titles and never lost a game. There was the memorable scoreless tie with Army in 1946 in which Lujack, playing safety, saved the Irish from defeat with an open-field tackle of Army fullback Doc Blanchard, the reigning Heisman winner. They played both ways in those days, and many believed Lujack was even better on defense than offense. The 1947 Notre Dame team is arguably the greatest in college football history, with Lujack as its Heisman-winning quarterback. As a pro with the Chicago Bears, Lujack threw for 468 yards in one game, intercepted a record eight passes on defense as a rookie, and led the team in scoring all four years.

LEON HART
END
1949 HEISMAN TROPHY

Only two linemen ever won the Heisman Trophy—Yale's Larry Kelley in 1936 and Notre Dame's Leon Hart in 1949. With Hart starting at right end for four years from 1946 to 1949, Notre Dame never lost a game. With college football teams nationwide adopting the two-platoon system, Hart was one of the last of the game's iron men. He was equally devastating to opponents on both sides of the ball. A three-year first-team All-American and two-time consensus pick, Hart made his name as a pass receiver—more than one-fourth of his catches went for touchdowns—but he was also adept as a blocker, tackler, and pass rusher. His 1949 honors included both the Heisman Trophy and the Maxwell Award as the nation's best player. Over his eight-year career with the Detroit Lions, Hart helped the team to three NFL titles and was an All-Pro on both offense and defense in 1951. He was enshrined in the College Football Hall of Fame in 1973.

JOHN LATTNER
HALFBACK
1953 HEISMAN TROPHY

John Lattner won the Heisman as a senior in 1953, Frank Leahy's last season as Notre Dame's coach. The Fighting Irish went 9–0–1 and were second in the final wire service polls. Lattner had finished fifth in Heisman voting as a junior and won the Maxwell Award as the nation's top player both seasons. Over his three-year career, Lattner averaged 4.9 yards per carry with 20 rushing touchdowns and intercepted 13 passes. His school record for all-purpose yards (rushing, receiving, and returns) stood for more than a quarter century. As a senior he averaged more than 40 yards on eight kickoff returns, running two back for touchdowns.

PAUL HORNUNG
QUARTERBACK
1956 HEISMAN TROPHY

In 1956 Notre Dame finished 2–8, and Paul Hornung became the first and only player to win the Heisman Trophy while playing for a losing team. As a junior in 1955, when Notre Dame went 8–2, Hornung came in fifth in Heisman voting after finishing fourth nationally in total offense with 1,215 yards. He accounted for 354 yards, the highest single-game total in the nation that year, against Southern California. He ran for a touchdown, threw for another, and intercepted two passes in the win against fourth-ranked Navy, and he kicked the winning field goal with the clock winding down against Iowa. As a senior in 1956, he led the Irish in rushing, passing, punting, kicking, and kick returns; finished second in tackles and interceptions; and he scored more than half of the team's points. He accumulated 1,337 yards of total offense, second most in the nation. As a member of the Green Bay Packers, Hornung led the NFL in scoring three straight years—1959, 1960, and 1961. He is a member of both the College and Pro Football Halls of Fame.

JOHN HUARTE
QUARTERBACK
1964 HEISMAN TROPHY

After a disastrous 2–7 campaign in 1963, Notre Dame hired Ara Parseghian as coach, and the Irish stormed to nine straight wins in 1964 before falling in the last minute and a half at Southern California to go 9–1. The quarterback was senior John Huarte, who had previously been hardly used. He teamed with receiver Jack Snow to form the nation's most potent pass-catch duo. Huarte opened the season with 270 yards passing, including touchdown throws of 61 and 42 yards to Snow, in an upset win over Wisconsin. For the season he completed 56 percent of his passes for 2,062 yards and 16 touchdowns, ranked third nationally in total offense with 2,069 yards, and collected Notre Dame's sixth Heisman Trophy.

TIM BROWN
FLANKER
1987 HEISMAN TROPHY

After a sensational junior campaign in 1986, Tim Brown won Notre Dame's seventh Heisman Trophy as a senior in 1987. Brown had finished his junior year with a 254-total-yard performance in the 38–37 come-from-behind upset of Southern California, with a 56-yard punt return to set up the winning field goal. He essentially secured the award when he returned back-to-back punts for touchdowns in the 1987 Michigan State game. As a junior he finished third nationally in all-purpose yardage and averaged 20 yards per catch. He averaged 22 yards per reception as a senior. For his career he caught 12 touchdown passes, ran for four more, scored three times on kickoff returns, and three more on punt returns. He also left Notre Dame as the school's all-time leader in receiving yardage (2,493). The sixth-overall pick in the 1988 NFL Draft, Brown was a nine-time Pro Bowler during his career with the Raiders.

Tim Brown spent 16 years with the Raiders in the NFL and was the last player from the team's stint in Los Angeles to remain with the organization. When he retired, he was third all time in NFL touchdowns behind Jerry Rice and Cris Carter.

Notre Dame in the Heisman Race

Year	Winner's Name, School	Notre Dame,	Finish
1935	Jay Berwanger, Chicago	Bill Shakespeare	3rd
1936	Larry Kelley, Yale	none	
1937	Clint Frank, Yale	none	
1938	Davey O'Brien, Texas Christian	Whitey Beinor	9th
1939	Nile Kinnick, Iowa	none	
1940	Tom Harmon, Michigan	none	
1941	Bruce Smith, Minnesota	Angelo Bertelli	2nd
1942	Frank Sinkwich, Georgia	Angelo Bertelli	6th
1943	Angelo Bertelli, Notre Dame	Creighton Miller	4th
		Jim White,	9th
1944	Les Horvath, Ohio State	Bob Kelly	6th
1945	Doc Blanchard, Army	Frank Dancewicz	6th
1946	Glenn Davis, Army	John Lujack	3rd
1947	John Lujack, Notre Dame	none	
1948	Doak Walker, Southern Methodist	none	
1949	Leon Hart, Notre Dame	Bob Williams	5th
		Emil Sitko,	8th
1950	Vic Janowicz, Ohio State	Bob Williams	6th
1951	Dick Kazmaier, Princeton	none	
1952	Billy Vessels, Oklahoma	John Lattner	5th
1953	John Lattner, Notre Dame	none	
1954	Alan Ameche, Wisconsin	Ralph Guglielmi	4th
1955	"Hopalong" Cassady, Ohio State	Paul Hornung	5th
1956	Paul Hornung, Notre Dame	none	
1957	John David Crow, Texas A&M	none	
1958	Pete Dawkins, Army	Nick Pietrosante	10th
1959	Bill Cannon, LSU	Monty Stickles	9th
1960	Joe Bellino, Navy	none	
1961	Ernie Davis, Syracuse	none	
1962	Terry Baker, Oregon State	none	
1963	Roger Staubach, Navy	none	
1964	John Huarte, Notre Dame	Jack Snow	5th
1965	Mike Garrett, Southern California	Bill Wolski	11th
1966	Steve Spurrier, Florida	Nick Eddy,	3rd
		Terry Hanratty	6th
1967	Gary Beban, UCLA	Terry Hanratty	9th
1968	O.J. Simpson, Southern California	Terry Hanratty	3rd
1969	Steve Owens, Oklahoma	Mike McCoy	6th
1970	Jim Plunkett, Stanford	Joe Theismann	2nd

1971	Pat Sullivan, Auburn	Walt Patulski	9th
1972	Johnny Rodgers, Nebraska	none	
1973	John Cappelletti, Penn State	none	
1974	Archie Griffin, Ohio State	Tom Clements	4th
1975	Archie Griffin, Ohio State	Steve Niehaus	12th
1976	Tony Dorsett, Pittsburgh	none	
1977	Earl Campbell, Texas	Ken MacAfee	3rd
		Ross Browner	5th
1978	Billy Sims, Oklahoma	none	
1979	Charles White, Southern California	Vagas Ferguson	5th
1980	George Rogers, South Carolina	none	
1981	Marcus Allen, Southern California	none	
1982	Herschel Walker, Georgia	none	
1983	Mike Rozier, Nebraska	Allen Pinkett	16th
1984	Doug Flutie, Boston College	none	
1985	Bo Jackson, Auburn	Allen Pinkett	8th
1986	Vinny Testaverde, Miami	none	
1987	Tim Brown, Notre Dame	none	
1988	Barry Sanders, Oklahoma State	none	
1989	Andre Ware, Houston	Tony Rice	4th
		Raghib Ismail, tie for	10th
1990	Ty Detmer, Brigham Young	Raghib Ismail	2nd
1991	Desmond Howard, Michigan	none	
1992	Gino Torretta, Miami	Reggie Brooks	5th
1993	Charlie Ward, Florida State	none	
1994	Rashaan Salaam, Colorado	none	
1995	Eddie George, Ohio State	none	
1996	Danny Wuerffel, Florida	none	
1997	Charles Woodson, Michigan	none	
1998	Ricky Williams, Texas	none	
1999	Ron Dayne, Wisconsin	none	
2000	Chris Weinke, Florida State	none	
2001	Eric Crouch, Nebraska	none	
2002	Carson Palmer, Southern California	none	
2003	Jason White, Oklahoma	none	
2004	Matt Leinart, Southern California	none	
2005	Reggie Bush, Southern California	Brady Quinn	4th
2006	Troy Smith, Ohio State	Brady Quinn	3rd
2007	Tim Tebow, Florida	none	
2008	Sam Bradford, Oklahoma	none	

THE LEGEND OF GEORGE GIPP

George Gipp might have been the most electrifying football player to ever play the game. His school career rushing record was not broken for 58 years, and on defense he never allowed a pass completion in his area—not one in four years.

Gipp went to Notre Dame in 1916 on a baseball scholarship, but coach Knute Rockne, an assistant at the time under Jesse Harper, spotted him playing around on the practice field in early September, in street clothes. The tall, lanky youngster was dropkicking the ball 50 yards and more with perfect ease, and Rock challenged the freshman to join the football team.

Gipp, who hailed from Laurium, Michigan, was the most versatile player of Rockne's coaching regime—he was skilled at running, passing, punting, kicking, and returning punts and kicks. He led the team in both rushing and passing in 1918, 1919, and 1920. As a senior he ran for 827 yards at 8.1 per carry with eight touchdowns, and completed 30 of 62 passes for 709 yards and three more scores. For his career he ran for 2,341 yards, averaging 6.3 per rush with 21 touchdowns. He passed for 1,769 yards and eight touchdowns and intercepted five passes. The Irish were undefeated in Gipp's last 20 games.

Gipp contracted strep throat during the Northwestern game on November 20, 1920, and died of complications on December 14 after a record-setting All-American career. On his deathbed (so the story goes), Gipp asked his coach to have a Notre Dame team "win one for the Gipper" some day.

Rockne agreed and fulfilled his promise on November 10, 1928. That injury-decimated Irish squad, that eventually finished the season 5–4 (as close to a losing record as Rockne would come), faced a powerful Army team.

In the locker room before the game, Rockne drew

his players around him, waited for the room to fall silent, and repeated Gipp's dying words: "I've got to go, Rock. It's all right. I'm not afraid. Some time, Rock, when the team is up against it, when things are wrong and the breaks are beating the boys, tell them to go in there with all they've got and win just one for the Gipper. I don't know where I'll be then, Rock. But I'll know about it, and I'll be happy." With his players choked with emotion, Rockne continued: "This is the day, and you are the team."

The doors nearly flew off their hinges as the team stormed out to the field. The Irish won 12–6 on a 1-yard touchdown run by Jack Chevigny ("That's one for the Gipper," he shouted from the end zone) and a 32-yard Butch Niemiec–to–Johnny O'Brien touchdown pass.

GEORGE GIPP CAREER STATISTICS

(Does not include defensive or special teams statistics)

		Rushing		Passing		
Year	**Carries**	**Yards**	**TD**	**Att.**	**Comp**	**Yards**
1917	63	244	0	8	3	40
1918	98	541	6	45	19	293
1919	106	729	7	72	41	727
1920	102	827	8	62	30	709
Total	369	2,341	21	187	93	1,769

THE FOUR HORSEMEN OF NOTRE DAME

The Notre Dame–Army series is no longer a part of the college football landscape but while it was it saw some of the most history-making games in the sport. There was the Dorais-to-Rockne game of 1913, the "Win one for the Gipper" game of 1928 and in between came perhaps the best known one of all. Here's Grantland Rice's legendary lead in the *New York Herald Tribune* describing the Notre Dame–Army game played on October 18, 1924:

"Outlined against a blue-gray October sky the four horsemen rode again. In dramatic lore they are known as famine, pestilence, destruction, and death. These are only aliases. Their real names are Stuhldreher, Miller, Crowley, and Layden. They formed the crest of the South Bend cyclone before which another fighting Army football team was swept over the precipice at the Polo Grounds yesterday afternoon as 55,000 spectators peered down on the bewildering panorama spread on the green plain below."

Thanks to Rice, the Notre Dame backfield of quarterback Harry Stuhldreher, left halfback Jim Crowley, right halfback Don Miller, and fullback Elmer Layden will live forever as the "Four Horsemen of Notre Dame".

It didn't hurt that Knute Rockne was their coach. Or that a student publicity aide named George Strickler, after reading Rice's piece, had them photographed in their uniforms astride horses from the livery stable in town. Or that they played behind a great line known as the Seven Mules, featuring Hall of Famers Adam Walsh at center and Rip Miller at tackle.

Miller, Crowley, and Layden combined for more than 5,000 rushing yards and 42 touchdown runs during their careers, while Stuhldreher was a cocky, fearless field general. He was accurate as a passer, intercepted three passes as a junior, and ran back a punt for a touchdown.

Other than the Army game, the Irish were never threatened with a loss during that 1924 season. They finished the regular season 9–0, then beat an undefeated Stanford 11 starring All-America fullback Ernie Nevers and coached by Glenn "Pop" Warner in the Rose Bowl. Layden scored three times, including interception returns of 78 and 70 yards, for a 27–10 victory, a 10–0 record. and Notre Dame's first consensus national title.

All four players are enshrined in the College Football Hall of Fame, with Layden a charter member (elected in 1951).

FOUR HORSEMEN CAREER STATISTICS

(Does not include the 1925 Rose Bowl)

	Rushing			Passing				Receiving		
Year	**Carries**	**Yds**	**TD**	**Att.**	**Comp**	**Yds**	**TD**	**No.**	**Yds**	**TD**
JIM CROWLEY										
1922	75	566	5	21	10	154	1	0	0	0
1923	88	536	4	36	13	154	1	1	44	0
1924	131	739	6	26	14	236	2	12	265	3
Totals	294	1,841	15	83	37	544	4	13	309	3
ELMER LAYDEN										
1922	80	453	0	17	9	173	2	4	57	1
1923	102	420	5	6	3	51	0	6	78	2
1924	111	423	5	6	1	18	0	1	10	0
Totals	293	1,296	10	29	13	242	2	11	145	3
DON MILLER										
1922	87	472	3	0	0	0	0	6	144	1
1923	89	689	9	0	0	0	0	9	149	1
1924	107	763	5	1	0	0	0	16	297	2
Totals	283	1,933	17	1	0	0	0	31	590	4
HARRY STUHLDREHER										
1922	26	49	5	15	8	68	3	6	95	1
1923	26	50	2	19	10	205	3	7	63	0
1924	17	19	3	33	25	471	4	5	52	0
Totals	69	118	10	67	43	744	10	18	210	1

COMBINED STATISTICS

Rushing: 939 attempts, 5,188 yards, 53 touchdowns

Passing: 180 attempts, 93 completions, 1,530 yards, 16 touchdowns

Receiving: 73 receptions, 1,254 yards, 11 touchdowns

Interceptions: 19 interceptions, 205 return yards

Punt returns: 99 returns, 834 yards

Kick returns: 31 returns, 637 yards
Scoring: 66 touchdowns, 50 points after touchdowns, 446 points

JOE COOL

"Joe was born to be a quarterback." These are the words of Joe Montana's high school coach, Jeff Petrucci. Montana wasn't particularly tall, certainly wasn't fast, and didn't have a particularly strong arm. Yet he is commonly referred to as the greatest quarterback of all time.

Frank Carideo (1928–1930) and Johnny Lujack (1943, 1946–1947), who played for Rockne and Leahy, respectively, are known to college football historians as the best quarterbacks who ever took the field for Notre Dame. Both were two-year unanimous All-Americans. Lujack won a Heisman (Carideo didn't have an opportunity; the award didn't exist yet), and both quarterbacked the Irish to back-to-back national titles. Montana didn't win a Heisman and he didn't make All-American, though he did win a national title as a junior in 1977. But after his NFL career with the San Francisco 49ers, he popular choice among fans bcame a as the best quarterback they ever saw play.

At Notre Dame, Montana was known as the "Comeback Kid." He started three games as a sophomore in 1975 for first-year Irish coach Dan Devine, then missed the 1976 season with an injury. When the 1977 season opened, he was No. 3 on the depth chart, and the Irish were already 1–1 before Devine inserted him into a game. The Irish were trailing Purdue 24–14 when Montana came off the bench with 11 minutes remaining and led the Irish to 17 points, throwing for 154 yards in the 31–24 win.

What Montana pulled off in the 1979 Cotton Bowl, also known as the "Chicken Soup Game," against

Houston could be called miraculous. It was also the greatest comeback win in Notre Dame history. The game was played in an ice storm, and Montana missed most of the third quarter with hypothermia. He was administered a dose of chicken soup to bring his body temperature up to normal. The Irish trailed the Cougars 34–12 midway through the fourth quarter when the Irish rallied for 23 unanswered points. Montana ran for a touchdown, threw for another, and also connected on a pair of two-point conversion passes, including one with no time left on the clock, for the 35–34 victory in the last game of his career.

But what most casual fans remember were his years as a pro, when he piloted the 49ers to four Super Bowl titles. "Joe Cool," as Montana became known, is still the only player in NFL history to win three Super Bowl MVP awards.

FIGHTING IRISH PLAYERS IN THE COLLEGE FOOTBALL HALL OF FAME

These players have been honored with induction into the College Football Hall of Fame, which, appropriately enough, now resides in South Bend, Indiana.

ANGELO BERTELLI
QUARTERBACK, 1941–1943
INDUCTED 1972

JIM CROWLEY
HALFBACK, 1922–1924
INDUCTED 1966

GEORGE GIPP
HALFBACK, 1917–1920
INDUCTED 1951

LEON HART
END, 1946–1949
INDUCTED 1973

PAUL HORNUNG
QUARTERBACK, 1954–1956
INDUCTED 1985

JOHN HUARTE
QUARTERBACK, 1961–1964
INDUCTED 2005

JOHN LATTNER
HALFBACK, 1951–1953
INDUCTED 1979

ELMER LAYDEN
FULLBACK, 1922–1924
INDUCTED 1951

JOHNNY LUJACK
QUARTERBACK, 1943, 1946–1947
INDUCTED 1960

DON MILLER
HALFBACK, 1922–1924
INDUCTED 1970

HARRY STUHLDREHER
QUARTERBACK, 1922–1924
INDUCTED 1958

HEARTLEY "HUNK" ANDERSON
GUARD, 1918–1921
INDUCTED 1974

Many people know Hunk Anderson succeeded Knute Rockne as Notre Dame's coach, but most don't realize he was a first-team All-American guard in 1921 while playing for Rockne. Anderson was a four-year starter, playing on Rockne's first team in 1918 and

Notre Dame star Frank Carideo loosens up in the Los Angeles Coliseum in 1930. He won every game he started over two seasons, winning national championships with the Irish in 1929 and 1930.

blocking for George Gipp for three years (1918–1920). The Irish were 31–2–2 during Anderson's playing days.

ROSS BROWNER
DEFENSIVE END, 1973, 1975–1977
INDUCTED 1999

Ross Browner was a four-year starter who played for two Notre Dame national champions, as a freshman in 1973 and as a senior in 1977. He was a two-time consensus All-American in 1976 and 1977. He won the Outland Trophy in 1976 and the Lombardi in 1977, when he finished seventh in the Heisman voting. He still holds Notre Dame career records for tackles for a loss in a single season (28 in 1976) and career (77) and career fumble recoveries (12). Browner also blocked two kicks and scored two safeties and one touchdown.

JACK CANNON
GUARD, 1927–1929
INDUCTED 1965

Jack Cannon was a consensus All-American guard for Knute Rockne's 1929 national champions. In the 1929 win over Army at Yankee Stadium, Cannon threw the key block for Jack Elder, who ran 96 yards for the winning touchdown. In 1947 famed sportswriter Grantland Rice declared Cannon the greatest guard in Notre Dame history.

FRANK CARIDEO
QUARTERBACK, 1928–1930
INDUCTED 1954

Frank Carideo is arguably the greatest quarterback in Notre Dame history. He certainly was Knute Rockne's best quarterback, and he was the field general for what Rock believed to be his best team, the 1930 national champions. Carideo was a starter for two seasons, 1929 and 1930, winning two national championships. He was a consensus All-American both years, and he won every game he started.

GEORGE CONNOR
TACKLE, 1946–1947
INDUCTED 1963

George Connor won the inaugural Outland Trophy in 1946 for Coach Frank Leahy's national champions. He was captain of the legendary 1947 team and was a consensus All-American both years he played. Notre Dame never lost a game during Connor's playing days and was national champion both years.

ZYGMONT "ZIGGY" CZAROBSKI
TACKLE, 1942–1943, 1946–1947
INDUCTED 1977

Ziggy Czarobski joined fellow Irish tackle starter George Connor as a first-team All-American in 1947. He started for Coach Frank Leahy's national champions in 1943, then spent two years in the military during World War II. He returned after the war to start at right tackle on the great 1946 and 1947 national title teams.

BOB DOVE
END, 1940–1942
INDUCTED 2000

Bob Dove was a two-year consensus All-American on Coach Frank Leahy's first two Irish squads, in 1941 and 1942. In 1939, Dove caught 15 passes for 187 yards from future Heisman Trophy winner Angelo Bertelli. In 1942 Dove won the Rockne Trophy (precursor to the Outland Trophy, including ends) as the nation's outstanding college lineman.

Legendary end Bob Dove is seen in this photo from 1941. A two-time All-American, Dove was a favorite target of Angelo Bertelli. He won the 1942 Rockne Award when the lineman award still included pass-catching ends like Dove.

RAY EICHENLAUB
FULLBACK, 1911–1914
INDUCTED 1972

Gus Dorais and Knute Rockne weren't the only All-Americans on Coach Jesse Harper's 1913 Notre Dame team. They were joined by bruising fullback Ray "Iron Eich" Eichenlaub. The four-year starter scored 12 touchdowns as a senior and finished with 176 career points. He was also a four-year letterman in track.

BILL "MOOSE" FISCHER
GUARD, 1945–1948
INDUCTED 1983

Moose Fischer was a consensus All-American in both his junior and senior years, 1947 and 1948. He was a three-year starter and captain of the 1948 national champions. In 1948, he became the second Notre Dame player to win the Outland Trophy in three years (along with George Connor in 1946).

JERRY GROOM
CENTER/LINEBACKER, 1948–1950
INDUCTED 1994

Jerry Groom was a consensus All-American and captain of the 1950 Irish team. He started both ways, at center and linebacker, his junior and senior years, and he was a key component of the 1949 national title team. Over his three-year career, he played 465 minutes—86 percent of the total possible time.

RALPH GUGLIELMI
QUARTERBACK, 1951–1954
INDUCTED 2001

Ralph Guglielmi was a three-year starter and was a unanimous All-American as a senior. He completed 208 of 435 career pass attempts for 3,073 yards and 18 touchdowns, ran for 12 more scores, intercepted

10 passes (and ran one back for a score), recovered two fumbles, and kicked five extra points. He finished fourth in the Heisman Trophy voting in 1954.

FRANK "NORDY" HOFFMAN
GUARD, 1930–1931
INDUCTED 1978

Frank Hoffman was a first-team All-American as a senior in 1931, while playing next to a fellow Hall of Famer, center Tommy Yarr. Hoffman led the 1931 Irish in interceptions with three.

JIM LYNCH
LINEBACKER, 1964–1966
INDUCTED 1992

Jim Lynch was captain of the 1966 national champions. He was a unanimous first-team All-American that season and also the recipient of the Maxwell Award as the nation's outstanding college football player.

KEN MACAFEE
TIGHT END, 1974–1977
INDUCTED 1997

Ken MacAfee was a three-time first-team All-American, from 1975 to 1977. He was a unanimous pick in his senior year of 1977, when he finished third in Heisman Trophy voting and became the first lineman to win the Walter Camp Player of the Year award. During that national championship season of 1977, MacAfee caught 54 passes from his tight end spot for 797 yards and six touchdowns. For his career, he caught 128 passes for 1,759 yards and 15 touchdowns but was just as good, if not better, as a blocker.

Bert Metzger anchored a powerful Irish offensive line in 1929 and 1930.

JIM MARTIN
END/TACKLE, 1946–1949
INDUCTED 1995

Jim Martin started for four years during the late 1940s, when the Fighting Irish did not lose a game and won three out of four national titles. Martin played both ways, his first three years at end and at tackle as a senior. He was co-captain of the 1949 national champions, and he led that squad in minutes played with 405.

BERT METZGER
GUARD, 1928–1930
INDUCTED 1982

A 5-foot-9, 149-pound guard on Rockne's last two teams, in 1929 and 1930, Bert Metzger was the spearhead of the line. Those two teams were unbeaten, untied, national champions both years, and outscored their opposition 410–112 with Metzger at right guard. He was a first-team All-American as a senior in 1930.

CREIGHTON MILLER
HALFBACK, 1941–1943
INDUCTED 1976

A nephew of Four Horseman Don Miller, Creighton Miller is the only Notre Dame player to lead the nation in rushing for a season. In 1943 Miller tallied 911 rushing yards, the second highest single-season total in school history at that time, and ran for 13 touchdowns. He was also a consensus All-American for the national champions, placing fourth in voting for the Heisman Trophy, which was won by teammate Angelo Bertelli.

EDGAR "RIP" MILLER
TACKLE, 1922–1924
INDUCTED 1966

Rip Miller was one of the famous Seven Mules, the line that cleared the way for the Four Horsemen. Over three years with Miller at right tackle, the Irish went

27–2–1, including 10–0 in 1924, when the Irish won their first consensus national championship.

FRED MILLER
TACKLE, 1926–1928
INDUCTED 1985

The grandson of MBC founder, Fred Miller was a three-year starter at left tackle for Knute Rockne's Fighting Irish. He was a first-team All-American in 1928 before graduating cum laude, establishing the highest scholastic average of any monogram winner at Notre Dame.

WAYNE MILLNER
END, 1933–1935
INDUCTED 1990

Wayne Millner caught the winning touchdown pass with less than two minutes remaining in the 1935 Ohio State game is regarded as one of the greatest that football games ever played. He was a three-year starter at left end and a consensus All-American as a senior.

ALAN PAGE
DEFENSIVE END, 1964–1966
INDUCTED 1993

Alan Page made 63 tackles for the 1966 Irish team that won the national title. He was a three-year starter at defensive right end and a consensus All-American as a senior. He posted 134 career tackles, recovered four fumbles, broke up two passes, and scored one touchdown. After football, he graduated law school, was named assistant attorney general of Minnesota, and in 1992 was elected to the state supreme court.

LOUIS "RED" SALMON
FULLBACK, 1900–1903
INDUCTED 1971

Red Salmon was Notre Dame's first All-American. His single-season scoring record of 105 points in 1903 and his 36 career touchdowns were school records that stood until 1984. He scored 250 career points, a school record that stood until 1985, even though touchdowns counted for only five points when he played.

MARCHY SCHWARTZ
HALFBACK, 1929–1931
INDUCTED 1974

Marchy Schwartz was a consensus All-American in 1930 and a unanimous pick as a senior in 1931. He led the team in rushing, passing, and scoring for both his junior and senior seasons. He was a key component of the 1930 national title run in Knute Rockne's final season. He ranked second to George Gipp in career rushing and ranks among the school's all-time leaders with 1,945 career yards and 5.5 per carry.

BILL SHAKESPEARE
HALFBACK, 1933–1935
INDUCTED 1983

Known as the "Bard of Staten Island", Bill Shakespeare started at left halfback for Coach Elmer Layden in 1934 and 1935 and was a first-team All-American as a senior. He is best known for throwing the winning touchdown pass to Wayne Millner in the classic 1935 showdown with Ohio State. He stood as Notre Dame's career punting leader for more than a half-century.

EMIL SITKO
HALFBACK/FULLBACK, 1946–1949
INDUCTED 1984

The media referred to him as "Six-yard" Sitko; his friends and schoolmates knew him as "Red". He was a two-time consensus All-American and a unanimous pick for the 1949 national champions. During the four years Sitko played for Coach Frank Leahy, the Fighting Irish never lost a game. He ran for 2,226 yards and 26 touchdowns over his career, averaging 6.1 yards per carry. He averaged 7.1 yards per carry with the immortal 1947 squad.

JOHN "CLIPPER" SMITH
GUARD, 1925–1927
INDUCTED 1975

Clipper Smith bounced around between fullback, halfback, and center before settling in at guard, where he was a starter as a junior and senior. He was a consensus All-American in 1927, when he also served as team captain.

JOE THEISMANN
QUARTERBACK, 1968–1970
INDUCTED 2003

Joe Theismann was a first-team All-American and runner-up to Stanford's Jim Plunkett in the Heisman derby of 1970, even though he was talked into changing the way his name is pronounced to help his chances of winning. He was voted team MVP after quarterbacking the Irish to a 10–0 record and a 24–11 victory over top-ranked Texas in the Cotton Bowl.

ADAM WALSH
CENTER, 1922–1924
INDUCTED 1968

Adam Walsh was captain of Notre Dame's 1924 national title team, spearheading the line known as the Seven Mules. He was a two-year starting center, blocking for the Four Horsemen in 1923 and 1924. Walsh played the Army game in 1924 with two broken hands, yet still intercepted a pass and led the team in tackles.

BOB WILLIAMS
QUARTERBACK, 1948–1950
INDUCTED 1988

Bob Williams' single-season 161.4 passing efficiency rating in 1949, when he was just 19, still ranks as the best in Notre Dame history. He completed 56 percent of his passes, setting a Notre Dame season record that lasted 19 years and promoted Coach Frank Leahy to proclaim: "This was as great a year as any Notre Dame quarterback has ever had." He was a consensus All-American, placing fifth in Heisman Trophy voting and was sixth as a senior in 1950.

TOMMY YARR
CENTER, 1929–1931
INDUCTED 1987

Tommy Yarr was the starting center on Knute Rockne's prized 1930 team. Against Southern Methodist, Yarr intercepted two passes in the game's closing minutes to ensure the win. In 1931 he was named team captain and a consensus All-American.

Joe Theismann's name pronunciation was unofficially changed when his hall mates in Zahm Hall hung a banner out a fourth-story window reading "Theisman [sic] for Heisman" late in the 1970 season.

First Team All-Americans

(SOURCE: NCAA. *CONSENSUS, #UNANIMOUS)

Gus Dorais, QB, *1913; Stan Cofall, HB, 1916; Frank Rydzewski, C, *1917; Roger Kiley, E, 1920, 1921; George Gipp, HB, *1920; Eddie Anderson, E, *1921; Hunk Anderson, G, 1921; Don Miller, HB, 1923; Harry Stuhldreher, QB, *1924; Jimmy Crowley, HB, *1924; Elmer Layden, FB, *1924; Bud Boeringer, C, *1926; John Smith, G, *1927; Christy Flanagan, HB, 1927; Fred Miller, T, 1928; Jack Cannon, G, *1929; Frank Carideo, QB, #*1929, #*1930; Marchy Schwartz, HB, *1930, *1931; Bert Metzger, G, 1930; Marty Brill, HB, 1930; Tommy Yarr, C, *1931; Joe Kurth, T, 1931, #*1932; Nordy Hoffman, G, 1931; Jack Robinson, C, *1934; Wayne Millner, E, *1935; Bill Shakespeare, HB, 1935; John Lautar, G, 1936; Chuck Sweeney, E, *1937; Ed Beinor, T, 1937, #*1938; Earl Brown, E, 1938; Bud Kerr, E, 1939; Bob Dove, E, *1941, *1942; Bernie Crimmins, G, 1941; Angelo Bertelli, QB, 1942, *1943; John Yonakor, E, *1943; Jim White, T, *1943; Pat Filley, G, *1943; Creighton Miller, HB, *1943; John Mastrangelo, G, 1945, 1946; George Strohmeyer, C, 1946; George Connor, T, *1946, *1947; John Lujack, QB, #*1946, #*1947; Leon Hart, E, 1947, *1948, #*1949; Bill Fischer, G, *1947, *1948; Ziggy Czarobski, T, 1947; Marty Wendell, G, 1948; Emil Sitko, B, *1948, #*1949; Bob Williams, QB, *1949, 1950; Jim Martin, T, 1949; Jerry Groom, C, *1950; Bob Toneff, T, 1951; Johnny Lattner, HB, #*1952, #*1953; Art Hunter, T, *1953; Ralph Guglielmi, B, #*1954; Frank Varrichione, T, 1954; Pat Bisceglia, G, 1955; Don Schaefer, FB, 1955; Paul Hornung, HB, *1955, QB, 1956; Al Ecuyer, G, *1957, 1958; Nick Pietrosante, FB, 1958; Monty Stickles, E, 1958, *1959; Jim Kelly, E, 1963; Jim Carroll, LB, 1964; Jack Snow, E, *1964; John Huarte, QB, *1964; Dick Arrington, G, #*1965; Nick Rassas, DB, *1965; Tom Regner, G, *1966; Nick Eddy, HB, #*1966; Alan Page, DE, *1966; Jim Lynch, LB, #*1966; Pete Duranko, DT, 1966; Tom Schoen, DB, *1967; Jim Seymour, E, 1967, 1968; Kevin Hardy, DE, 1967; George Kunz, T, *1968; Terry Hanratty, QB, *1968; Mike McCoy, DT, #*1969; Jim Reilly, OT, 1969; Larry DiNardo, OG, 1969, *1970; Tom Gatewood, SE, *1970; Joe Theismann, QB, 1970; Clarence Ellis, DB, 1970, *1971; Walt Patulski, DE, #*1971; Greg Marx,

DT, #*1972; Dave Casper, TE, *1973; Mike Townsend, DB, *1973; Pete Demmerle, SE, *1974; Gerry DiNardo, G, *1974; Tom Clements, QB, 1974; Mike Fanning, DT, 1974; Greg Collins, LB, 1974; Steve Niehaus, DT, #*1975; Ken MacAfee, TE, 1975, *1976, #*1977; Ross Browner, DE, #*1976, #*1977; Luther Bradley, DB, *1977; Dave Huffman, C, *1978; Bob Golic, LB, #*1978; Vagas Ferguson, RB, *1979; Tim Foley, OT, 1979; Scott Zettek, DL, 1980; John Scully, C, #*1980; Bob Crable, LB, *1980, *1981; Dave Duerson, DB, 1982; Mark Bavaro, TE, 1984; Tim Brown, FL, 1986, #*1987; Andy Heck, OT, 1988; Mike Stonebreaker, LB, *1988, #*1990; Frank Stams, DE, *1988; Chris Zorich, DT, *1989, DL #*1990; Todd Lyght, DB, #*1989, *1990; Raghib Ismail, KR, 1989, #*1990; Derek Brown, TE, 1991; Mirko Jurkovic, OL, *1991; Aaron Taylor, OL, *1992, #*1993; Jeff Burris, DB, *1993; Bryant Young, DL, 1993; Bobby Taylor, DB, 1993, *1994; Mike Rosenthal, OL, 1998; Jeff Faine, OL, 2002; Shane Walton, DB, #*2002; Jeff Samardzija, WR, *2005, 2006

ACADEMIC ALL-AMERICANS (COSIDA)

Joe Heap, HB, 1952–54; Don Schaefer, FB, 1955; Bob Wetoska, E, 1958; Bob Lehmann, G, 1963; Tom Regner, G, 1966: Jim Lynch, LB, 1966; Jim Smithberger, DB, 1967; George Kunz, T, 1968; Jim Reilly, T, 1969; Joe Theismann, QB, 1970; Larry DiNardo, G, 1970; Tom Gatewood, SE, 1970–71; Greg Marx, DT, 1971–72; Bob Thomas, K, 1973; Gary Potempa, LB, 1973; Pete Demmerle, SE, 1974; Reggie Barnett, CB, 1974; Ken MacAfee, TE, 1977; Dave Vinson, G, 1977; Joe Restic, S, 1977–78; Bob Burger, G, 1980; Tom Gibbons, S, 1980; John Krimm, CB, 1981; Greg Dingens, DT, 1985; Vince Phelan, P, 1987; Ted Gradel, K, 1987; Tim Ruddy, C, 1992–93; John Carlson, TE, 2006

ALL-TIME DRAFT SELECTIONS

YEAR, ROUND, NAME, POSITION, TEAM, (OVERALL PICK WHEN AVAILABLE)

1936: 1. Bill Shakespeare, B, Pittsburgh (3); 3. Andy Pilney, B, Detroit (26); 7. Marty Peters, E, Pittsburgh (57); 7. Wally Fromhart, B, Green Bay (61); 8. Wayne Millner, E, Boston (65)

1938: 5. Chuck Sweeney, E, Green Bay (37); 10. Pat McCarty, C, Pittsburgh (84); 12. Joe Kuharich, G, Pittsburgh (104)

1939: 6. Ed Beinor, T, Brooklyn (46); 8. Paul Kell, T, Green Bay

(69); 9. Earl Brown, E, Chicago Cardinals (71); 17. Ed Longhi, C, Pittsburgh (152); 19. Ed Simonich, B, Chicago Bears (176); 21. Bill Hofer, B, Green Bay (194); 21. Mario Tonelli, B, N.Y. Giants (195)

1940: 14. Bud Kerr, E, Green Bay (129); 19. Tad Harvey, T, Pittsburgh (173); 22. Steve Sitko, B, Washington (198)

1941: 11. Milt Piepul, B, Detroit (95); 16. Bob Osterman, C, Chicago Bears (148); 17. Bob Saggau, B, Green Bay (157)

1942: 13. John Kovatch, E, Washington (116); 21. Steve Juzwik, B, Washington (191)

1943: 3. Fred "Dippy" Evans, B, Chicago Bears (24); 5. Bob Dove, E, Washington (40); 6. Wally Ziemba, C, Washington (50); 7. Lou Rymkus T, Washington (60); 13. Tom Brock, C, Green Bay (118); 13. Harry Wright, G, Washington (120); 26. Bob Neff, T, Philadelphia (242); 30. Dick Creevy B, Chicago Bears (289)

1944: 1. Angelo Bertelli, QB, Boston (1); 1. Creighton Miller, B, Brooklyn (3); 9. Matt Bolger, E, Detroit (79); 12. Pat Filley, G, Cleveland (119); 19. Bob McBride, G, Cleveland (196); 21. John Creevey, B, Cleveland (218); 25. John McGinnis, E, Chicago Cardinals (253); 27. Bill Earley, B, Chicago Cardinals (275); 27. Russell (Pete) Ashbaugh, B, Pittsburgh (283); 32. Stan Kudlacz, C, Cleveland (329)

1945: 1. Frank Szymanski, C, Detroit (6); 1. John Yonakor, E, Philadelphia (9); 3. John "Tree" Adams, T, Washington (23); 4. Jack Zilly, E, L.A. Rams (32); 6. Corwin "Cornie" Clatt, B, Chicago Cardinals (45); 6. Jim Mello, B, Boston (47); 6. Gerry Cowhig, B, Cleveland (48); 7. Ziggy Czarobski, T, Chicago Cardinals (55); 10. Bill Huber, E, Chicago Cardinals (88); 12. Herb Coleman, C, Boston (113); 15. George Connor, T, Pittsburgh (145); 16. John Creevey, B, Chicago Bears (159); 22. Bob Livingstone, B, Chicago Bears (225); 23. Luke Higgins, T, Cleveland (235); 30. Paul Limont, E, Detroit (313)

1946: 1. Frank Dancewicz, QB, Boston (1); 1. Johnny Lujack, QB, Chicago Bears (4); 1. George Connor, T, N.Y. Giants (5); 1. Emil Sitko, B, L.A. Rams (10); 3. Elmer Angsman, B, Chicago Cardinals (16); 7. Ed Mieszkowski, T, Boston (52); 7. Pete Berezney, T, Detroit (58); 9. Bob Skoglund, E, Washington (79); 10. Joe Signaigo, G, L.A. Rams (90); 13. George Strohmeyer, C, L.A. Rams (120); 14. Bob Palladino, B, L.A. Rams (130); 15. Fred Rovai, G, Chicago Cardinal; 17. Gasper Urban, G, L.A. Rams (160); 17. Jerry Ford, E, L.A. Rams (180); 20. Bill Heywood, B, Chicago Cardinals (181); 20. Frank Ruggerio, B, Boston (182)

1947: 3. John Mastrangelo, G, Pittsburgh (16); 6. George Sullivan, T, Boston (37); 10. Bob Kelly, B, Green Bay (81); 13. Bob Skoglund, E, Green Bay (111); 15. John Fallon, T, N.Y. Giants (134); 26. Ralph Stewart, C, N.Y. Giants (244); 27. Bob Palladino, B, Green Bay (250); AAFC — 1. George Sullivan, T, Chicago Rockets (4); 2. Gerry Cohwig, B, Cleveland (16); 5. John Mastrangelo, G, Buffalo (34); 6. Jack Zilly, E, San Francisco (46); 8. Matt Bolger, E, Chicago Rockets (60); 8. George Strohmeyer, C, N.Y. Yankees (63); 14. Bob Livingstone, B, Chicago Rockets (108); 14. Joe Signaigo, B, Cleveland (112); 16. Frank Kosikowski, E, Buffalo (122); Johnny Lujack, QB, Chicago Rockets

1948: 6. Joe Gasperella, B, Pittsburgh (43); 8. Marty Wendell, G, Philadelphia (63); 16. George Ratterman, QB, Boston (139); 17. Jack Fallon, G, Chicago Bears (152); 18. Bill O'Connor, G, L.A. Rams (160); 24. Floyd Simmons, B, Pittsburgh (223); 25. Coy McGee, B, Detroit (227); 29. John Panelli, B, Green Bay (271); 21. Art Statuto, C, Philadelphia (292); 32. Bill Fischer, G, Chicago Cardinals (300); AAFC — 3. Bill Gompers, B, Buffalo (16); 4. Bill O'Connor, E, Buffalo (24); 5. Bill Walsh, C, Chicago Rockets (25); 6. Marty Wendell, G, Buffalo (33); 18. Doug Waybright, E, Buffalo (119); 19. Russell (Pete) Ashbaugh, B, Cleveland (129); 26. John Panelli, B, N.Y. Yankees (184)

1949: 1. Frank Tripuka, QB, Philadelphia (9); 1. Bill Fischer, G, Chicago Cardinals (10); 2. John Panelli, B, Detroit (12); 3. Bill Walsh, C, Pittsburgh (26); 5. Terry Brennan, B, Philadelphia (51); 8. Bill Wightkin, E, Chicago Bears (79); 20. Frank Gaul, T, Boston (193); 24. Don McAuliffe, B, N.Y. Giants (235); AAFC — 2. John Panelli, B, N.Y. Yankees (13); 5. Frank Gaul, G, Buffalo (35)

1950: 1. Leon Hart, E, Detroit (1); 2. Jim Martin, E, Cleveland (26); 4. Larry Coutre, B, Green Bay (43); 5. Mike Swistowicz, B, N.Y. Bulldogs (55); 5. Frank Spaniel, B, Washington (58); 5. Ernie Zalejski, B, Chicago Bears (62); 7. Bill Gay, B, Chicago Cardinals (85); 10. Walt Grothaus, C, Chicago Cardinals (125); 11. John Helwig, G, Chicago Bears (140); 18. Ray Espenan, E, Chicago Cardinals (229); 19. Gus Cifelli, T, Detroit (239); 19. Frank Gaul, T, Pittsburgh (242); 30. Ed Hudak, T, Pittsburgh (386)

1951: 1. Bob Williams, QB, Chicago Bears (2); 1. Jerry Groom, C, Chicago Cardinals (6); 12. Jack Landry, B, Chicago Cardinals (139); 20. Fred Wallner, G, Chicago Cardinals (235); 29. Bob Livingstone, B, Chicago Cardinals (343)

1952: 2. Bob Toneff, T, San Francisco (22); 7. John Petitbon,

B, N.Y. Yankees (74); 10. Chet Ostrowski, E, Washington (115); 12. Jim Mutscheller, E, N.Y. Yankees (134); 13. Dave Flood, B, Pittsburgh (150); 16. Paul Burns, G, N.Y. Giants (191); 28. Billy Barrett, B, Green Bay (327)

1953: 8. Don Beck, B, N.Y. Giants (94); 15. Bob O'Neil, E, Pittsburgh (173); 29. Jack Alessandrini, G, Baltimore (338); 30. Bill Gaudreau, B, Chicago Cardinals (351)

1954: 1. Art Hunter, T, Green Bay (2); 1. Johnny Lattner, B, Pittsburgh (7); 1. Neil Worden, B, Philadelphia (9); 2. Jim Schrader, C, Washington (20); 4. Frank Paterra, B, Chicago Bears (42); 4. Minnie Mavraides, G, Philadelphia (45); 6. Tom McHugh, B, Chicago Cardinals; 10. Joe Katchik, E, L.A. Rams; 15. Sam Palumbo, G, San Francisco; 18. Don Penza, E, Pittsburgh; 28. Joe Bush, G, Pittsburgh

1955: 1. Ralph Guglielmi, QB, Washington (3); 1. Frank Varrichione, T, Pittsburgh (6); 1. Joe Heap, B, N.Y. Giants (8); 2. Dick Szymanski, C, Baltimore (16); 3. Tony Pasquesi, T, Chicago Cardinals (32); 4. Paul Reynolds, B, Cleveland (41); 4. Sam Palumbo, C, Cleveland (49); 6. Dan Shannon, E, Chicago Bears (63); 24. Bob Ready, T, Washington (279)

1956: 3. Don Schaefer, B, Philadelphia (28); 9. Wayne Edmonds, G, Pittsburgh (100); 13. Jim Mense, C, Green Bay (152); 14. John McMullan, G, N.Y. Giants (165); 15. Dick Fitzgerald, B, Chicago Bears (178); 19. Ray Lemek, G, Washington (227); 21. Gene Martell, T, Pittsburgh (244); 21. Gene Kapish, E, Cleveland (253); 22. George Nicula, T, Washington (262); 29. Pat Bisceglia, G, Washington (347)

1957: 1. Paul Hornung, B, Green Bay (1); 12. Ed Sullivan, C, Green Bay (135); 13. Jim Morse, B, Green Bay (148); 20. Byron Beams, T, L.A. Rams (232)

1958: 6. Dick Lynch, B, Washington (66); 9. Frank Kuchta, C, Washington (102); 10. Aubrey Lewis, B, Chicago Bears (113)

1959: 1. Nick Pietrosante, B, Detroit (6); 5. Bob Wetoska, T, Washington (49); 5. Frank Geremia, T, San Francisco (54); 7. Don Lawrence, T, Washington (76); 10. Ron Toth, T, Washington (113); 10. Bronko Nagurski, T, San Francisco (114); 18. Al Ecuyer, G, N.Y. Giants (214); 27. Norm Odyniec, B, Washington (316); 28. Bob Williams, B, Chicago Bears (332); 29. Dick Loncar, T, Pittsburgh (343); 30. Angelo Mosca, T, Philadelphia (350)

1960: 1. George Izo, B, Chicago Cardinals (2); 1. Monty Stickles, E, San Francisco (11); 3. Bob Scholtz, C, Detroit (27); 12. Jim Crotty,

HB, Washington/Dallas (136); 17. Mike Graney, E, Philadelphia/Buffalo (200); AFL—George Izo, B, N.Y. Titans; Monty Stickles, E, L.A. Chargers; Bob Scholtz, C, L.A. Chargers; Jim Crotty, HB, Dallas Texans; Mike Graney, E, Buffalo

1961: 2. Myron Pottios, LB, Pittsburgh (19); 10. Joe Scibelli, HB, L.A. Rams (130); 10. Bill "Red" Mack, B, Pittsburgh (131); 20. Ray Ratkowski, B, Green Bay (218); AFL— 3. Myron Pottios, LB, Oakland; 9. Bob Scarpitto, HB, L.A. Chargers; 10. Joe Scibelli, HB, N.Y. Titans; 23. Bill "Red" Mack, B, Buffalo; 27. Ray Ratkowski, B, Boston

1962: 2. Joe Carollo, T, L.A. Rams (16); 2. Bob Bill, T, N.Y. Giants (26); 5. Mike Lind, HB, San Francisco (64); 9. John Powers, E, Pittsburgh (117); 13. Joe Perkowski, B, Chicago Bears (175); AFL—4. Bob Bill, T, San Diego (31); 13. Nick Buoniconti, G, Boston (102); 18. Joe Carollo, T, L.A. Dallas Texans (139); 19. Mike Lind, HB, San Diego (152)

1963: 10. Ed Hoerster, LB, Chicago Bears (137); 12. Daryle Lamonica, QB, Green Bay (168); 16. John Slafkosky, T, St. Louis (213); AFL—9. Ed Burke, T, Houston (70); 16. Ed Hoerster, LB, Buffalo (124); 24. Daryle Lamonica, QB, Buffalo (188)

1964: 2. Jim Kelly, E, Pittsburgh (28); 4. Paul Costa, B, Green Bay (55); 4. Frank Budka, HB, Chicago Bears (56); 5. Jim Snowden, FB, Washington (59); 8. George Bednar, G, St. Louis (104); 13. Tom MacDonald, B, Washington (171); 17. Dave Humenik, T, N.Y. Giants (236); AFL—2. Jim Kelly, E, Boston (13); 3. George Bednar, G, Oakland (23); 15. John Simon, E, Kansas City (50); 10. Clay Stephens, E, Kansas City (73); 14. Paul Costa, B, Kansas City (106); 15. Jim Snowden, FB, Kansas City (114); 17. Bob Lehmann, G-LB, N.Y. Jets (131); 23. Dave Humenik, T, N.Y. Jets (180)

1965: 1. Jack Snow, E, Minnesota (8); 6. Tony Carey, HB, Chicago Bears (73); 6. John Huarte, QB, Philadelphia (76); 8. John Meyer, LB, St. Louis (110); 12. Jim Carroll, LB, N.Y. Giants (155); 14. Dave Pivec, E, Chicago Bears (185); 14. Tom Longo, B, Philadelphia (188); 18. Dick Arrington, G, Cleveland (251); AFL—2. John Huarte, QB, N.Y. Jets; 4. Dick Arrington, G, Boston; 7. Jack Snow, E, San Diego; 9. Tony Carey, HB, San Diego; 14. Tom Longo, B, Philadelphia/Oakland

1966: 2. Nick Rassas, DB, Atlanta (17); 2. Nick Eddy, HB, Detroit (24); 3. Phil Sheridan, E, Atlanta (48); 4. Pete Duranko, DE-LB, Cleveland (61); 5. Bill Wolski, HB, Atlanta (65); 8. Tom Talaga, E,

Cleveland (123); 16. Arunas Vasys, LB, Philadelphia (234); AFL—1. (redshirt) Nick Eddy, HB, Denver; 2. Nick Rassas, DB, San Diego; 2. Pete Duranko, DE-LB, Denver; 4. Phil Sheridan, E, N.Y. Jets; 10. Bill Wolski, HB, N.Y. Jets; 18. Tom Talaga, E, Denver

1967: 1. Paul Seiler, G, N.Y. Jets (12); 1. Alan Page, DE, Minnesota (15); 1. Tom Regner, G, Houston (23); 2. Larry Conjar, FB, Cleveland (46); 2. Jim Lynch, LB, Kansas City (47); 3. George Goeddeke, C, Denver (59); 4. Tom Rhoads, DE, Buffalo (70); 16. Allen Sack, LB, L.A. Rams (408); Paul Hornung, HB, New Orleans (Expansion); Bob Scholtz, T, New Orleans (Expansion)

1968: 1. Kevin Hardy, DE, New Orleans (7); 3. Mike McGill, LB, Minnesota (76); 5. Jim Smithberger, DB, Boston (116); 6. Dave Martin, DB, Philadelphia (157); 8. Dick Swatland, G-T, New Orleans (195); 8. Tom Schoen, DB, Cleveland (212); 11. John Pergine, LB, L.A. Rams (297); 16. Rocky Bleier, RB, Pittsburgh (417)

1969: 1. George Kunz, T, Atlanta (2); 1. Jim Seymour, SE, L.A. Rams (10); 2. Terry Hanratty, QB, Pittsburgh (30); 4. Bob Kuechenberg, G, Philadelphia (80); 5. Jim Winegardner, TE, Chicago Bears (119); 6. Ed Tuck, G, Miami (141); 8. Bob Gladieux, RB, Boston (186); 11. Eric Norri, DT, Washington (269); 12. Bob Belden, QB, Dallas (308); 12. John Lavin, LB, Kansas City (309); 13. Tom Quinn, DB, Chicago Bears (325)

1970: 1. Mike McCoy, DT, Green Bay (2); 3. Jim Reilly, G, Buffalo (57); 5. Bob Olson, LB, Boston (107); 5. Mike Oriard, C, Kansas City (130); 7. Terry Brennan, T, Philadelphia (158)

1971: 4. Joe Theismann, QB, Miami (99); 5. Tim Kelly, LB, Boston (106); 7. Larry DiNardo, G, New Orleans (158); 15. Jim Wright, LB, N.Y. Giants (382)

1972: 1. Walt Patulski, DE, Buffalo (1); 1. Clarence Ellis, DB, Atlanta (15); 1. Mike Kadish, DT, Miami (25); 3. Fred Swendsen, DE, Buffalo (53); 4. Eric Patton, LB, Green Bay (86); 5. Tom Gatewood, WR, N.Y. Giants (107); 7. Ralph Stepaniak, DB, Buffalo (157); 7. Mike Zikas, DT, N.Y. Giants (177)

1973: 2. Greg Marx, DT, Atlanta (39); 6. Mike Creaney, C, Chicago Bears (138); 9. John Dampeer, G, Cincinnati (224); 12. Jim O'Malley, LB, Denver (296); 13. John Cieszkowski, RB, Chicago Bears (320); 15. Ken Schlezes, DB, Philadelphia (367)

1974: 2. Dave Casper, TE, Oakland (45); 4. Mike Townsend, DB, Minnesota (86); 9. Brian Doherty, P, Buffalo (226); 11. Tim Rudnick, DB, Baltimore (285); 14. Frank Pomarico, G, Kansas

(353); 15. Bob Thomas, K, L.A. Rams (388); 17. Cliff Brown, RB, Philadelphia (427); 17. Willie Townsend, WR, L.A. Rams (440)

1975: 1. Mike Fanning, DT, L.A. Rams (9); 2. Greg Collins LB, San Francisco (35); 3. Drew Mahalic, LB, Denver (69); 5. Kevin Nosbusch, DT, San Diego (111); 5. Wayne Bullock, RB, San Francisco (114); 10. Steve Sylvester, T, Oakland (259); 13. Pete Demmerle, WR, San Diego (320); 13. Eric Penick, RB, Denver (329); 14. Reggie Barnett, DB, San Diego (345); 16. Tom Fine, TE, Buffalo (406)

1976: 1. Steve Niehaus, DT, Seattle, (2); 7. Ed Bauer, G, New Orleans, (201)

1977: Supplemental: 4. Al Hunter, RB, Seattle

1978: 1. Ken MacAfee, TE, San Francisco (7); 1. Ross Browner, DT, Cincinnati (8); 1. Luther Bradley, DB, Detroit (11); 2. Willie Fry, DE, Pittsburgh (49); 3. Ernie Hughes, G, San Francisco (79); 5. Ted Burgmeier, DB, Miami (111); 9. Steve McDaniels, T, San Francisco (249); 10. Doug Becker, LB, Pittsburgh (258)

1979: 2. Dave Huffman, C, Minnesota (43); 2. Bob Golic, LB, New England (52); 3. Joe Montana, QB, San Francisco (82); 8. Steve Heimkreiter, LB, Baltimore (197); 9. Jerome Heavens, RB, Chicago Bears (230); 9. Kris Haines, WR, Washington (233); 9. Jeff Weston, DT, Miami (244); 10. Joe Restic, DB, Chicago Bears (257); 10. Mike Calhoun, DT, Dallas, (274); 12. Jim Browner, DB, Cincinnati (304)

1980: 1. Vagas Ferguson, RB, New England (25); 2. Dave Waymer, DB, New Orleans (41); 2. Tim Foley, T, Baltimore (51); 4. Rusty Lisch, QB, St. Louis (89); 8. Bobby Leopold, LB, San Francisco (210); 10. Rob Martinovich, T, Kansas City

1981: 4. John Scully, C, Atlanta (109); 7. Pete Holohan, TE, San Diego (189); 8. Scott Zettek, DT, Chicago Bears (205); 9. Jim Stone, RB, Seattle (223); 9. Tim Huffman, T, Green Bay (227); 12. John Hankerd, LB, Denver (317)

1982: 1. Bob Crable, LB, N.Y. Jets (23); 3. John Krimm, DB, New Orleans (76); 5. Phil Pozderac, T, Dallas (137)

1983: 1. Tony Hunter, TE, Buffalo (12); 3. Dave Duerson, DB, Chicago Bears (64); 4. Tom Thayer, C, Chicago Bears (91); 5. Larry Moriarty, RB, Houston (114); 9. Mark Zavagnin, LB, Chicago Bears (235); 9. Bob Clasby, T, Seattle (236)

1984: 1. Greg Bell, RB, Buffalo (26); 6. Chris Brown, DB, Pittsburgh (164); 6. Stacey Toran, DB, L.A. Raiders (168); 9. Neil Maune, G, Dallas (249); 11. Blair Kiel, QB, Tampa Bay (281)

1985: 2. Mike Gann, DE, Atlanta (45); 3. Mike Kelley, C, Houston (82); 4. Mark Bavaro, TE, N.Y. Giants (100); 10. Mike Golic, DT, Houston (255); 10. Larry Williams, G, Cleveland (259)

1986: 1. Eric Dorsey, DE, N.Y. Giants (19); 3. Allen Pinkett, RB, Houston (61); 8. Tony Furjanic, LB, Buffalo (202); 8. Mike Perrino, T, San Diego (209)

1987: 2. Wally Kleine, T, Washington (48); 4. Steve Beuerlein, QB, L.A. Raiders (110); 7. Robert Banks, DT, Houston (176); 8. Joel Williams, TE, Miami (210)

1988: 1. Tim Brown, WR, L.A. Raiders (6); 3. Tom Rehder, T, New England (69); 3. Chuck Lanza, C, Pittsburgh (70); 6. Cedric Figaro, LB, San Diego (152); 9. Brandy Wells, DB, Cincinnati (226)

1989: 1. Andy Heck, T, Seattle (15); 2. Frank Stams, DE, L.A. Rams (44); 5. Mark Green, RB, Chicago (130); 6. Wes Pritchett, LB, Miami (147); 11. George Streeter, S, Chicago (304)

1990: 2. Anthony Johnson, FB, Indianapolis (36); 2. Tim Grunhard, OG, Kansas City (40); 2. Jeff Alm, DT, Houston (41); 2. Pat Terrell, FS, L.A. Rams (49); 4. Mike Brennan, OT, Cincinnati (92); 5. Stan Smagala, CB, L.A. Raiders (122); 6. Ned Bolcar, LB, Seattle (146); 10. D'Juan Francisco, SS, Washington (262); 12. Dean Brown, OT, Indianapolis (316)

1991: 1. Todd Lyght, CB, L.A. Rams (5); 2. Ricky Watters, RB, San Francisco (45); 2. Chris Zorich, NT, Chicago (49); 3. Bob Dahl, DT, Cincinnati (72); 4. Raghib Ismail, FL, L.A. Raiders (100); 5. Tim Ryan, OG, Tampa Bay (136); 7. Andre Jones, OLB, Pittsburgh (185); 8. Scott Kowalkowski, OLB, Philadelphia (216); 9. Michael Stonebreaker, ILB, Chicago (245); 10. Mike Heldt, C, San Diego (257)

1992: 1. Derek Brown, TE, N.Y. Giants (14); 2. Rod Smith, DB, New England (35); 4. Rodney Culver, FB, Indianapolis (85); 4. Tony Brooks, FB, Philadelphia (92); 4. Gene McGuire, C, New Orleans (95); 6. Tony Smith, SE, Kansas City (159); 6. George Williams, DT, Cleveland (163); 9. Mirko Jurkovic, OG, Chicago (246)

1993: 1. Rick Mirer, QB, Seattle (2); 1. Jerome Bettis, FB, L.A. Rams (10); 1. Tom Carter, CB, Washington (17); 1. Irv Smith, TE, New Orleans (20); 2. Demetrius DuBose, LB, Tampa Bay (34); 2. Reggie Brooks, TB, Washington (45); 4. Devon McDonald, LB, Indianapolis (107); 5. Lindsay Knapp, OG, Kansas City (130); 8. Craig Hentrich, PK-P, N.Y. Jets (200)

1994: 1. Bryant Young, DT, San Francisco (7); 1. Aaron Taylor, OG, Green Bay (16); 1. Jeff Burris, FS, Buffalo (27); 2. Tim Ruddy, C, Miami (65); 3. Jim Flanigan, DT, Chicago (74); 3. Willie Clark, CB, San Diego (82); 3. Lake Dawson, SE, Kansas City (92); 5. John Covington, SS, Indianapolis (133); 5. Anthony Peterson, LB, San Francisco (153); 7. Pete Bercich, LB, Minnesota (211)

1995: 2. Ray Zellars, FB, New Orleans (44); 2. Bobby Taylor, CB, Philadelphia (50); 4. Oliver Gibson, NG, Pittsburgh (120); 5. Michael Miller, FL, Cleveland (147); 7. Travis Davis, SS, New Orleans (242)

1996: 2. Derrick Mayes, SE, Green Bay (56); 4. Paul Grasmanis, NG, Chicago (116); 6. Shawn Wooden, CB, Miami (189); 6. Dusty Zeigler, G, Buffalo (202)

1997: 1. Renaldo Wynn, DL, Jacksonville (21); 2. Marc Edwards, RB, San Francisco (55); 3. Bert Berry, LB, Indianapolis (86); 3. Kinnon Tatum, LB, Carolina (87); 5. Pete Chryplewicz, TE, Detroit (135)

1998: 3. Allen Rossum, DB, Philadelphia (85)

1999: 1. Luke Petitgout, OT, N.Y. Giants (19); 5. Jerry Wisne, OG, Chicago (143); 5. Mike Rosenthal, OT, N.Y. Giants (149); 5. Malcolm Johnson, SE, Pittsburgh (166); 7. Hunter Smith, P, Indianapolis (210); 7. Autry Denson, TB, Tampa Bay (233); 7. Kory Minor, LB, San Francisco (234)

2000; 7. Jarious Jackson, QB, Denver Broncos (214)

2001: 3. Mike Gandy, OG, Chicago (68); 3. Brock Williams, CB, New England (86); 4. Jabari Holloway, TE, New England (119); 6. Tony Driver, FS, Buffalo (178); 6. Dan O'Leary, TE, Buffalo (195); 7. Anthony Denman, ILB, Jacksonville (213)

2002: 2. Anthony Weaver, DT, Baltimore (52); 4. Rocky Boiman, OLB, Tennessee (133); 5. John Owens, TE, Detroit (138); 6. Tyreo Harrison, ILB, Philadelphia (198); 6. Javin Hunter, WR, Baltimore (206); 7. David Givens, WR, New England (253)

2003: 1. Jeff Faine, C, Cleveland (21); 5. Jordan Black, OT, Kansas City (153); 5. Sean Mahan, OG, Tampa Bay (168); 5. Shane Walton, CB, St. Louis (170); 6. Gerome Sapp, SS, Baltimore (182); 6. Arnaz Battle, WR, San Francisco (197); 6. Brennan Curtin, OT, Green Bay (212)

2004: 2. Julius Jones, RB, Dallas (43); 2. Courtney Watson, LB, New Orleans (60); 4. Glenn Earl, FS, Houston (122); 6. Vontez

Duff, CB, Houston (170); 7. Jim Molinaro, OT, Washington (180)

2005: 3. Justin Tuck, DE, NY Giants (74); 5. Jerome Collins, TE, St. Louis (144)

2006: 2. Anthony Fasano, TE, Dallas (53); 3. Maurice Stovall, WR, Tampa Bay (90); 6. Dan Stevenson, OG, New England (205)

2007: 1. Brady Quinn, QB, Cleveland (22); 2. Victor Abiamiri, DE, Philadelphia (57); 3. Ryan Harris, OT, Denver (70); 5. Derek Landri, DT, Jacksonville (166); 6. Mike Richardson, CB, New England (202); 7. Dan Santucci, OL, Cincinnati (230); 7. Chinedum Ndukwe, S, Cincinnati (253)

2008: 2. John Carlson, TE, Seattle (38); 2. Trevor Laws, DT, Philadelphia (47); 2. Tom Zbikowski, S, Baltimore (86); 6. John Sullivan, C, Minnesota (187)

2009: 4. David Bruton, S, Denver (114)

Justin Tuck holds three key Notre Dame defensive records: 24.5 career sacks, 43 tackles for a loss, and 13.5 sacks in a single season. He did all of this despite battling injuries and only playing three seasons in South Bend.

John Carlson holds onto a pass despite the coverage of a Penn State tackler. The highest draft pick from the Fighting Irish in 2008, he led the Seattle Seahawks in both catches and receiving yards as a rookie, a feat not accomplished since Hall of Famer Steve Largent in 1976.

First-Round Draft Picks

YEAR: NAME, POSITION, TEAM (OVERALL PICK)

1936: Bill Shakespeare, B, Pittsburgh (3)

1944: Angelo Bertelli, QB, Boston (1); Creighton Miller, B, Brooklyn (3)

1945: Frank Szymanski, B, Detroit (6); John Yonakor, E, Philadelphia (9)

1946: Frank Dancewicz, QB, Boston (1); John Lujack, QB, Chicago (4); George Connor, T, New York Giants (5); Emil Sitko, B, Los Angeles Rams (10)

1949: Frank Tripucka, QB, Philadelphia (9); Bill Fischer, G, Phoenix (10)

1950: Leon Hart, E, Detroit (1)

1951: Bob Williams, B, Chicago (2); Jerry Groom, C, Phoenix (6)

1954: Art Hunter, T, Green Bay (2); John Lattner, B, Pittsburgh (7); Neil Worden, B, Philadelphia (9)

1955: Ralph Guglielmi, QB, Washington (3); Frank Varrichione, T, Pittsburgh (6); Joe Heap, B, New York Giants (8)

1957: Paul Hornung, B, Green Bay (1)

1959: Nick Pietrosante, B, Detroit (6)

1960: George Izo, QB, New York Jets, Phoenix (2); Monty Stickles, E, San Diego, San Francisco (11)

1965: Jack Snow, WR, Minnesota (8)

1967: Paul Seiler, G, New York Jets (12): Alan Page, DT, Minnesota (15); Tom Regner, G, Houston (23)

1968: Kevin Hardy, DE, New Orleans (7)

1969: George Kunz, T, Atlanta (2); Jim Seymour, E, Los Angeles Rams (10)

1970: Mike McCoy, DT, Green Bay (2)

1972: Walt Patulski, DE, Buffalo (1); Clarence Ellis, DB, Atlanta (15); Mike Kadish, DT, Miami (25)

1975: Mike Fanning, DT, Los Angeles Rams (9)

1976: Steve Niehaus, DT, Seattle (2)

1978: Ken MacAfee, TE, San Francisco (7); Ross Browner, DE, Cincinnati (8); Luther Bradley, DB, Detroit (11)

1980: Vagas Ferguson, RB, New England (25)

1982: Bob Crable, LB, New York Jets (23)

1983: Tony Hunter, TE, Buffalo (12)

1984: Greg Bell, RB, Buffalo (26)

1986: Eric Dorsey, DT, New York Giants (19)

1988: Tim Brown, WR, Los Angeles Raiders (6)

1989: Andy Heck, T, Seattle (15)

1991: Todd Lyght, CB, Los Angeles Rams (5)

1992: Derek Brown, TE, New York Giants (14)

1993: Rick Mirer, QB, Seattle (2); Jerome Bettis, FB, Los Angeles Rams (10); Tom Carter, CB, Washington (17); Irv Smith, TE, New Orleans (20)

1994: Bryant Young, DT, San Francisco (7); Aaron Taylor, G, Green Bay (16); Jeff Burris, S, Buffalo (27)

1997: Renaldo Wynn, DE, Jacksonville (21)

1999: Luke Petitgout, T, New York Giants (19)

2003: Jeff Faine, C, Cleveland (21)

2007: Brady Quinn, QB, Cleveland (22)

All-Century Team

(Selected by *Blue & Gold Illustrated* in 2000)

Offense: G Heartley "Hunk" Anderson, 1918–21; G Bill Fischer, 1945–48; T George Connor, 1946–47; T Jim Martin, 1946–49; C Adam Walsh, 1922–24; TE Dave Casper, 1971–73; WR Tim Brown, 1984–87; WR Raghib Ismail, 1988–90; QB Joe Montana, 1975, 1977–78; TB George Gipp, 1917–20; FB Jerome Bettis, 1990–92; K John Carney, 1983–86

Defense: DE Leon Hart, 1946–49; DE Ross Browner, 1973, 1975–77; DT Alan Page, 1964–66; DT Chris Zorich, 1988–90; LB Jim Lynch, 1964–66; LB Bob Golic, 1975–78; LB Bob Crable, 1978–81; DB Luther Bradley, 1973, 1975–77; DB John Lattner, 1951–53; DB Todd Lyght, 1987–90; DB John Lujack, 1943, 1946–47; P Craig Hentrich, 1989–92; Utility Paul Hornung, 1954–56

RECORDS/LEADERS

Rushing Yards

Game

Name	Carries	Yds	Opponent	Date
1. Julius Jones	24	262	at Pittsburgh	Oct. 11, 2003
2. Vagas Ferguson	30	255	at Georgia Tech	Nov. 18, 1978
3. Phil Carter	40	254	at Michigan State	Oct. 4, 1980
4. Reggie Brooks	19	227	at S. California	Nov. 28, 1992
5. Jim Stone	38	224	vs. Miami	Oct. 11, 1980
6. Julius Jones	33	221	vs. Navy	Nov. 8, 2003
7. Vagas Ferguson	18	219	vs. Navy	Nov. 4, 1978
8. Julius Jones	23	218	at Stanford	Nov. 29, 2003
9. Allen Pinkett	36	217	at Penn State	Nov. 12, 1983
10. Jim Stone	33	211	vs. Navy	Nov. 1, 1980

Season

Name	Year	Carries	Yards
1. Vagas Ferguson	1979	301	1,437
2. Allen Pinkett	1983	252	1,394
3. Reggie Brooks	1992	167	1,343
4. Julius Jones	2003	229	1,268
(tie) Autry Denson	1997	264	1,268
6. Darius Walker	2006	255	1,267
7. Darius Walker	2005	253	1,196
8. Vagas Ferguson	1978	211	1,192
9. Autry Denson	1996	202	1,179
10. Autry Denson	1998	251	1,176

Career

Name	Carries	Yards	TDs
1. Autry Denson (1995–98)	854	4,318	43
2. Allen Pickett (1982–85)	889	4,131	49
3. Vagas Ferguson (1976–79)	673	3,472	32
4. Darius Walker (2004–06)	693	3,249	17

5. Julius Jones (1999–01)	634	3,018	26
6. Jerome Heavens (1975–78)	590	2,682	15
7. Phil Carter (1979–82)	557	2,409	4
8. George Gipp (1917–20)	369	2,341	21
9. Randy Kinder (1993–96)	404	2,295	18
10. Tony Brooks (1987–91)	423	2,274	12

Passing Yards

Game

Name	Yards	Opponent	Date
1. Joe Theismann	526	at Southern California	Nov. 28, 1970
2. Brady Quinn	487	vs. Michigan State	Sept. 17, 2005
3. Brady Quinn	467	vs. Brigham Young	Oct. 22, 2005
4. Brady Quinn	440	at Purdue	Oct. 1, 2005
5. Brady Quinn	432	vs. Purdue	Oct. 2, 2004
(tie) Brady Quinn	432	at Stanford	Nov. 26, 2005
7. Jimmy Clausen	401	vs. Hawaii	Nov. 24, 2008
8. Jimmy Clausen	383	at North Carolina	Oct. 11, 2008
9. Terry Hanratty	366	at Purdue	Sept. 30, 1967
10. Joe Montana	358	at Southern California	Nov. 25, 1978

Season

Name	Yards	Year
1. Brady Quinn	3,919	2005
2. Brady Quinn	3,426	2006
3. Jimmy Clausen	3,172	2008
4. Jarious Jackson	2,753	1999
5. Brady Quinn	2,586	2004
6. Joe Theismann	2,529	1970
7. Steve Beuerlein	2,211	1986
8. Rick Mirer	2,117	1991
9. Ron Powlus	2,078	1997
10. John Huarte	2,062	1964

Career

Name	Yards	Years
1. Brady Quinn	11,762	2003–06
2. Ron Powlus	7,602	1994–97
3. Steve Beuerlein	6,527	1983–86
4. Rick Mirer	5,997	1989–92
5. Jarious Jackson	4,820	1996–99
6. Jimmy Clausen	4,426	2007–08
7. Joe Theismann	4,411	1968–70
8. Terry Hanratty	4,152	1966–68
9. Joe Montana	4,121	1975–78
10. Blair Kiel	3,650	1980–83

Receiving

Game

Name	Yards	Opponent	Date
1. Jim Seymour	276	vs. Purdue	Sept. 24, 1966
2. Jack Snow	217	at Wisconsin	Sept. 26, 1964
3. Bobby Brown	208	at Pittsburgh	Nov. 13, 1999
(tie) Jim Morse	208	at Southern California	Nov. 26, 1955
5. Maurice Stovall	207	vs. Brigham Young	Oct. 22, 2005
6. Tom Gatewood	192	vs. Purdue	Sept. 26, 1970
7. Jeff Samardzija	191	at Stanford	Nov. 26, 2005
8. Kris Haines	179	at Southern California	Nov. 25, 1978
9. Maurice Stovall	178	vs. Michigan State	Sept. 17, 2005
10. Jeff Samardzija	177	vs. North Carolina	Nov. 4, 2006
(tie) Golden Tate	177	vs. Hawaii	Dec. 24, 2008

Season

Name	Yards	Year
1. Jeff Samardzija	1,249	2005
2. Maurice Stovall	1,149	2005
3. Tom Gatewood	1,123	1970
4. Jack Snow	1,114	1964

5. Golden Tate	1,080	2008
6. Jeff Samardzija	1,017	2006
7. Tim Brown	910	1986
8. Rhema McKnight	907	2006
9. Derrick Mayes	881	1995
10. Jim Seymour	862	1966

Career

Name	**Yards**	**Years**
1. Jeff Samardzija	2,593	2003–06
2. Derrick Mayes	2,512	1992–95
3. Tim Brown	2,493	1984–87
4. Tom Gatewood	2,283	1969–71
5. Rhema McKnight	2,277	2002–06
6. Maurice Stovall	2,195	2002–05
7. Jim Seymour	2,113	1966–68
8. Tony Hunter	1,897	1979–82
9. Ken MacAfee	1,759	1974–77
10. Malcolm Johnson	1,737	1995–98

Other Records

Points, game: 37 Art Smith vs. Loyola (Chicago), 1911 (seven touchdowns worth five points each & two point-after-touchdown conversions)

Points, season: 120 Jerome Bettis, 1991

Points, career: 320 Allen Pinkett, 1982–85

All-purpose yards, game: 361 Willie Maher vs. Kalamazoo, 1923 (107 rushing, 80 punt return, 174 kick return)

All-purpose yards, season: 1,937 Tim Brown, 1986 (254 rushing, 910 receiving, 75 punt return, 698 kick return)

All-purpose yards, career: 5,462 Julius Jones, 1999–2001, 2003 (3,108 rushing, 250 receiving, 426 punt return, 1,678 kick return)

Interceptions, game: 3 by 13 players

Interceptions, season: 10 Mike Townsend, 1972 (39 yards)

Interceptions, career: 17 Luther Bradley, 1973, 1975–77 (218 yards)

Tackles, game: 26 (tie), Bob Golic vs. Michigan, Sept. 23, 1978, and Bob Crable vs. Clemson, Nov. 17, 1979

Tackles, season: Bob Crable, 187 (1979)

Tackles, career: Bob Crable, 521 (1978–81)

Sacks, game: 4 (tie), Justin Tuck (twice) and Victor Abiamiri

Sacks, season: 13.5, Justin Tuck, (2003)

Sacks, career: 24.5, Justin Tuck (2002–04)

Luther Bradley still holds the Notre Dame record for career interceptions. After playing in the NFL for four seasons, he moved on to the USFL where he was the league's all-time interception leader.

THE COACHES

Head Coaches

Year(s)	Coach	W-L-T	Pct.
1894	J.L. Morrison	3–1–1	.700
1895	H.G. Hadden	3–1–0	.750
1896–98	Frank E. Hering	12–6–1	.658
1899	James McWeeney	6–3–1	.650
1900–01	Patrick O'Dea	14–4–2	.750
1902–03	James Faragher	14–2–2	.833
1904	Louis Salmon	5–3–0	.625
1905	Henry J. McGlew	5–4–0	.556
1906–07	Thomas Barry	12–1–1	.893
1908	Victor M. Place	8–1–0	.889
1909–10	Frank C. Longman	11–1–2	.857
1911–12	John L. Marks	13–0–2	.933
1913–17	Jesse C. Harper	34–5–1	.863
1918–30	Knute Rockne	105–12–5	.881
1931–33	Hunk Anderson	16–9–2	.630
1934–40	Elmer Layden	47–13–3	.770
1941–43, 46–53	Frank Leahy	87–11–9	.855
1944	Ed McKeever	8–2–0	.800
1945, 1963	Hugh Devore	9–9–1	.500
1954–58	Terry Brennan	32–18–0	.640
1959–62	Joe Kuharich	17–23–0	.425
1964–74	Ara Parseghian	95–17–4	.836
1975–1980	Dan Devine	53–16–1	.764
1981–1985	Gerry Faust	30–26–1	.535
1986–1996	Lou Holtz	100–30–2	.765
1997–2001	Bob Davie	35–25–0	.583
2002–2004	Tyrone Willingham	21–15–0	.583
2004	Kent Baer (interim)	0–1–0	.000
2005–	Charlie Weis		

The two most recent head coaches at Notre Dame chat at a 2005 game in Seattle. Tyrone Willingham was let go after just three seasons in South Bend, and he struggled to find success in his next stop at Washington before being fired in 2008.

Jesse Harper
1913–1917

Contrary to popular misconception, Notre Dame football was not an unknown quantity until Knute Rockne's reign as coach. Rockne played end at Notre Dame, and the school made a huge splash during Rock's 1913 senior season, Jesse Harper's first as coach. It's best remembered for quarterback Gus Dorais and his roommate, Rockne, teaming up to shock mighty Army 35–13 at West Point.

The Irish finished undefeated. In five years at Notre Dame, Harper's teams lost only five games.

Harper played football under the immortal Amos Alonzo Stagg at the University of Chicago, when it was a national powerhouse. He enjoyed successful coaching stints at Alma College in Michigan and Wabash College in Indiana before taking the Notre Dame job. He retired from coaching in 1917 at the age of 33. In 1971 he was elected to the College Football Hall of Fame.

Harper at Notre Dame
34–5–1

Year	Record
1913	7–0
1914	6–2
1915	7–1
1916	8–1
1917	6–1–1

Knute Rockne
1918–1930

Notre Dame's Knute Rockne may have been the greatest football coach in history. He seized the public's imagination and helped popularize the game nationwide.

Rockne's teams won with deception, finesse and speed, inspiring spectators and opponents. On average, his teams outscored their opponents by more than four to one. During Rockne's tenure in South Bend, attendance figures across the nation began to skyrocket and at Notre Dame games they multiplied almost tenfold.

Rockne was born on March 4, 1888, in Voss, Norway, and immigrated to the United States with his family when he was five. They settled in Chicago and supposedly young Knute fell in love with the game while watching the great Walter Eckersall play in high school.

As a Notre Dame player from 1910 to 1913, Rockne was instrumental in thrusting his school into the nation's football consciousness. By the end of his all-too-brief coaching career from 1918 to 1930, he had led the Notre Dame football program into elite status.

The *anybody, anywhere, anytime* character of Rockne's early teams helped inspire the phenomenon known as the "subway alumni," people who never went to college but could identify with a school, especially if considered an underdog. By the end of his reign, Rockne's Ramblers (a nickname with which Rock himself was not particularly enamored) had become known as the "Fighting Irish."

While watching the performance of a chorus line, Rockne conceived the idea of what came to be known as the "Notre Dame Shift." The backs would line up in a T formation, then shift rapidly into a single wing (Rockne's version was called the "box" formation), with all four backs in motion at the snap before the defense could get set. The Notre Dame Shift is the reason the rules now require a full-second stop after a shift and prohibit more than one man in motion when the ball is snapped.

During that time substitutions were strictly limited, precluding the use of two platoons. So Rockne employed what he called his "shock troops," an entire team of back-ups who started games and wore down their opponents before giving way to the real first string.

Rockne played end for Notre Dame under coaches Frank Longman, John Marks, and Jesse Harper. During Harper's first year at the helm (1913), Rockne teamed with his roommate, quarterback Gus Dorais, to help revolutionize the game.

Rockne and Dorais worked as janitors and busboys at a beachfront hotel in Cedar Point, Ohio, in the summer of 1913 and during their off hours practiced at a nearby athletic field at perfecting a new weapon that had been legalized in 1906, the forward pass. Their grand unveiling came in at Army November.

Before that day, a receiver would run a designated distance downfield, turn to face his quarterback, wait for the ball to come to him and cradle it away in his arms. What they did was run established pass routes and timing patterns. The quarterback would lead the receiver, who caught the ball on the run with his hands. Dorais completed an unheard of 14 of 17 passes for 243 yards, and his 40-yard completion to Rockne was the longest pass play at that time. Notre Dame stunned the Cadets 35–13, changing the way the forward pass was viewed.

Rockne worked his way through school, was a star in track as well as football, and graduated magna cum laude. He accepted a graduate assistantship in chemistry while also serving as an assistant on Harper's coaching staff. He was named head coach upon Harper's resignation in early 1918.

In his 13 seasons as Notre Dame's coach, Rockne compiled a record of 105–12–5, with six perfect seasons and five national titles. Three of them (in 1924, 1929, and 1930) were consensus selections. His winning percentage of .881 is the highest in history, college or pro. He is the only person ever coach 10 or more years to person and had few career losses than seasons coached.

Rockne produced 20 first-team All-Americans, including some of the game's most legendary figures.

Coach Knute Rockne spends time with his sons in this undated photo. Rockne had been visiting the two oldest boys at their boarding school before his tragic plane crash in 1930.

The Four Horsemen and the Seven Mules finished the 1924 season 10–0 and captured the national title. They concluded the campaign as 27–10 Rose Bowl victors over an undefeated Stanford 11 led by All-America fullback Ernie Nevers and coached by Glenn "Pop" Warner.

George Gipp, one of the greatest football players who ever lived, was another Rockne product. Gipp's school career record of 2,341 rushing yards from 1917 to 1920 stood for more than a half century, and the Irish were undefeated in his last 20 games.

Gipp can also be credited with a famous historic win eight years after he died of strep throat on December 14, 1920, with Rockne at his bedside. On November 10, 1928, against Army, Rockne exhorted his outmanned troops to win one for the Gipper. Fulfilling Gipp's dying request, the Irish won 12–6. The Irish finished the campaign at 5–4, and a loss to Army that day would have hung Rockne with the only losing record of his career.

Rockne's last two teams, in 1929 and 1930, were his best. Quarterback Frank Carideo was a consensus All-American both seasons and won every game he started. In 1929, with Notre Dame Stadium under construction, Rockne's Ramblers played the entire schedule away from home and finished a perfect 9–0. The 13–12 win over Southern California was played in front of a crowd of approximately 120,000 at Chicago's Soldier Field. Rock's 10–0 team in 1930 was his last.

On March 31, 1931, Rockne boarded Transcontinental-Western Flight 599 in Kansas City bound for Los Angeles, where he was scheduled to film a football demonstration movie. A friend, playwright Albert C. Fuller, was there to see him off. "Happy landing, Rock!" Fuller said as he waved goodbye. "Thanks, Al," Rockne replied, "but I'd prefer just an ordinary soft landing." Just after takeoff, the plane encountered a storm, iced over, and crashed into a

Captain Jerry Groom (50) and Coach Frank Leahy pause during practice on September 5, 1950.

wheat field near Bazaar, Kansas, killing everyone onboard. Rockne was 43.

Foreign dignitaries, including the king of Norway, attended Rockne's funeral at the Cathedral of the Sacred Heart on the Notre Dame campus. President Herbert Hoover declared Rockne's death "a national loss." Thousands of mourners were turned away, unable to fit inside. More than one hundred thousand lined the procession route from Rockne's house on Wayne Street to the Cathedral.

Many years later Elmer Layden, the fullback of the Four Horsemen backfield, remembered the shock surrounding his coach's passing: "It was almost the size of President Kennedy's impact. It was amazing. They turned out on the train and at the funeral. He was a national hero."

During his time as a football coach, Rockne also served as Notre Dame's athletics director, track coach, ticket distributor, and equipment manager. He was a published author with three books to his credit, and he designed Notre Dame Stadium. Consequently, Rockne was a charter member of the College Football Hall of Fame in 1951.

Rockne at Notre Dame
105–12–5

Year	Record	Bowl
1913	7–0	
1918	3–1–2#	
1919*	9–0	
1920*	9–0	
1921	10–1	
1922	8–1–1	
1923	9–1	
1924**	10–0	Rose
1925	7–2–1	
1926	9–1	

1927	7–1–1
1928	5–4
1929**	9–0
1930**	10–0
#season abbreviated due to influenza epidemic	
*national champions	
**consensus national champions	

Frank Leahy
1941–1943, 1946–1953

He was known as the master. Frank Leahy's winning percentage of .855 at Notre Dame ranks second only to Knute Rockne's in Division I-A (Bowl Subdivision) history. Add his two years from Boston College in 1939 and 1940, and his career percentage rises to .864. Consequently, Leahy and Rockne are the only coaches of 10 or more years to have no more losses than seasons coached (11 losses in 11 seasons at Notre Dame; 13 losses in 13 seasons total).

Leahy played tackle for Rockne in 1928 and 1929 but missed his senior season (1930) due to injuries. Following his graduation, he embarked on a career as a line coach, first at Georgetown in 1931, then at Michigan State in 1932. He spent from 1933 to 1938 on the staff at Fordham under head coach Jim Crowley, a halfback in Notre Dame's Four Horsemen backfield of 1924. From 1935 to 1937, Leahy's Fordham line earned fame as the "Seven Blocks of Granite", one of whom was future legendary Green Bay Packer coach Vince Lombardi.

In 1939 Leahy moved to Boston College for his first head coaching gig and guided the Eagles through the greatest two-year run in school history, with a record of 20–2, which included a 19–13 victory over Tennessee in the 1941 Sugar Bowl. The Volunteers, coached by the legendary Bob Neyland, had not lost a regular-season game in more than three years, and Leahy's win landed him back at his alma mater.

In 1941, his inaugural season at Notre Dame, the Fighting Irish went 8–0–1 with a No. 3 national ranking, and Leahy was named Coach of the Year. Two seasons later, in 1943, the Fighting Irish were national champions with quarterback Angelo Bertelli winning Notre Dame's first Heisman Trophy.

Leahy spent 1944 and 1945 in the navy during World War II, and upon his return the Fighting Irish dominated college football. After losing their season finale in 1945, Notre Dame didn't lose again until 1950. An entire class of students went through four years of school and graduated without the football team losing a single game. That has never again happened in major college football. Those Leahy-coached juggernauts of the late '40s claimed three national titles (1946, 1947, and 1949), two Heisman Trophies (Johnny Lujack in 1947, Leon Hart in 1949) and two Outland Trophies (George Connor in 1946, Bill Fischer in 1948).

In 1997 *Sports Illustrated* published an extensive article on what the greatest college football team of all time was, choosing between the 1946 and 1947 teams. However, many historians believe it was Leahy's 1949 team. At the time many thought that Notre Dame's backups could probably beat anybody else's starters.

Football practices at Notre Dame during the Leahy years, particularly the full contact midweek scrimmages, were so grueling that to the players the games themselves were considered easier. Leahy drove them, and himself, relentlessly.

He addressed his players as a group as "lads," and individually by their formal given names—Frank Tripuka was "Francis;" Ziggy Czarobski was "Zygmont." He was quoted in the press before every season saying things like, "We'll be lucky to make a first down," then proceed to win another national title. He refused to run up gaudy scores against his opponents.

Leahy retired for health reasons after the 1953 season. More than half of his teams finished undefeated, and five won national championships. He produced 20 consensus All-Americans and four Heisman Trophy winners (Bertelli, Lujack, Hart, and Johnny Lattner in 1953). Leahy was inducted into the National Football Foundation Hall of Fame in 1970.

Leahy at Notre Dame
87–11–9

Year	record
1941	8–0–1
1942	7–2–2
1943**	9–1
1946**	8–0–1
1947**	9–0
1948	9–0–1
1949*	10–0
1950	4–4–1
1951	7–2–1
1952	7–2–1
1953*	9–0–1
*national champions	
** consensus national champions	

Ara Parseghian
1964–1974

Ara Parseghian cut his teeth as an assistant from 1950 to 1955 on Woody Hayes' staff at Miami, Ohio, his alma mater. He was the head coach at Northwestern for eight years (1956–1963) before arriving at Notre Dame. His Wildcat teams played the Irish four times and won all four. So after a 2-7 season they hired him.

During his first season, the Irish came within a minute and a half of a perfect 10–0 record and the national title. For his efforts, Parseghian was named Coach of the Year.

Coach Parseghian celebrates in the locker room by hoisting the Sugar Bowl Trophy after his Fighting Irish upset top-ranked Alabama on New Year's Eve, 1973. The win vaulted the Irish to 11–0 and made them national champions.

In 11 years at the Irish helm, he won two consensus national championships, in 1966 and 1973, and parts of two others. He compiled a record of 95–17–4. His winning percentage under the Dome of .836 is the third highest of all Irish coaches who stayed more than two years—behind only legendary Knute Rockne and Frank Leahy.

Before retiring after the 1974 season due to health reasons, Parseghian produced three bowl champions (1971 Cotton, 1973 Sugar, 1975 Orange), 21 consensus All-Americans, and a Heisman Trophy winner—quarterback John Huarte in 1964. He was inducted into the National Football Foundation Hall of Fame in 1980.

Parseghian at Notre Dame
95–17–4

Year	Record	Bowl
1964*	9–1	
1965	7–2–1	
1966**	9–0–1	
1967*	8–2	
1968	7–2–1	
1969	8–2–1	Cotton
1970*	10–1	Cotton
1971	8–2	
1972	8–3	Orange
1973**	11–0	Sugar
1974	10–2	Orange

*national champions

**consensus national champions

Lou Holtz
1986–1996

Before arriving at Notre Dame, Lou Holtz had been the head coach at William & Mary (1969–1971), North Carolina State (1972–1975), Arkansas (1977–1983), and Minnesota (1984–1985) and had fashioned himself as something of a program rebuilder. That's what Notre Dame needed in 1986 when he was hired. The Irish were coming off a 5–6 record in 1985, finishing the season with the worst loss in program history—58–7 at Miami.

Holtz's record of 5–6 in '86 wasn't an improvement mathematically, but everyone around the program could sense the wheels were in motion. By his third year in South Bend (1988) the Irish were national champions, and Holtz was Coach of the Year.

Holtz coached more games (132) than any other coach in school history and won more than any other (100) except Rockne. At Notre Dame, Holtz coached 14 consensus All-Americans. He led Notre Dame to nine straight New Year's Day bowl games from 1987 through 1995. Three of his Irish teams played the nation's most difficult schedule, and five finished sixth or better in the final Associated Press poll.

Over the course of his career he won 249 games, ranking him eighth all time on the NCAA Division I-A list. Against top 25 competition he was 32–20–2.

Holtz at Notre Dame
100–30–2

Year	Record	Bowl
1986	5–6	
1987	8–4	Cotton
1988**	12–0	Fiesta
1989*	12–1	Orange
1990	9–3	Orange
1991	10–3	Sugar

Lou Holtz signals to the crowd after his Fighting Irish knocked off the Miami Hurricanes en route to the national championship in 1988. Only Knute Rockne has won more games at Notre Dame than Holtz, and no coach has been at the helm for more games.

1992	10–1–1	Cotton
1993*	11–1	Cotton
1994	6–5–1	Fiesta
1995	9–3	Orange
1996	8–3	
*national champions		
**consensus national champions		

Coaches' Awards

AFCA (American Football Coaches Association) Award: 1941 Frank Leahy; 1964 Ara Parseghian (tie with Frank Broyles of Arkansas)
Eddie Robinson Award: 1964 Ara Parseghian; 1988 Lou Holtz; 2005 Charlie Weis
Home Depot Award: 2002 Tyrone Willingham
Paul W. "Bear" Bryant Award: 1988 Lou Holtz

2009 Coaching Staff

Charlie Weis	Head Coach
Corwin Brown	Defensive Coordinator/Defensive Backs
Michael Haywood	Offensive Coordinator/Running Backs
Rob Ianello	Receivers Coach/Recruiting Coordinator
John Latina	Assistant Head Coach (Offense)/Offensive Line
Jappy Oliver	Defensive Line
Bernie Palmalee	Tight Ends
Brian Polian	Special Teams
Ron Powlus	Quarterbacks
Jon Tenuta	Assistant Head Coach (Defense)/Linebackers
Patrick Graham	Defensive Graduate Assistant
Kevin Loney	Offensive Graduate Assistant

THE RIVALRIES

Notre Dame vs. Michigan

It isn't anywhere close to being one of college football's oldest rivalries, and the two schools aren't in the same state or conference, but Michigan vs. Notre Dame has become one of college football's benchmark series.

First of all, the game has always been played early in the season. For the independent Fighting Irish, it's a sudden-death playoff atmosphere, because one loss can end Notre Dame's annual national championship quest. The message in South Bend the week of the Michigan game frequently is: lose this one and play out the string.

Oh, and Michigan needs the victory too, if it wants to aspire to anything more than the Big Ten title.

"It sets the tone for the season," said Mike Trgovac, who played for Michigan under Coach Bo Schembechler but later became a defensive line coach for Notre Dame. "After we beat them (in 1978), I think it was tough for them to recover, and it kind of propelled us. It lets you know right away where you are as a team. In '91 Desmond Howard makes that catch (Michigan 24, Notre Dame 14), and we have a bad year (10–3)."

Second, it's the proximity of the two schools, which are a two-hour drive apart. That's one reason many top players visit both schools during recruiting. Quarterback Rick Mirer grew up a Michigan fan but wound up at Notre Dame. Irish star Jerome Bettis hails from Detroit.

Then, there are the players and the unforgettable plays. Rocket Ismail streaking through the rain to return two kickoffs for touchdowns, giving Notre Dame a 24–19 victory in Ann Arbor in 1989. Mirer engineering a late 76-yard drive to lead a 28–24 Irish comeback win in 1990 in his first start as a sophomore. Howard

Rick Mirer turns to hand off in the 1993 Cotton Bowl. One in a long line of fantastic quarterbacks to wear no. 3 at Notre Dame, Mirer had grown up a Michigan fan but decided to attend Notre Dame in a recruiting coup for Coach Lou Holtz.

making "The Catch" in 1991 to put Michigan on top 24–14 and himself in front of the Heisman Trophy race that he eventually won.

Last, but not least, is the pageantry that comes with the two all-time winningest programs in college football in both total victories and winning percentage. They even have great fight songs: Notre Dame's "Victory March" vs. Michigan's "The Victors."

"The Michigan–Notre Dame game epitomizes the best in college football," said Schembechler, who compiled a 4–6 record against the Irish before retiring after the 1989 season.

"You have two big-time schools that understand where football belongs in the scheme of things," Schembechler said. "There's no hanky-panky in recruiting. Almost every top player has visited both schools. They're both classy institutions. You like that kind of competition."

Notre Dame vs. Michigan

(Michigan leads series 20-15-1)

Year	Site	Winner	Score
1887	South Bend	Michigan	8–0
1888	South Bend	Michigan	26–6
1888	South Bend	Michigan	10–4
1898	Ann Arbor	Michigan	23–0
1899	Ann Arbor	Michigan	12–0
1900	Ann Arbor	Michigan	7–0
1902	Toledo	Michigan	23–0
1908	Ann Arbor	Michigan	12–6
1909	Ann Arbor	Notre Dame	11–3
1942	South Bend	Michigan	32–20
1943	Ann Arbor	Notre Dame	35–12
1978	South Bend	Michigan	28–14
1979	Ann Arbor	Notre Dame	12–10
1980	South Bend	Notre Dame	29–27

1981	Ann Arbor	Michigan	25–7
1982	South Bend	Notre Dame	23–17
1985	Ann Arbor	Michigan	20–12
1986	South Bend	Michigan	24–23
1987	Ann Arbor	Notre Dame	26–7
1988	South Bend	Notre Dame	19–17
1989	Ann Arbor	Notre Dame	24–19
1990	South Bend	Notre Dame	28–24
1991	Ann Arbor	Michigan	24–14
1992	South Bend	Tie	17–17
1993	Ann Arbor	Notre Dame	27–23
1994	South Bend	Michigan	26–24
1997	Ann Arbor	Michigan	21–14
1998	South Bend	Notre Dame	36–20
1999	Ann Arbor	Michigan	26–22
2002	South Bend	Notre Dame	25–23
2003	Ann Arbor	Michigan	38–0
2004	South Bend	Notre Dame	28–20
2005	Ann Arbor	Notre Dame	17–10
2006	South Bend	Michigan	47–21
2007	Ann Arbor	Michigan	38–0
2008	South Bend	Notre Dame	35–17

Notre Dame vs. Southern California

It's considered the oldest and most prestigious intersectional rivalry in the country, and over the years many national championships have been certified or lost based on the outcome of the game that was first played in 1926.

It's a matchup that has enhanced the candidacy of Heisman Trophy winners. For Notre Dame they are Angelo Bertelli, Johnny Lujack, Leon Hart, John Lattner, Paul Hornung, John Huarte, and Tim Brown. For Southern California the names are Mike Garrett, O.J. Simpson, Charles White, Marcus Allen, Carson Palmer, Matt Leinart, and Reggie Bush.

Southern California's Troy Polamalu got juked on this play, leaving him stuck watching Carlyle Holiday run by. Though USC has had the edge on Notre Dame in recent years, the Fighting Irish still hold a comfortable lead in the all-time series.

It's matched legendary coaches: Notre Dame's Knute Rockne, Frank Leahy, and Ara Parseghian, against Howard Jones, John McKay, and John Robinson.

It's attracted the largest crowd in the history of college football, an estimated 120,000 for the 1927 meeting at Soldier Field in Chicago. The 1947 game at the Los Angeles Coliseum drew 104,953, still a stadium record.

Yet if it hadn't been for the persuasiveness of the bride of a young Southern California graduate manager and a famous coach's wife, there might not have been a Notre Dame-Southern California rivalry.

In 1925, Notre Dame was already an established college football power under Rockne. On January 1 that year, the Fighting Irish with the Four Horsemen had galloped over Stanford 27–10 in the Rose Bowl. Meanwhile, the Trojans had emerged as a West Coast power.

"I knew that Notre Dame was going to break its series with Nebraska (after the 1925 game) and that there would be an opening on its schedule," Southern California graduate manager Gwynn Wilson said. "Notre Dame was to play Nebraska on Thanksgiving Day, and I thought if I went back there and talked to Rockne, there might be a chance for us to get a game with them next year."

Wilson had an ally in Howard Jones, who had been hired in 1925 and wanted to make a national impact. While coaching at Iowa in 1921, his team had snapped a 22-game Notre Dame unbeaten streak. He had agreed to give Rockne a rematch sometime. Southern California had played few intersectional games, the most notable being a 14–3 win over Penn State in the Rose Bowl in 1923, and hadn't traveled east.

The key, though, may have been Wilson, 26, bringing his wife to Lincoln for his meeting with Rockne.

In front of the largest crowd in college football history—an estimated 120,000 at Chicago's Soldier Field—USC's Morley Drury escapes the Notre Dame defense and heads up field. Today the stadium would barely seat half of the crowd that watched this 1927 classic.

"I went to the hotel where the Notre Dame team was staying, but Rockne told me he didn't have enough time to talk about my proposal there," Wilson said. "He said he'd get a ticket to Chicago for me and my wife and he'd talk to me about it on the train."

It didn't help Wilson's cause that Notre Dame was shut out by Nebraska 17–0. Nonetheless, the Wilsons were still hopeful.

"I really didn't get a chance to talk to Rockne until the afternoon after the game, when we went into the observation car," Wilson said. "He told me that he couldn't meet Southern Cal because Notre Dame was already traveling too much, and the team had gotten the nickname "Ramblers", which he didn't like. He also said he was now getting some games with the Big Ten.

"I thought the whole thing was off, but as Rock and I talked Marion was with Mrs. Rockne, Bonnie, in her compartment. Marion told Bonnie how nice Southern California was and how hospitable the people were.

"Well, when Rock went back to the compartment, Bonnie talked him into the game. He came out, looked me up and said, 'What kind of proposition do you have?' I said, 'We'll give you a $20,000 guarantee.' He said he would talk to Father Matthew J. Walsh (Notre Dame president). He did, and the series was on, with the first game to be played on December 4, 1926.

"But if it hadn't been for Mrs. Wilson talking to Mrs. Rockne, there wouldn't have been a series."

After allowing just one touchdown in the first eight games of the 1926 season, Notre Dame was shocked by Carnegie Tech, 19-0, in Pittsburgh. Meanwhile, the Trojans were also 8-1, having lost only to Stanford, 13–12.

A sellout crowd of 74,378 saw the game at the Coliseum, later enlarged for the 1932 Olympics. Southern California led 12–7 late in the game when Rockne sent in Art Parisien, a 5-foot-7, 148-pound

Vagas Ferguson (32) advances for a short gain against the USC defense on November 27, 1978, in Los Angeles.

senior reserve quarterback, with Notre Dame in possession on its 42-yard line.

Six weeks previously, Parisien had suffered a chest injury against Northwestern. Doctors had advised Rockne not to let him play. The Irish coach had brought him west only as a gesture of kindness. He ended up thowing two touchdown passes to win the game, 13-12.

One of the most memorable games in the series took place in 1964 at the Coliseum when Southern California, trailing 17–0 at halftime, deprived previously unbeaten Notre Dame of the national championship with a 20–17 victory on quarterback Craig Fertig's fourth-down pass to halfback Rod Sherman with 1:33 remaining. Instead Alabama claimed the title, and in apprecaiation Coach Paul W. "Bear" Bryant awarded letters to Fertig and Sherman.

In the aftermath of that game, the Reverend Theodore Hesburgh, Notre Dame president from 1952 to 1987, congratulated Rich McKay, saying, "That wasn't a very nice thing for a Catholic (McKay) to do."

Replied McKay, "Father, it serves you right for hiring a Presbyterian (Parseghian)."

In 1977 Coach Dan Devine momentarily delayed a run of Trojan dominance with a strategy that wasn't related to football. His team wore blue jerseys while warming up for the game in South Bend, went back to the dressing room and reappeared in emerald green jerseys for the kickoff. It was a startling transformation, and the aroused Irish routed the Trojans 49–19.

The last time Notre Dame won the national championship, in 1988 under Lou Holtz, the Fighting Irish were ranked No. 1 and the Trojans No. 2 when they squared off in the Coliseum. Both teams carried 10–0 records into the contest, but Holtz sent running backs Ricky Watters and Tony Brooks home for being late to the team dinner the night before the game. With

Rodney Peete as their quarterback, the Trojans outgained the Irish, but Notre Dame prevailed 27–10 behind a 65-yard touchdown run by quarterback Tony Rice and a 64-yard interception return for another touchdown by cornerback Stan Smagala.

In 2005 Reggie Bush won the Heisman after running for 160 yards and touchdowns of 36, 45, and 9 yards against the Irish, but the game came down to one play. After four lead changes in the fourth quarter, the Irish led 31–28 with Southern California facing fourth-and-9 from its own 26. Leinart connected with Dwayne Jarrett for a 61-yard pass, and with three seconds remaining the quarterback managed to reach the end zone from a yard out (with help from the "Bush Push") for the 34–31 win.

Notre Dame vs. Southern California

(Notre Dame leads series 42-33-5)

Year	Site	Winner	Score
1926	Los Angeles	Notre Dame	13–12
1927	Soldier Field	Notre Dame	7–6
1928	Los Angeles	Southern California	27–14
1929	Soldier Field	Notre Dame	13–12
1930	Los Angeles	Notre Dame	27–0
1931	South Bend	Southern California	16–14
1932	Los Angles	Southern California	13–0
1933	South Bend	Southern California	19–0
1934	Los Angeles	Notre Dame	14–0
1935	South Bend	Notre Dame	20–13
1936	Los Angeles	Tie	13–13
1937	South Bend	Notre Dame	13–6
1938	Los Angeles	Southern California	13–0
1939	South Bend	Southern California	20–12
1940	Los Angeles	Notre Dame	10–6
1941	South Bend	Notre Dame	20–18
1942	Los Angeles	Notre Dame	13–0

1946	South Bend	Notre Dame	26–6
1947	Los Angeles	Notre Dame	38–7
1948	Los Angeles	Tie	14–14
1949	South Bend	Notre Dame	32–0
1950	Los Angeles	Southern California	9–7
1951	Los Angeles	Notre Dame	19–12
1952	South Bend	Notre Dame	9–0
1953	Los Angeles	Notre Dame	48–14
1954	South Bend	Notre Dame	23–17
1955	Los Angeles	Southern California	42–20
1956	Los Angeles	Southern California	28–20
1957	South Bend	Notre Dame	40–12
1958	Los Angeles	Notre Dame	20–13
1959	South Bend	Notre Dame	16–6
1960	Los Angeles	Notre Dame	17–0
1961	South Bend	Notre Dame	30–0
1962	Los Angeles	Southern California	25–0
1963	South Bend	Notre Dame	17–14
1964	Los Angeles	Southern California	20–17
1965	South Bend	Notre Dame	28–7
1966	Los Angeles	Notre Dame	51–0
1967	South Bend	Southern California	24–7
1968	Los Angeles	Tie	21–21
1969	South Bend	Tie	14–14
1970	Los Angeles	Southern California	38–28
1971	South Bend	Southern California	28–14
1972	Los Angeles	Southern California	45–23
1973	South Bend	Notre Dame	23–14
1974	Los Angeles	Southern California	55–24
1975	South Bend	Southern California	24–17
1976	Los Angeles	Southern California	17–13
1977	South Bend	Notre Dame	49–19
1978	Los Angeles	Southern California	27–25
1979	South Bend	Southern California	42–23

1980	Los Angeles	Southern California	20–3
1981	South Bend	Southern California	14–7
1982	Los Angeles	Southern California	17–13
1983	South Bend	Notre Dame	27–6
1984	Los Angeles	Notre Dame	19–7
1985	South Bend	Notre Dame	37–3
1986	Los Angeles	Notre Dame	38–37
1987	South Bend	Notre Dame	26–15
1988	Los Angeles	Notre Dame	27–10
1989	South Bend	Notre Dame	28–24
1990	Los Angeles	Notre Dame	10–6
1991	South Bend	Notre Dame	24–20
1992	Los Angeles	Notre Dame	31–23
1993	South Bend	Notre Dame	31–13
1994	Los Angeles	Tie	17–17
1995	South Bend	Notre Dame	38–10
1996	Los Angeles	Southern California	27–20 (OT)
1997	South Bend	Southern California	20–17
1998	Los Angeles	Southern California	10–0
1999	South Bend	Notre Dame	25–24
2000	Los Angeles	Notre Dame	38–21
2001	South Bend	Notre Dame	27–16
2002	Los Angeles	Southern California	44–13
2003	South Bend	Southern California	45–14
2004	Los Angeles	Southern California	41–10
2005	South Bend	Southern California	34–31
2006	Los Angeles	Southern California	44–24
2007	South Bend	Southern California	38–0
2008	Los Angeles	Southern California	38–3

TRADITIONS

No other school in the nation can approach the number of significant, time-honored traditions that encase Notre Dame football. They're part of the vernacular: Touchdown Jesus, the Golden Dome, the Victory March.

Here's a small sample of what makes the Fighting Irish unique.

The Fighting Irish

During the 1800s, Notre Dame's football team bore the nickname "Catholics." Sometime during the early decades of the 20th century the moniker "Fighting Irish" took hold, though the exact process by which this happened is unknown. During the early 1920s, the team was known as the "Ramblers," or sometimes "Rockne's Ramblers," but the change was already in the works.

It may have been Northwestern's fans shouting "kill the fighting Irish!" during the matchup in 1899 or the exhortation from a Notre Dame player to his teammates—"What's wrong with you guys? You're all Irish and you're not fighting worth a lick!" during the 1909 Michigan game—or any number of other possible explanations. The roster was dominated by Irish surnames, and by the end of the Rockne regime "Ramblers" had gradually evolved into "Fighting Irish."

Gold and Blue (and sometimes green)

When Father Edward Sorin, a 28-year-old French priest of the Congregation of Holy Cross, founded the University of Notre Dame du Lac in 1842, he adopted yellow and blue as the official school colors. After the dome and statue of the Blessed Mother surmounting the Administration Building were gilded, the colors changed to gold and blue.

Green jerseys have been used as a psychological

The Notre Dame mascot leads the team out on the field against Michigan in September 2006.

Student manager Meghan Callahan sprays helmets in 2003. One of the most recognizable symbols in college football, Notre Dame's helmets are still painted weekly by the managers.

ploy by Notre Dame coaches since the Knute Rockne years and were a prominent feature of Frank Leahy's teams. Though the team hasn't had much success in green of late, it's likely that we haven't seen the last of them.

Pep Rallies

The Friday evening pep rallies are an integral part of the Notre Dame football tradition. Historically, the band led the student body through campus to the Field House. But growing interest in the event over the last several years prompted a move to the more spacious Joyce Center. On September 5, 1997, the pep rally was held in Notre Dame Stadium, in conjunction with the expansion and rededication of the facility. Some of the recognizable people who have spoken at the event include Dick Vitale, Tommy Lasorda, and Regis Philbin.

Gold Dust

The gold helmets worn by the Notre Dame football players on game days are emblematic of the Golden Dome over the school's Administration building. Student managers mix real gold dust into the paint that they then apply to the helmets on Friday nights before home games and Thursday nights before road games.

Campus Landmarks

Golden Dome

The University of Notre Dame du Lac was founded in 1842 by Father Edward Sorin, of the Congregation of Holy Cross, who had come over from France for just that purpose.

In 1879 a fire destroyed the Main Building. After it was rebuilt, it was topped with a dome that was gilded, not painted. Atop the dome a 19-foot tall statue of the Blessed Mother, for whom the school is named and to whom it is dedicated, was placed. The statue is illuminated at night.

Irish players walk to spring practice in 2004 under the gaze of "Touchdown Jesus."

The Main Building with the Golden Dome serves as the backdrop for photographs of new alumni on graduation day and a rallying point for pregame activities during football season. It is the stepping-off point for the Band of the Fighting Irish as it leads the students into the stadium on game day.

Touchdown Jesus

The 132-foot stone mosaic on the south side of the Hesburgh Library is visible from inside Notre Dame Stadium. It is patterned after a painting by Millard Sheet called *The Word of Life*. In it, Jesus is surrounded by his apostles and others and is standing with his hands upraised. This posture of the main figure has given the world the football icon known as "Touchdown Jesus."

We're No. 1 Moses

Just outside the Hesburgh Library stands a bronze statue depicting Moses having just descended to the foot of Mount Sinai, chastising the Israelites who have taken to worshiping idols in his absence. He is cradling the stone tablets containing the Ten Commandments with his left arm and pointing to the sky with his right forefinger. Hence the nickname, "We're No. 1 Moses."

Fair Catch Corby

During the Civil War, Father William J. Corby, C.S.C., of the University of Notre Dame, served as a chaplain in the Union Army. A statue placed in front of Corby Hall depicts Father Corby with his hand raised, giving absolution to the men of the Irish Brigade as they prepare to go into action on the second day of the Battle of Gettysburg, July 2, 1863.

The raised hand suggests a punt returner signaling for a fair catch, and the piece is therefore known to students and alumni as "Fair Catch Corby."

Notre Dame Stadium

Notre Dame has been playing football in "The House that Rockne Built" since 1930. The football team's previous home was Cartier Field, just north of the current stadium. But the old venue could hold no more than 30,000 spectators and with Coach Knute Rockne at the helm, that just wasn't enough.

Rockne himself drew up the blueprints for Notre Dame Stadium, and the new facility was dedicated on October 4, 1930, with a 20–14 victory over Southern Methodist. Tragically, Rockne got to coach only one season in the new stadium before he was killed in a plane crash on March 31, 1931.

Since 1966, every game at Notre Dame but one has been a sellout. The only exception was a Thanksgiving Day 1973 contest against Air Force, a scheduling accommodation for television on a holiday when the students were away from campus.

Notre Dame Stadium was expanded from 59,075 capacity to 80,232 by the start of the 1997 season. In 2001 that number was upped to 80,795.

"When Irish Backs Go Marching By"

Rah! Rah! Rah!
Up! Notre Dame men answer the cry
Gathering foemen fling to the sky
Fight! Fight! Fight!
Brave hosts advancing challenging your name
March to the battle, Notre Dame!
And when the Irish backs go marching by
The cheering thousands shout their battle cry:
For Notre Dame men are marching into the game,
Fighting the fight for you, Notre Dame.
And when the Irish line goes smashing through
They'll sweep the foemen's ranks away;
When Notre Dame men fight for Gold and Blue,
Then Notre Dame men will win the day.

The Band of the Fighting Irish

The Notre Dame marching band, officially known as the Band of the Fighting Irish, is the oldest such aggregation in existence. Founded in 1845, the band has been present at every home football game in school history.

The Band of the Fighting Irish was one of the first in the nation to include pageantry, precision drill, and picture formations. In 1970 the band began to include women from Saint Mary's College before the university went coeducational in 1972.

On game day there is the "Concert on the Steps" at Bond Hall. From there the band marches through campus, leading the students to the stadium. The band marches into the tunnel, waits for the whistle to blow, and explodes out onto the playing field for the pregame festivities.

"Victory March"

Rally sons of Notre Dame
Sing her glory and sound her fame
Raise her gold and blue
And cheer with voices true:
Rah, rah for Notre Dame
We will fight in every game,
Strong of heart and true to her name
We will ne'er forget her
And will cheer her ever
Loyal to Notre Dame
Cheer, cheer for old Notre Dame,
Wake up the echoes cheering her name,
Send a volley cheer on high,
Shake down the thunder from the sky.
What though the odds be great or small
Old Notre Dame will win over all,
While her loyal sons are marching
Onward to victory.

The Irish Guard marches onto the field at Notre Dame Stadium before the 2002 game against Stanford. One of the proudest traditions at Notre Dame, over 60 students annually vie for the 10 Irish Guard positions.

Irish Guard

The Irish Guard leads the band into the tunnel and out to the field at Notre Dame Stadium for every home game. Each member of the guard is dressed in an Irish kilt. Including the bearskin shako atop each of their heads, they stand eight feet tall.

The guardsmen are selected on the basis of marching ability, appearance, and spirit. The colors of the kilt make up "Notre Dame plaid," with the school colors of gold and blue, and the green representing the Irish.

"Alma Mater (Notre Dame, Our Mother)"

Notre Dame, our mother
Tender, strong and true
Proudly in the heavens,
Gleams thy gold and blue.
Glory's mantle cloaks thee
Golden is thy fame,
And our hearts forever,
Praise thee, Notre Dame.
And our hearts forever,
Love thee, Notre Dame.

Mascots

From the 1930s through the 1950s, the mascot of the Fighting Irish was a succession of Irish terriers. The first, named Brick Top Shaun Rhu, was donated to Knute Rockne in 1930 by Cleveland native Charles Otis. Through the years, most of the terrier mascots bore the name Clashmore Mike. In 1965 the leprechaun replaced Clashmore Mike as the school's official mascot. The leprechaun is consistent with the Notre Dame nickname and is now an integral part of the game-day atmosphere.

"Moose"

Edward "Moose" Krause served as Notre Dame's athletics director for more than 30 years, from 1949 to 1981. Before graduating from Notre Dame in 1934, he had become an All-American in both football and basketball. He was Notre Dame's head basketball coach from 1942 to 1947, leading the Irish to a 98–48 record.

During his time as athletics director, Notre Dame's football team won four consensus national championships. On September 17, 1999, the day before that year's Notre Dame-Michigan State game, a bronze sculpture of Moose was dedicated in front of the Joyce Center. He sits on a bench looking toward Notre Dame Stadium.

Movies

Knute Rockne All American

In 1940 *Knute Rockne All American* debuted in theaters across the country. The film starred Pat O'Brien as the legendary coach and future U.S. president Ronald Reagan as George Gipp. In 1997 the Library of Congress designated *Knute Rockne All American* as a part of the National Film Registry, qualifying it as an "irreplaceable part of America's cinematic heritage."

Rudy

Rudy, a movie telling the story of Dan "Rudy" Ruettiger, was released in 1993. Rudy, a walk-on football player during the Ara Parseghian and Dan Devine coaching tenures, played 27 seconds in the 1975 Georgia Tech game, the last game of his senior year, after two years of sacrifice helping to prepare the team for each game.

Shillelagh

Each year a trophy is awarded to the winner of the Notre Dame-USC game—a jeweled shillelagh. A shillelagh is a Gaelic war club made of either oak or blackthorn saplings, purportedly because they are the only things tougher than an Irish skull. The foot-long shillelagh has ruby-adorned Trojan heads with the year and score of the Southern California wins, while emerald-studded shamrocks represent Notre Dame wins. According to legend, the original shillelagh was flown from Ireland by Howard Hughes' pilot and was first presented in 1952 by the Notre Dame Club of Los Angeles. The rivals are currently on their second shillelagh, the first one having been retired and put on display permanently at Notre Dame.

Actually, there are two shillelagh trophies in Notre Dame football tradition. The second has passed back and forth to the winner of the Notre Dame-Purdue game since 1957. It was donated by the late Joe McLaughlin, a merchant seaman and Notre Dame fan who brought the club back from Ireland. Following each contest between the two teams, a football with the winner's initials and the final score is attached to the stand.

The Notre Dame Alumni Club of Los Angeles donated the jeweled shillelagh in 1952, stating "this shillelagh will serve to symbolize in part the high tradition, the keen rivalry, and above all the sincere respect which these two great universities have for each other."

Notre Dame's 1924 offense lines up for a photo. The Four Horsemen are seen in the background, but they could not do it alone. The linemen, known as the "Seven Mules", helped open up holes for the four stars all season long.

THE NATIONAL CHAMPIONSHIPS

There are almost too many Notre Dame national championships to elaborate fully on all of them. Eleven times the Fighting Irish have stood alone atop the college football world, and 10 more times the Irish have earned a piece of the title. National championships and Notre Dame have been companions since Rockne arrived in South Bend.

Consensus National Titles

1924

The 1924 Notre Dame team will always be known for the backfield immortalized in the game recap that Grantland Rice filed with the *New York Herald Tribune* the day after the Army game, the story that led off with these words: "Outlined against a blue-gray October sky, the Four Horsemen rode again."

Quarterback Harry Stuhldreher, halfbacks Don Miller and Jim Crowley, and fullback Elmer Layden had been playing together as a unit since the end of their sophomore year The Championships in 1922. In the words of their coach, Knute Rockne, the backfield was "a product of destiny." They operated behind a line known as the "Seven Mules", featuring ends Ed Hunsinger and Chuck Collins, tackles Rip Miller and Joe Bach, guards Noble Kizer and John Weibel, and center Adam Walsh.

Another component of the team mostly forgotten by now were the shock troops, a complete unit of second-stringers that started every game and wore down the opponents for the first stringers.

The great 1924 team, Notre Dame's first consensus

national champion, outscored its nine regular-season opponents 258–44. It beat Army 13–3, Northwestern 13–6, and otherwise was not seriously challenged. Following the season, Rockne convinced university officials to permit his team to travel to California to play undefeated Stanford in the Rose Bowl game. The Indians were led by All-America fullback Ernie Nevers and coached by the immortal Glenn "Pop" Warner. Notre Dame won the game 27–10, thanks to fullback Elmer Layden's three touchdowns—a 3-yard run and interception returns of 78 and 70 yards. It was Notre Dame's first and only postseason appearance until 1970.

1929

"Fair. Just fair," was Knute Rockne's reply to questions regarding his team's chances entering the 1929 season. But that fall junior Frank Carideo became a starter and established himself as the greatest quarterback in Notre Dame history, with the possible exception of Johnny Lujack years later. Carideo started for two years and won the national championship both years, as well as every game he started.

Rockne's Ramblers played every game on the road, with Notre Dame Stadium under construction. Some 551,112 fans turned out to see the 1929 Irish play.

Carideo was a unanimous first-team All-American that year, as was guard Jack Cannon.

Behind the running of Jack Elder, Joe Savoldi, Marty Brill, Larry "Moon" Mullins, and Marchy Schwartz, the Irish dispatched all nine opponents. Savoldi made a name for himself in the Wisconsin game at Soldier Field in Chicago with touchdown runs of 71 and 40 yards.

The season finale, against Army on November 30, was played on a frozen surface at Yankee Stadium.

With the game scoreless in the second quarter, Elder intercepted a pass by Army's Red Cagle and returned it 93 yards for a touchdown. The Irish won the game 7–0 and the national title with a 9–0 record, playing the entire season without a home.

1930

In a way the 1929 Notre Dame team was a precursor to the 1930 squad, which Knute Rockne considered to be his best. Rockne's Irish finally had a home in Notre Dame Stadium. Carideo was back at quarterback and was a unanimous first-team All-American for the second straight year.

Carideo and fellow All-Americans Marchy Schwartz, Marty Brill, and Jumpin' Joe Savoldi as a unit brought back memories of the Four Horsemen of six years earlier. The line was a formidable group led by All-Americans Bert Metzger, Tommy Yarr, and Joe Kurth.

Notre Dame began the season 3–0 after a three-game homestand. Even after taking to the road, the Irish continued to roll. In Game 6, they trounced Penn, 60–20, when Brill, a Penn transfer, scored on runs of 45, 52, and 65 yards.

The Irish were 8–0 with Army and Southern California remaining. Schwartz scored on a 54-yard run to take a 7–0 lead over the Cadets. When Army scored soon after on a blocked punt, the Irish blocked the extra point, and the game ended in a 7–6 win. Second-string halfback Bucky O'Connor ran for two touchdowns, including an 80-yard sprint, against the Trojans in the 27–0 season-ending victory. Rockne's masterpiece finished 10–0 and repeated as national champions.

1943

Coach Frank Leahy's 1942 Fighting Irish finished 7–2–2 and returned only two starters for 1943. But that didn't deter this Irish team, as it finished with a 9–1 record after playing what may have been the most difficult schedule in school history. Seven of 10 opponents finished in the final Associated Press top 13.

Angelo Bertelli had moved from tailback to quarterback the season before, as Leahy changed his offense from the single wing to the T formation. Improvement was evident as the 1943 Irish increased their scoring by 156 points over 1942. In all, the 1943 national champions outscored their opponents 340–69.

Going into the final four games of the season, the Irish were rolling along unchallenged, with wins over Pittsburgh 41–0, Georgia Tech 55–13, Michigan 35–12, Wisconsin 50–0, Illinois 47–0, and Navy 33–6. Then the Marine Corps called up quarterback Angelo Bertelli, Notre Dame's first Heisman Trophy winner, for service in World War II.

Sophomore Johnny Lujack took over at quarterback and threw two touchdown passes, ran for another, and intercepted a pass in his first start, a 26–0 win over Army.

The 19–14 loss to Great Lakes Naval Training Station in the finale marred the record, but the title was in place. Halfback Creighton Miller led the nation in rushing that season with 911 yards and joined Bertelli, end John Yonakor, tackle Jim White, guard Pat Filley, and center Herb Coleman as All-Americans.

Georgia Tech Coach Bill Alexander said of the 1943 Irish, "They had speed, power, and deception in their attack, and they looked like one of the best teams I have seen in years."

1946

After World War II was over, Coach Frank Leahy and Notre Dame took control of college football and would not let go. After dropping the 1945 finale to Great Lakes 39–7, the Fighting Irish did not lose another game until 1950. From 1946 1949 the Irish went 38–0–2 and win three national titles.

In 1946 Johnny Lujack returned after two years of wartime service in the navy and became, along with 1929 and 1930 starter Frank Carideo, one of the greatest quarterbacks in school history. End Jim Martin, tackles George Connor and Ziggy Czarobski, guards John Mastrangelo and Bill "Moose" Fischer, center George Strohmeyer, and running backs Terry Brennan and Emil "Red" Sitko, were among the foremost stars on the team.

The 1946 Irish outscored the opposition 271–24, with five shutouts, including four in a row. But one of those shutouts was the infamous 0–0 tie with Army. Four Heisman Trophy winners played in that game—fullback Doc Blanchard (1945) and halfback Glenn Davis (1946) for the two-time defending national champion Cadets; Lujack (1947) and end Leon Hart (1949), who as a freshman backed up Jack Zilly in 1946, for the Irish.

The inaugural Outland Trophy was awarded in 1946, and Connor, arguably the greatest interior lineman in school history, was the recipient. Mastrangelo and Strohmeyer joined Lujack and Connor as All-Americans.

1947

The 1947 Notre Dame Fighting Irish were possibly the greatest football team of all time. Forty-two players from that team went on to play pro football, including some who couldn't even make the traveling squad. They played both ways back then, so that's just about four deep, and some starters, such as Terry Brennan, opted not to even try out for the pros.

In 1947 Notre Dame outscored its nine opponents 291–52, never trailed in any game, and only once allowed more than one touchdown.

Johnny Lujack was back at quarterback and won the Heisman Trophy for his 1947 performance; Connor, the reigning Outland winner, also returned, as did Brennan, Sitko, Hart, Martin, Czarobski, and Fischer.

The Irish opened the season with an easy 40–6 win at Pittsburgh. After brushing off Purdue 22–7, the Irish pitched three consecutive shutouts over Nebraska (31–0), Iowa (21–0), and Navy (27–0). Against Army the following week, Terry Brennan returned the opening kickoff 97 yards for a touchdown to spark a 27–7 Irish win. The following week, Northwestern became the only team on the schedule to come within two touchdowns of Notre Dame but fell to the Irish 26–19.

The season ended with wins of 59–6 over Tulane and 38–7 at Southern California.

Six members of the 1947 team—Lujack, Sitko, Hart, Connor, Czarobski, and Fischer—are in the College Football Hall of Fame, as is Leahy, their coach. The *Boston Herald* called the 1947 Irish "the greatest Notre Dame squad of all time. Its third string could whip most varsities." According to Grantland Rice: "College football never before has known a team so big, so fast, and so powerful." He forgot to mention deep.

Head coach Frank Leahy took a moment to smile for the camera in this photo. He had lots to smile about during his tenure at Notre Dame, especially his dominant 1947 squad.

1949

"We'll have the worst team Notre Dame has ever had," Coach Frank Leahy said before the 1949 season. The Fighting Irish had won national titles in 1946 and 1947 and finished second in 1948. They hadn't been beaten in three years and were about to make it four.

Junior Bob Williams quarterbacked the club in 1949 and made first-team All-American, as did fullback Emil "Six-yard" Sitko, end Leon Hart, and Jim Martin, who had moved from end to tackle for his senior year. Hart won the Heisman Trophy, something no other lineman has been able to accomplish since.

The 1949 Irish beat their 10 opponents by an average score of 36–9. notre Dame took over the No. 1 ranking after a 35–12 win over Purdue in Week 3, celebrated with a 46–7 thumping of fourth-ranked Tulane in Week 4, and easily held on to the top spot for the remainder of the season.

According to Braven Dwyer of the *Los Angeles Times* following the 32–0 Irish win over Southern California on November 26, "Make mistakes against the average team and you're in trouble. Make mistakes against Notre Dame and it's suicide. Even a perfect team couldn't have turned back this great Irish squad."

Southern Methodist and its great backfield starring Doak Walker, who had won the Heisman Trophy the previous season, and Kyle Rote gave Notre Dame its only real challenge of the season in the December 3 finale, but the Irish still prevailed 27–20.

"It's the greatest college team I've ever seen," said Red Grange regarding the 1949 Fighting Irish.

1966

In 1964, during his first season, Ara Parseghian came within a minute and a half of the national championship, and in 1966 he continued the tradition of Notre Dame coaches capturing the title in their third year.

Quarterback Terry Hanratty and end Jim Seymour opened the 1966 campaign as starters. In the nationally televised season opener against eighth-ranked Purdue, Hanratty and Seymour connected on 13 passes for 276 yards and three touchdowns and acquired the nickname "Touchdown Twins".

The All-America teams were heavily populated with Irish players that fall, including Hanratty, Seymour, halfback Nick Eddy, fullback Larry Conjar, offensive tackle Paul Seiler, guard Tom Regner, center George Goeddeke, defensive end Alan Page, defensive tackles Kevin Hardy and Pete Duranko, linebacker Jim Lynch, and safety Tom Schoen. Eddy, Regner, Page, and Lynch were consensus first-team picks. Eddy came in third in that year's Heisman race. Further down the roster, halfback Rocky Bleier and guard Bob Kuechenberg were future NFL stars.

The Irish shut out six opponents, including three straight in October.

Parseghian's players took their 8–0 record and No. 1 ranking to East Lansing for the enormously hyped showdown with Michigan State. Eddy was unavailable for the contest with a shoulder injury, Spartan defensive end Bubba Smith had knocked Hanratty and Goeddeke out of the game in the first quarter, and the game ended in a 10–10 tie. After the game, Smith said of the Irish, "Man, those cats hit and stick to you. That game was rough."

"The Super Bowl was not as big as that Michigan State Notre Dame game," said Lynch, who played in Super Bowl IV as a linebacker for the Kansas City Chiefs.

Tom Clements may have been lost to history as far as individual play is concerned, but being sandwiched between Joe Theismann and Joe Montana is a tough hurdle to overcome. Clements was still a stellar leader on the field, quarterbacking the 1973 national champions. He went on to a coaching career and was considered for the Notre Dame job in 2004.

The following week, the Irish traveled to Los Angeles to take on Southern California in the season finale, having left Hanratty, Eddy, and Goeddeke back in South Bend, and rolled over the Pac-8 champions 51–0. It was all the pollsters had to see, and the Irish were national champions.

1973

The Irish won their second consensus national title under Ara Parseghian in 1973. That Notre Dame team outscored the opposition 358–66. Tight end Dave Casper and cornerback Mike Townsend were consensus All-Americans, with a half dozen or more youngsters on the club destined for the All-America designation the following season.

With junior Tom Clements at quarterback, the offense was based on misdirection plays, with four backs sharing the rushing load. Fullback Wayne Bullock led with 752 rushing yards, halfback Art Best followed with 700, halfback Eric Penick added 586, and Clements pitched in with 360.

The Irish were 5–0 and ranked eighth in the nation going into the game with sixth-ranked USC. Penick ran for 118 yards, 50 more than the entire Southern California team, and scored on a dazzling 85-yard run as the Irish snapped the Trojans' 23-game unbeaten streak with the 23–14 victory.

Notre Dame cruised through the rest of the slate before traveling to New Orleans for the Sugar Bowl matchup with Alabama on New Year's Eve. What transpired was one of the greatest showdowns in history, pitting Paul W. "Bear" Bryant's top-ranked Crimson Tide against Parseghian's second-ranked Irish.

"It was the kind of game you could sink your teeth into," Bryant said.

The lead changed hands six times before Notre Dame prevailed 24–23 and claimed the school's ninth consensus national championship.

1977

Dan Devine got into the national title act during his third year at Notre Dame with a team featuring tight end Ken MacAfee, guard Ernie Hughes, defensive ends Ross Browner and Willie Fry, linebacker Bob Golic, and defensive backs Jim Browner and Luther Bradley.

And, oh yes, quarterback Joe Montana.

He didn't take over as the starter until Game 4, after there had already been a loss, 20–13, in Week 2 at Ole Miss. The following Saturday, with the Irish trailing Purdue 24–14, Montana came off the bench to throw for 154 yards and a touchdown, leading the Irish to a 31–24 win. From that point on, he never relinquished the job.

Notre Dame was ranked 11th nationally when Southern California visited. Wearing green jerseys, the Irish rolled to a 49–19 victory and topped it with a 48–10 trouncing of Miami.

On New Year's Day 1978, Notre Dame met No. 1 Texas in the Cotton Bowl. After finishing the first quarter tied at 3–3, the Irish scored three touchdowns before halftime and slowed Heisman Trophy–winning running back Earl Campbell enough for a 38–10 victory.

1988

Almost predictably, Notre Dame won the national title in Lou Holtz's third year, although it didn't seem likely during fall camp. There were no starters back on either the offensive or defensive line, and 1987 Heisman Trophy winner Tim Brown had graduated.

However, the backfield returned intact; quarterback Tony Rice, fullback Anthony Johnson, and tailback Mark Green, along with a strong group of linebackers, particularly Ned Bolcar and All-Americans Michael Stonebreaker and Wes Pritchett. Flanker Ricky Watters, offensive tackle Andy Heck, defensive end Frank Stams, and nose tackle Chris Zorich also graced the All-American teams of 1988.

The season began with a thrilling 19–17 win over ninth-ranked Michigan, propelling the Fighting Irish from 13th to eighth in the Associated Press poll. On October 15, No. 1–ranked Miami came to Notre Dame Stadium and left on the short end of a 31–30 score. Irish safety Pat Terrell knocked down a two-point conversion pass by Miami quarterback Steve Walsh with 45 seconds remaining to preserve the win.

By November the Irish had claimed the top spot. In the finale, Notre Dame visited the Los Angeles Coliseum for the annual showdown with Southern California with the teams ranked no.1 and no. 2. The Irish defense made life miserable for Trojans quarterback Rodney Peete. Rice scored on a 65-yard run, and Stan Smagala ran back an interception 64 yards for another touchdown in the 27–10 victory.

Finally came undefeated, third-ranked West Virginia and star quarterback Major Harris in the Fiesta Bowl. Notre Dame mauled the Mountaineers, holding their vaunted rushing game to 118 yards. The Irish held early leads of 16–0 and 23–3 and held on to win 34–21. The perfect 12–0 slate came with the national title.

According to Holtz: "I think this team is underrated even if we are No. 1."

The Other Ten

1919–1920

Knute Rockne won national titles, or at least portions thereof, in his second and third years after taking the helm from his own coach and predecessor, Jesse Harper. These were the last two seasons for George Gipp, and end Roger Kiley joined Gipp as an All-American. The Irish finished both seasons 9–0 with the Gipper averaging 6.9 yards per rush in 1919 and 8.1 yards in 1920 in addition to his exploits on defense and special teams.

1927

With Knute Rockne still at the controls, the Irish won a piece of the national title with halfback Christie Flanagan, tackle John Polisky, and guard John Smith all earning All-America honors. The season finale, a 7–6 win over Southern California, was played at Soldier Field in front of a crowd estimated at 120,000, the largest in college football history.

1938

The Dickinson System awarded the 8–1 Irish the national title in 1938. With former Four Horseman Elmer Layden as coach, Notre Dame held its nine opponents to a combined 39 points for the season, shutting out four of them. Steve Sitko quarterbacked the Irish that year, with Bob Saggau leading the team in both passing and rushing. The line was anchored by consensus All-American Joe Benoir.

Bob Saggau misses an extra point against Army in 1938. The Fighting Irish beat the Cadets at Yankee Stadium and won a share of the national championship with an 8–1 record.

1953

Frank Leahy concluded his coaching tenure in style with an undefeated (though once tied) campaign in 1953. It may have been the greatest backfield in Notre Dame history. Hall of Famer Ralph Guglielmi was the quarterback, and fullback Neil Worden led the team in rushing, with Joe Heap and Heisman Trophy winner Johnny Lattner at halfback. Art Hunter was a consensus All-American at tackle. Leahy's final two games as Notre Dame's coach were victories of 48–14 at Southern California and 40–14 over Southern Methodist.

1964

Ara Parseghian took the coaching reins on the heels of a 2–7 campaign and won his first nine games to top the rankings. But on November 28 Southern California scored 20 unanswered points in the second half to beat Notre Dame, costing it the consensus title (although a number of services still had the Irish No. 1). Quarterback Johnny Huarte won the Heisman Trophy, while receiver Jack Snow, linebacker Jim Carroll, defensive back Tony Carey, and sophomore defensive tackle Kevin Hardy were All-Americans.

1967

The Irish were defending national champion and opened with a resounding 41–8 win over Cal, but two losses in the next three games knocked Notre Dame out of the rankings. Parsegian's team finished with six straight victories, including wins over Pitt, Georgia Tech, and Miami to close out the season. End Kevin Hardy and safety Tom Schoen were consensus All-Americans.

1970

The one blemish was a 38–28 loss to Southern California in the regular-season finale. A 24–11 win over top-ranked Texas in the Cotton Bowl merited national title honors by a few services, especially after Darrell Royal's Longhorns had won 30 straight games and hadn't been beaten since the second game of the 1968 season. The Irish outscored opponents 330–97 during the regular season, including three shutouts. Quarterback Joe Theismann and wide receiver Tom Gatewood set numerous school records. Guard Larry DiNardo and cornerback Clarence Ellis joined them as All-Americans.

1989

Heading into the finale at Miami the defending national champions were nursing a 23-game winning streak, only to see it come to an end against the Hurricanes, 27-10. Led by quarterback Tony Rice and receiver Rocket Ismail, the combined score of Notre Dame's regular-season games was 406–173. The defense featured linemen Jeff Alm and Chris Zorich, linebacker Ned Bolcar, and consensus All-American cornerback Todd Lyght. A 21–6 Orange Bowl win over Colorado salvaged a piece of the national title.

1993

After winning its showdown with No. 1 Florida State, 10-0 Notre Dame came out flat against Boston College and lost 41–39 on a last-second field goal. As a result, the Associated Press awarded Florida State the national title, but some services still preferred Notre Dame after its 24–21 win over No. 4 Texas A&M in the Cotton Bowl. Offensive linemen Tim Ruddy and Aaron Taylor, defensive tackle Bryant Young, and defensive backs Bobby Taylor and Jeff Burris were named All-Americans.

Notre Dame has consistently gotten the better of Stanford, and Rashon Powers-Neal proved it with his 108 yard performance in a big win in 2002. The result was much the same as in the Four Horsemen's swan song in the Rose Bowl, a big Irish win.

THE GREATEST GAMES

Notre Dame 35, Army 13
November 1, 1913

The forward pass had been legalized in 1906 and utilized primarily as a desperation measure by teams fighting to overcome late-game deficits. But on November 1, 1913, the passing game was used for the first time as a team's modus operandi and Army had no answer.

Coach Jesse Harper and the Irish arrived at West Point with 18 players and 14 pairs of cleats, and the Cadets were licking their chops. After Notre Dame fumbled the ball away on the first series, quarterback Gus Dorais opened it up, with end Knute Rockne as his primary target. Having spent all summer on the beach at Cedar Point, Ohio, perfecting their revolutionary technique of quarterback leading receiver and receiver catching the ball on the run, Dorais and Rockne sliced Army to shreds.

Dorais missed on his first two passes but connected on 14 of his next 15, including a then-unheard-of 40-yarder to Rockne. When the Cadets were looking for the pass, Irish All-America fullback Ray Eichenlaub enjoyed vast expanses of running room.

The Irish returned home 35–13 victors, having exploded onto the national scene and having changed the game of football forever.

Notre Dame 27, Stanford 10
1925 Rose Bowl

It was the last game the Four Horsemen would play together and the last bowl game Notre Dame would play in for another 45 years. Knute Rockne's opportunistic Irish would not let Pop Warner's undefeated

Stanford team off the hook for its mistakes.

The Indians drew first blood with a 27-yard field goal and a 3–0 lead after one quarter of play. In the second stanza, Notre Dame's lean, slashing fullback Elmer Layden took over, scoring on a 3-yard run and a 78-yard interception return to put the Irish up 13–3 at the half.

Late in the third quarter, Layden punted and the Stanford return man fumbled. Irish end Ed Hunsinger scooped up the loose ball and returned it 20 yards for a touchdown.

With the Irish leading 20–10 with 30 seconds remaining, Layden returned another interception 70 yards for a touchdown to make the final score 27–10. Both of Layden's picks came off the arm of Stanford All-America fullback Ernie Nevers.

Notre Dame 12, Army 6
November 10, 1928

This was the "Win One for the Gipper" game. Rockne's roster had been decimated by injuries and almost became the only losing team of his career. It finished 5–4, and if it weren't for some Rockne psychology before the Army game, it would have finished 4–5.

After pregame warmups, Rockne called his team together in the locker room. He told them about George Gipp, the greatest Notre Dame player of all time, who had died during his senior year. Then he told them about Gipp's deathbed request to exhort a Notre Dame team to overcome great odds and win a game just for him, "for the Gipper."

"This is the day, and you are the team," Rock said.

There was no way Notre Dame would lose. The Irish fell behind 6–0 in the third quarter but won the game 12–6 on a 1-yard plunge by Jack Chevigny and a 32-yard pass from Butch Niemiec to Johnny O'Brien.

"That's one for the Gipper," Chevigny supposedly said after his score.

"That's one for the Gipper, too," O'Brien said after he scored.

The Irish lost their remaining two games, to Carnegie Tech and Southern Calfironia, but the losing record was averted.

Notre Dame 18, Ohio State 13
November 2, 1935

Notre Dame has been involved in some great football games over the years, but this one beats them all. Both Notre Dame and Ohio State were undefeated, but Notre Dame was a heavy underdog. One sportswriter picked Ohio State by 40.

In front of 81,000 fans in Ohio Stadium, the Buckeyes took a 13–0 halftime lead. The dire predictions appeared to be accurate. The Irish attack had been completely stunted. The Buckeye line made it almost impossible for Notre Dame to throw the ball or even get a punt off.

"I've never seen a Notre Dame offense so completely stopped," said writer Francis Wallace.

Irish Coach Elmer Layden, who had been the fullback of the Four Horsemen backfield, decided to start the second string in the second half. In the third quarter Notre Dame backup halfback Andy Pilney caught fire. The score was still 13–0 after three quarters, but the Irish were on the Ohio State 12.

On the first play of the fourth quarter, Pilney hit Francis Gaul with a pass to the 2, and from there Steve Miller scored on the next play to make the score 13–6.

On the next Notre Dame possession, Miller fumbled into the end zone, where Ohio State recovered for a touchback. But the Irish weren't finished.

Notre Dame took possession on its own 20 with three minutes to go. Some dazzling runs by Pilney and

With Army threatening in the fourth quarter, Emil Sitko picked off this Cadet pass to end the scoring chance; Johnny Lujack holds his hands out waiting for a potential lateral. Neither team got on the scoreboard, and this classic ended in a scoreless tie.

a 33-yard touchdown pass from Pilney to Mike Layden brought the score to 13–12.

Coach Layden called for an onside kick, which the Buckeyes recovered, but the Irish recovered a fumble by Buckeye Dick Belz at midfield. After a 30-yard scramble, Pilney was knocked out of bounds and out of the game at the Ohio State 19.

Bill Shakespeare replaced Pilney with less than half a minute left and threw a pass that was almost intercepted by Belz, who could have redeemed himself for his earlier miscue. On the next play, Shakespeare threw the winning touchdown pass to end Wayne Millner, and the Irish escaped Columbus with the unforgettable 18–13 victory.

Notre Dame 0, Army 0
November 9, 1946

World War II had ended the previous year. Army had won 25 straight games and two straight national titles. They had beaten the Irish 59–0 in 1944 and 48–0 in 1945. But Notre Dame Coach Frank Leahy and many of his players had returned from the service and were back on the football field. The Notre Dame-Army game had been sold out since June, even though tickets didn't publicly go on sale until August 1.

The Irish plowed through their five opponents heading into the Army game. "Fifty-nine and forty-eight, this is the year we retaliate," was the chant heard around campus the week before the game. The Notre Dame student body called itself the SPATNC—the Society for the Prevention of Army's Third National Championship.

The game itself was hard fought and brutal, but it failed to produce a winner. Leahy and his Army counterpart, Earl "Red" Blaik, both went conservative, playing not to lose.

In the second quarter, Notre Dame drove to the Army 4-yard line but turned the ball over on downs after two quarterback sneaks and two running plays to the left were stopped short of the goal line.

Army's great backs, Doc Blanchard and Glenn Davis, were contained all day except for a single play. Blanchard broke free on one run, cut toward the sideline, and had clear sailing. But Irish quarterback Johnny Lujack cut Blanchard off and tackled him by the ankles at the Notre Dame 37. The Cadets moved the ball to the Irish 12, but Davis threw an interception. Irish halfback Terry Brennan returned the pickoff to the 30, and Army's scoring threat was stopped. Consequently, the game of the year ended in an unsatisfying tie.

Notre Dame 7, Oklahoma 0
November 16, 1957

Oklahoma boasted the longest winning streak in NCAA football history at 47 games. The Sooners had trounced the Irish 40–0 the previous season in South Bend and hadn't lost since they dropped the 1953 season opener to the Fighting Irish, 28–21. Oklahoma was a 19-point favorite entering the game.

The Sooners drove to the Notre Dame 13-yard line on their opening drive, but the Irish defense held. That was the deepest penetration the Sooners would manage all day.

Both defenses controlled the game until, with 3:50 left to play, Notre Dame faced fourth-and-goal at the three. Quarterback Bob Williams faked a handoff to Nick Pietrosante into the middle and pitched the ball to Dick Lynch around right end for the score. Monte Stickles added the PAT and the Irish held on for the 7–0 win.

Irish Coach Terry Brennan credited his defense with the victory. The unit had held Oklahoma's powerful running game to 98 yards.

Oklahoma's Carl Dodd looks for daylight in the team's 1957 matchup with Notre Dame. Dodd and the rest of the Oklahoma offense struggled to get going all day, and the Irish defense held them to just 98 yards on ground. The 7–0 Irish win snapped Oklahoma's record 47-game winning streak.

Notre Dame 10, Michigan State 10
November 19, 1966

It was one of the most eagerly anticipated games in college football history—an epic No. 1 versus No. 2 matchup. Both teams were loaded with star players. For Notre Dame they included quarterback Terry Hanratty, split end Jim Seymour, running backs Nick Eddy and Rocky Bleier, offensive guard Tom Regner, center George Goeddeke, defensive end Alan Page, defensive tackles Kevin Hardy and Pete Duranko, linebackers Jim Lynch and John Pergine, and safety Tom Schoen. Michigan State boasted quarterback Jimmy Raye, running backs Clinton Jones, Regis Cavender, and Bob Apisa, split end Gene Washington, offensive linemen Jerry West and Joe Pryzbicki, defensive end Bubba Smith, defensive tackle Patrick Gallinagh, linebacker Charlie Thornhill, and rover George Webster. They were arguably two of the greatest teams ever to play the game.

But the Irish played the entire game without Eddy, who finished third in the Heisman voting that year, because of a shoulder injury and lost both Hanratty and Goeddeke in the first quarter, compliments of Bubba Smith.

After a four-yard run by Cavender and a 47-yard Dick Kenney field goal, the Spartans led 10–0 in the second quarter. Coley O'Brien, Hanratty's backup, hit Bob Gladieux, Eddy's backup, on a perfect 34-yard touchdown pass to cut the deficit to three; then a 28-yard Joe Izzaro field goal tied the score at 10 on the first play of the fourth quarter.

With time running out, Notre Dame got the ball on its own 30. Coach Ara Parseghian decided to play it safe and go for the tie, for which he would be criticized. The 51–0 victory over Pac-8 champion Southern California in Los Angeles the following week secured the controversial national championship.

Notre Dame 24, Texas 11
1971 Cotton Bowl

Coach Darrell Royal's Longhorns finished the 1970 regular season 10–0, defending their 1969 national title. They had won 30 games in a row and hadn't been beaten since the second game of the 1968 season. One of the 30 games in the Texas winning streak was a 21–17 victory over the Irish in the 1970 Cotton Bowl.

Irish quarterback Joe Theismann threw a 26-yard touchdown pass to Tom Gatewood and ran for two more scores, all within the first 16:32 of the game, and that was all Notre Dame needed for the 24–11 upset.

Texas actually drew first blood with a 23-yard field goal by Happy Feller for a short-lived 3–0 lead. Then Theismann went to work, putting the Irish up 21–3 in short order. Texas running back Jim Bertelsen closed the score to 21–9 with a two-yard run, and a two-point conversion pass from Eddie Phillips to Danny Lester made it 21–11. Irish kicker Scott Hemphill split the uprights on a 36-yard field goal with the first half drawing to a close for the 24-11 lead, which held.

The Longhorns outgained Notre Dame 426–359, but the Irish forced nine Texas fumbles and recovered five. It was Notre Dame's first bowl victory in 46 years; the Irish had abstained from postseason play since the 1925 Rose Bowl before taking on Texas in Dallas the previous year.

Notre Dame 24, Alabama 23
1973 Sugar Bowl

It was a historic matchup, the first between Notre Dame and Alabama, (not to mention Ara Parseghian against Paul W. "Bear" Bryant) and lived up to its billing.

A Sugar Bowl-record crowd of 85,161 saw the lead change hands six times.

The Irish defense held Alabama without a yard of

offense in the first quarter. A six-yard run by fullback Wayne Bullock put the Irish up 6–0. A botched snap on the extra-point attempt kept it at 6–0. Midway through the second quarter, Alabama went up 7–6 on a six-yard Randy Billingsley run, but Notre Dame's Al Hunter took the ensuing kickoff 93 yards for a touchdown, and the two-point conversion pass gave the Irish a 14–7 lead. A 39-yard field goal by Alabama's Bill Davis made it 14–10 at the half.

In the third quarter, the Crimson Tide took a 17–14 lead after an 11-play, 93-yard drive ended in a five-yard touchdown run by Wilbur Jackson.

An Alabama fumble recovered by linebacker Drew Mahalic gave Notre Dame the ball on the Tide 12, from where halfback Eric Penick scored on the first play, giving the Irish the lead again, 21–17. Early in the fourth quarter, Alabama had the ball on the Notre Dame 25 when quarterback Richard Todd handed off to Mike Stock, who turned and threw the ball back to Todd, who loped down the sideline into the end zone. But the extra-point attempt failed, and the Tide held a two-point, 23–21 lead.

Notre Dame's Bob Thomas countered with a 19-yard field goal to cap an 11-play, 79-yard drive. With three minutes to play, Bryant decided to punt and Greg Gantt's 69-yard kick pinned Notre Dame on its 1. Roughing the kicker was called, which would have given the Tide a fourth-and-five, so Bryant opted to decline the penalty and hope his defense would get the offense another chance.

It didn't. On third down, Notre Dame quarterback Tom Clements dropped back into his end zone and fired a 38-yard pass to backup tight end Robin Weber for the first down. From there the Irish ran out the clock for the national championship.

Notre Dame's Ken MacAfee walks along the sideline at the 1978 Cotton Bowl in Dallas.

Notre Dame 38, Texas 10
1978 Cotton Bowl

When the 1978 Cotton Bowl began, Texas was they only undefeated team in college football, Texas. Notre Dame forced six Texas turnovers and scored off five of them en route to the 38–10 rout to seize the national title.

Longhorn running back Earl Campbell had won that year's Heisman Trophy and ran for 116 yards, but he was unable to dominate the game thanks to defensive ends Ross Browner and Willie Fry, linebacker Bob Golic, and defensive backs Jim Browner and Luther Bradley.

After an exchange of field goals tied the score at 3 to end the first quarter, the Fighting Irish took command with three touchdowns, on runs of 6 and 10 yards by Terry Eurick and a 17-yard Joe Montana-to-Vagas Ferguson pass.

Texas cut the deficit to 24–10 with a Randy McEachern pass to Mike Lockett as time expired in the first half, but Ferguson added touchdown runs of 3 and 26 yards in the second half.

Notre Dame 35, Houston 34
1979 Cotton Bowl

It is known as the "Chicken Soup Game". The Cotton Bowl against Southwest Conference champion Houston was Joe Montana's last with Notre Dame and was played in an ice storm. The temperature at kick-off was 20 degrees with a fierce wind chill. Notre Dame took a 12–0 first-quarter lead on a 3-yard Montana run, a 1-yard Pete Buchanan run, and two failed conversion attempts. The Cougars countered with two touchdowns and two field goals to take a 20–12 halftime lead.

Houston tacked on two more touchdowns in the third quarter, and with a hypothermic Montana on the sideline unable to continue, the situation looked bleak for the Fighting Irish. But a heads-up Notre Dame assistant administered chicken soup to the ailing quarterback, bringing his body temperature back up to normal and allowing Montana to mount an unforgettable rally.

With 7:37 remaining in the game and Dan Devine's team trailing 34–12, freshman Tony Belden blocked a Houston punt, and freshman Steve Cichy scooped the ball up and returned it 33 yards for a touchdown. Montana hit Vagas Ferguson with a two-point conversion pass, bringing the score to 34–20.

The Irish defense forced another punt, giving Notre Dame the ball at its 39 with 5:40 to play. After completing three straight passes to three different receivers, Montana swept around the left end for a 2-yard touchdown. He connected with split end Kris Haines for the two-point conversion pass to make it 34-28.

The Irish were driving again with 2:05 to play when Montana fumbled the ball away at the Houston 20 after a 16-yard run. But the Irish held and took over on downs at the Houston 29 with 28 seconds remaining. The quarterback ran for 11 yards, then found Haines for a 10-yard gain. An incomplete pass intended for Haines in the end zone left just 2 seconds on the clock, so he called the same play and this time made the completion to tie the game at 34. Joe Unis' extra-point kick with no time remaining was nullified by a penalty, so he did it again for the 35-34 victory.

Notre Dame 31, Miami 30
October 15, 1988

Defending national champion Miami took its 36-game regular-season winning streak into South Bend to face the No. 4 Irish, and the Hurricanes had outscored Notre Dame by a combined 133–20 in the four previous meetings.

Notre Dame struck first with a 7-yard touchdown run by quarterback Tony Rice capping off a 75-yard, 12-play drive. Early in the second quarter, the visi-

Coach Lou Holtz smiles as he hoists the Paul "Bear" Bryant Coach of the Year Award in 1988. Holtz had plenty of reason to smile after the win against Miami and a bowl victory over West Virginia that led the Irish to the national championship.